MIDNIGHT FLIGHT TO NUREMBERG

Be it enacted by the Senate and House of Representatives of the United States of America in Congress Assembled, that the Act entitled "An act for making further and more effectual provision for the national defense, and other purposes," approved June 3, 1916, as amended, be, and the same is hereby, amended so that the Air Service referred to in that Act and all subsequent Acts of Congress shall be known as the Air Corps.

Public Law 69-446, 2 July 1926

From the author of *Left for Dead at Nijmegen*, 2019 Nonfiction Book of the Year.

"We found the narrative compelling." Julie Huggins, *Smithsonian Books*

MIDNIGHT FLIGHT TO
NUREMBERG

The Capture of the Nazi who put Adolf Hitler into Power

MARCUS A. NANNINI

AIR WORLD

AIR WORLD

MIDNIGHT FLIGHT TO NUREMBERG
The Capture of the Nazi who put Adolf Hitler into Power

First published in Great Britain in 2021 by
Air World
An imprint of
Pen & Sword Books Ltd
Yorkshire – Philadelphia

ISBN 978 1 52679 273 0

Typeset by SJmagic DESIGN SERVICES, India.
Printed and bound in the UK by CPI Group (UK) Ltd, Croydon, CR0 4YY.

Pen & Sword Books Limited incorporates the imprints of Atlas, Archaeology,
Aviation, Discovery, Family History, Fiction, History, Maritime, Military, Military
Classics, Politics, Select, Transport, True Crime, Air World, Frontline Publishing, Leo
Cooper, Remember When, Seaforth Publishing, The Praetorian Press, Wharncliffe
Local History, Wharncliffe Transport, Wharncliffe True Crime and White Owl.

For a complete list of Pen & Sword titles please contact

PEN & SWORD BOOKS LIMITED
47 Church Street, Barnsley, South Yorkshire, S70 2AS, England
E-mail: enquiries@pen-and-sword.co.uk
Website: www.pen-and-sword.co.uk

Or
PEN AND SWORD BOOKS
1950 Lawrence Rd, Havertown, PA 19083, USA
E-mail: Uspen-and-sword@casematepublishers.com
Website: www.penandswordbooks.com

Contents

Prologue

These are the World War II experiences of C-47 Pilot/Instructor, First Lieutenant Harry E. Watson Jr., a veteran of twenty-seven combat missions, recipient of three Air Medals, and seven Battle Stars. Conversations and speeches have been recreated to the best of Harry's excellent memory.

Harry's wife Donna is my editor's aunt and was the reason we drove from Phoenix, Arizona, to visit them at their California home. I was mildly aware Harry was a World War II veteran. It didn't take long for us to hit it off. After all, I was writing World War II stories, and he'd served in the war. We spent several long weekends with them at their home in Riverside, California, across two years.

Harry and I would sit together for hours on end while I took notes, and he relived his experiences, beginning as a child and continuing right through the war. I knew Harry and Donna were devout Christians, we went to their church with them, but Harry seldom went to a formal church service before the war. It was a subject he was hesitant to speak of. But my interview process is based on patience and establishing a close rapport with my interviewee as we develop a friendship.

In between visits, I researched Harry's story as I sought to verify myriad details. We spoke and emailed almost daily as I worked on the initial, full draft. Then we'd drive to California for a long weekend when Harry and I would hammer out the various aspects of his story. As with all my previous interviews with World War II vets, the best details were the most elusive.

Eventually, Harry revealed he'd been skeptical concerning the existence of a supreme being; that is, until the day of his initial solo flight. I worked through the sequences of that flight numerous times until he announced that what I had written had made him relive the experience as if it were happening again. Only after achieving such a degree of accuracy did he begin to feel comfortable enough to share some very private thoughts about his wartime experience.

In loving remembrance of my mother,
Esther Pierina Paganelli Nannini Biagini
And my dear friend,
Captain Harry E. Watson

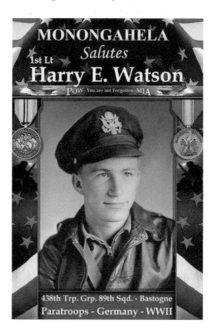

A special thank-you to my editor,
Susanne C. Johnson, M.A.

Chapter 1

Fueling Patton's Tanks
September 6–7, 1944

First Lieutenant Harry Watson, eyes closed, his body sunk deep into his bunk at Greenham Common Airbase, England, was enjoying a slow start to what was scheduled as his first day off in a week. A copy of *Stars and Stripes* was propped on his knees, but his thoughts were drifting to a future life as the pilot of a Pan-Am clipper flying boat, soaring over the peaceful expanses of the Pacific Ocean. It was his childhood dream, a dream he never considered possible until the opportunity to join the U.S. Army Air Corps presented itself.

The day before, he'd been flying under miserable weather conditions for hours on end while routinely intercepting radio traffic alerting him to the fact German fighter planes were sharing the sky with him. The enemy activity compounded the stress he was experiencing following a week of running supply missions, frequently in foul weather, and often landing in hastily mown fields.

It wasn't long before his respite was interrupted by the all too familiar sound of a Jeep grinding to a halt over loose gravel. He slowly sat up, swung his legs over the side of the bunk while simultaneously tossing the paper to the side. Harry was considering how he might intimidate some hapless young private he assumed was about to intrude upon him when, to his surprise, he heard his co-pilot, Al, calling to him.

"Harry, are you in there?" Harry recognized Al's usually upbeat tone was missing and lost no time responding as he jumped to action and quickly scurried to the front of the tent.

"Al, I'm here," he said, while deftly slipping through the unfastened canvas flaps. He blinked his eyes a few times as he adjusted to the midday sun before returning his attention to Al. "What's the big deal?"

Al appeared to be both annoyed and anxious as he explained Colonel Donalson wanted to see him, "as-in right now, and it sure didn't sound like he's going to invite you to a dance party, so let's get a move-on!"

Al paused a moment, tossed his cigarette onto the gravel, ground it with the toe of his right boot to make sure it was out, then removed a fresh cigarette from a pocket in his brown leather flight jacket and lit it. Harry recognized the behavior as indicating Al was worried. *Truly* worried because Al only smoked when he was nervous, anxious, or both, and ever since their unorthodox flight to Orly Airport in August, just the mention of Donalson was enough to put both men on edge.

"Well, hell," Harry replied, "I haven't done anything out-of-the-ordinary, at least for me anyway, and our plane's waiting for a new number one engine. Just like you predicted, they couldn't fix it, so I don't have the faintest idea what the fuss is all about." Harry thought for a moment and continued: "There's no way he can blame me for that engine, it was flak damage, plain and simple."

Harry took a deep breath, put his hand on his head, and realized he'd forgotten his cap. "Hold on a minute while I get my cap."

"Shake a leg Harry, you don't want to make things any worse!"

Harry disappeared into the tent and momentarily returned, cap in hand.

The two men jumped into the Jeep, and as Harry began to adjust his cap, Al hit the gas, catching him by surprise. The hat went flying behind them, forcing Al to turn around to retrieve it. Al leapt out, picked it up, and plopped back into the driver's seat. Just as he was about to place it into Harry's outstretched hand, he came to an abrupt halt. His mouth dropped open as he stared at Harry's uncovered hair.

"Geez Harry, I never realized your hair's turned half grey, when did that happen?"

"I first noticed it after the Orly trip, and I've been trying to keep my cap on ever since."

Harry grasped the cap from Al's hand, firmly placed it on his head, and, with a wry smile said: "If you don't mind, I'd prefer not to keep Donalson waiting any longer, so if you'd floor it, I'd be most obliged."

"I wouldn't worry too much, Donalson probably wants you to instruct some new arrivals on night landings. I doubt he's still holding a grudge, or we'd both be out of here and hauling freight over the 'Hump' in Burma. But then, why does he still list us as MIA on that forsaken blackboard of his?"

"I don't pay any attention to it, though I got to admit I'm always worried he might change his mind about that court-martial," replied Harry.

The two men were silent until Al slammed the brakes and slid to a halt in front of Colonel Donalson's Quonset hut. Harry jumped out and wasted no time making his way to Staff Sergeant Kane, who was staffing the desk outside Donalson's office. Kane, buried behind a mountain of paperwork, peered around the stacks of files when he heard Harry hurriedly walking towards him, the noise from his hard, rubber-heeled, leather boots reverberating on the plank flooring alerting him to Harry's approach.

"Hi lieutenant," said Kane, smiling, "where've you been? I sent for you more than an hour ago." Kane didn't expect a reply and continued. "Doesn't matter, you're here now so I'll tell the colonel." Kane walked to the door, lightly tapped two times, and waited for permission to enter before disappearing into the office.

Harry began wishing he hadn't skipped noon chow and noticed his palms were sweaty, for he was beginning to suspect his plans for the remainder of the day were about to change, and probably not in a good way. He tried to relax by reasoning that Kane had smiled at him, but was it a smile or more of a smirk? Did he really summon Harry an hour ago, or was he bullshitting? The one thing Harry knew for sure was Donalson wasn't one to be kept waiting.

Soon enough, the door opened, and Kane beckoned him to enter. Harry walked in and confidently approached Donalson who, his back to Harry, was examining a wall-size map of the European Theatre of Operations. Harry held his salute, but Donalson was lost in thought.

Harry felt a bit odd, for Donalson wasn't much for formalities such as saluting. Still, since his Orly mission, he always played it safe and saluted any senior officer he happened upon. After a few moments Donalson noticed Harry was obediently standing nearby and turned to face him.

"At ease, Harry, have yourself a seat." He motioned to a chair in front of his desk. "I've got a special mission for you," Donalson said, "and it ought to be right up your alley." Kane knocked on the door and stuck his head into the opening. "Colonel, your plane will be ready to go in 15!" Donalson nodded an acknowledgment, and Kane returned to his desk, softly closing the door behind him.

Addressing Harry by his first name should have been enough to place him at ease for the simple reason Donalson never called him by anything other than 'lieutenant', or 'Watson.' Harry realized it was the first time Donalson ever addressed him by his first name, and until that moment, he wasn't sure Donalson even knew what it was.

Inexplicably he began to feel nervous all over again when the thought occurred to him that Donalson might have addressed him as Harry because he was about to deliver awful news. He considered the possibility some big-shot general had learned of his Orly trip and decided to bring him up on charges. His palms were sweating so severely he realized he'd been unconsciously rubbing them on his slacks.

Donalson, still standing, turned and pointed to a speck on the map and motioned for Harry to approach him. "See this area?" He didn't expect an answer. "The Luftwaffe had been using a makeshift airfield as an auxiliary to their main base in Reims, located right about here." Harry moved alongside Donalson as he followed his finger, and they jointly began to carefully examine the specific point on the map.

"One of Patton's recon units has been exploiting a breach in the German lines and managed to run out of fuel. They're dug-in near this field, and I need you to fly them a plane-load of Jerry cans so they don't get themselves massacred. HQ tells me there are some shell-holes scattered about the landing area, so be sure to do a fly-over before you go in, this is not a paved runway." Donalson took a deep breath.

"As you can imagine, there's a significant degree of urgency here. You've already demonstrated an uncanny ability to locate just about anything when it's foggy and rainy, and today you'll be looking at both, except today there won't be any electronic guides for you. This mission's going to be good old-fashioned, 100 percent seat-of-the-pants flying." He paused as he looked Harry in the eyes and, with a slight smile, said: "As I said, this ought to be right up your alley."

Donalson lit a cigarette and offered one to Harry. "Thank you Sir, but I don't smoke."

"Sorry, I forgot. In fact, if I remember correctly, you don't spend any money on cigarettes or booze, and you send practically all your pay home to your mom and wife. I admire that, it tells me you're responsible, though after that Orly affair, I had reason to wonder about you." Donalson paused a few moments to gather his thoughts. "You're from Pennsylvania coal country, right?"

"That's correct, Sir."

"Lots of good folks back where you come from, hard workers, and tough as nails, so I know where you get it."

"Thank-you Sir." Harry tried to conceal his surprise at the compliment but did let a hint of a smile slip. If Donalson noticed, he didn't let on.

They both returned to studying the map.

"Colonel, I'm sure I can locate the airstrip, especially with these topographical features over here being so obvious." Harry pointed to various locations on the map surrounding the landing strip, "The only problem is, my C-47 is missing an engine."

"That's why you'll be flying mine. It's being loaded as we speak and will be ready when you are. And Watson, I'd appreciate returning it to me in one piece, I don't want you running into one of those shell-holes and ripping her up." Donalson smiled and motioned Harry to return to his chair.

Harry sat on the edge of the seat and began looking at a few reconnaissance photos of the landing strip scattered across the desktop. He was still staring at them when Donalson continued.

"There's nobody else I dare send in there, not under these conditions. The weather report calls for continuous fog and rain, without let-up, possibly right through daybreak tomorrow. And as you can see from the map, a precise location of the landing strip isn't exactly clear-cut, but these recon photos are only a day old. Feel free to take them with you. Watson, you're the best damn navigator and foul weather pilot I've got, which is why this critical mission falls to you. We don't want our boys caught by surprise with no fuel for their Sherman tanks. Time is of the essence Watson, any questions?"

While Donalson was speaking, Harry's thoughts were racing. He considered the supplies he'd need; survival kits, firearms, ammo, food, water, bedrolls, and more. Once the essentials were covered, his mind wandered. Supply needs were replaced by an image of a Messerschmitt 109 pouring fire into his plane. Exploding Jerry cans engulfed the cabin, trapping him and Al, a scene interrupted when he realized Donalson was waiting for an answer. Quickly recovering, he replied:

"Just one. Have the troops on the ground been told I could use a little guidance after I've landed?"

"Good question. You can anticipate ground flares, but don't count on it. You're flying right into the front lines, and you just can't be sure what to expect once you're on the ground. If they don't use signal flares, assume it's because it's too dangerous. However, on the bright side, there is a small hangar there. It's a good landmark, but don't be alarmed when you land and see it's occupied by a Messerschmitt 262. It's out of commission, but other than the jet, G2 tells me the Germans have cleared out and believe you should be fine. As usual, maintain strict radio silence because, as you know, the Luftwaffe hasn't exactly given up yet."

"Sir, I'll get the fuel there no sweat, but it might be risky to take-off again if the weather, more specifically, the fog gets too heavy." Harry paused as he further considered the situation. "I might need to delay my return flight and wait for better conditions because the very last thing I want to do is find myself bogged down in the mud, or worse, so I'll play it by ear." Harry paused as another thought came to mind. "Will I be taking out any casualties?"

"No word on casualties, at least not as of now. But if there are casualties to ferry back, you'll be advised where to take them. And Watson, I don't want any more bad weather shenanigans on your part, so use your head. If you find yourself sopped-in, don't attempt to return until it's safe, even if you have a planeload of wounded. Transporting casualties is not a ticket to take unwarranted risks, and by that, I'm referring to your excursion to Orly last month."

Harry stood as Donalson reached across the desk and shook his hand. "Oh, and as far as getting your crew together, don't sweat it, I've attended to that. Good luck, and remember I don't want you doing anything stupid. I want my plane back in one piece and you and your crew with it." Donalson returned to his seat as Harry replied, "Yes Sir!"

It was just past 1600 hours and they'd been flying for more than two hours at altitudes between 200 and 500 feet. Once in a while Harry or Al would spot patches of farm fields and, much to their relief, they occasionally recognized geographical features confirming they were on course. Fog and low-lying clouds eventually merged into one, further hampering their visibility. It had been some time since they last spotted a landmark, and Al was growing more anxious by the moment.

"Harry, did you hear that?" Al said excitedly.

Harry acknowledged overhearing the radio message alerting them a formation of C-47s somewhere "out there" reported they'd been engaged by German fighters and were ducking into the clouds. He cautioned Al to "simmer down", assuring him there was no chance they could be spotted in this "pea soup". Harry recalls making a conscious effort not to reveal so much as a hint of trepidation.

About half an hour after the radio intercept, Al mentioned he couldn't see more than about a mile ahead through the "muck" and wondered if they dared take her a little lower. Al had been making continuous attempts to view the landscape by poking his head out the side window.

At one point, as he was sticking his head through the open side-window, Al shouted he was catching glimpses of what looked to him to be nothing but endless farm fields. His tone of voice conveyed his frustration. He failed to locate any of the landmarks Harry had noted on the map and again urged Harry to take her lower.

Harry's plane, 'Wee Junie', on the homeward leg of a successful supply mission.

Harry said they were already below 300 feet, and as near as he could tell, they should be on top of the landing site any minute. He told Al they didn't dare drop any lower because the recon photos had revealed hills and forested areas surrounded the landing field, so dropping any lower would be a dangerous proposition.

The two men were soon joined by their also antsy crew chief, "Chief," all of whom were intently watching the landscape whenever it would

7

Possibly the airfield and hangar Harry encountered. Note the forest in the background.

appear through occasional openings in the clouds and nearly relentless fog. Suddenly, Al practically jumped out of his seat and excitedly shouted: "Over there, at one o'clock!" He was pointing through the windscreen, excited as a kid who had just hit a home run in his little league game.

"Before you get yourself all riled up, I'm going to circle round first and get us a closer look. Whatever you do, don't lose sight of it!" Harry ordered.

He dipped the right-wing into a hard bank and began to maneuver toward the airstrip, flying a bit south before turning back.

Harry dropped to about 200 feet as they overflew the landing strip, such as it was. Al leaned forward as hard as he could as he searched for bomb craters.

"There's a ton of craters down there. And there's a couple of real doozies near the hangar, so we'd better keep to the left, I think it's our best shot," said Al.

"Got it. I'll just make one more swing around to be sure, then it's time to hold onto your cap!" Harry said.

The radio again sprung to life with another sighting of German fighter planes somewhere in their general vicinity. Al mentioned it would be nice if they had a better idea where the Germans were – it could be a few miles from here, or fifty, "I'd just like to know."

Harry conducted a final fly-over, circled the field, and set up an approach to "take her in on the left side" of the landing strip, which wasn't much more than a mostly flat, grassy field. The bomb craters would have seemed unexpected, save for the appearance of the lone hangar indicating the meadow was an airfield and, therefore, a legitimate military target.

Harry lowered the landing gear and held his breath as he waited to learn whether he had brought them around, in the near-zero visibility, to where they needed to be for a proper landing.

"That a-way!" exclaimed Chief as he pointed straight ahead, directly at the landing strip. "I'll be damned if you don't get us lined up first time, every damn time! Good goin'!"

As they drew closer to the landing strip, it was apparent there was "nary a soul" to be seen. There was no signal flare, let alone any trucks to haul away the Jerry cans. Nobody was rushing out to greet them, which Harry considered to be odd. He'd assumed there'd be some sort of ad-hoc reception waiting for them and found himself growing anxious. He briefly considered the possibility he was putting them down onto the wrong field and fought-off the thought he might be landing behind enemy lines.

Once on the ground, he taxied toward the hangar, being careful to avoid several large shell craters in the process, as both he and Al found it necessary to poke their heads out the side windows to determine what obstacles might be waiting from them. When he was about 50 feet from the front of the hangar, he brought the plane to a halt and ordered Al not to cut the engines just yet.

The recon photos didn't disclose sufficient detail to determine whether the hangar doors were open – which they were. One of the two doors was bent and twisted, while the other door displayed evidence of significant shrapnel damage. Sitting inside was a disabled Messerschmitt 262 "Swallow" jet fighter painted in a summer camouflage pattern. It was the lone occupant of an otherwise empty hangar and served as confirmation that Harry had landed at the correct location.

Harry stared at what was his first "up-close look" at a Messerschmitt 262. He was momentarily transfixed as his eyes locked-in on the four cannons mounted in the nose of the plane. He thought to himself he'd been awful lucky to have never come up against one as he'd heard how fast and well-armed they were. He noticed the sides of the left engine had been stripped open and concluded it was likely undergoing repairs when the German occupants abandoned the place. He mused that they must have been in one hell of a hurry because they didn't take the time to destroy the valuable jet fighter.

Harry knew they were sitting ducks. They remained stationary, engines idling, for what seemed like an hour, but was probably no more than a long minute. Just about the time Harry began thinking they might have a problem, he noticed someone cautiously peeking his head from around the far side of the hangar. When the man recognized the Army Air Force markings on the fuselage he, along with four other infantrymen, came running towards the plane wearing huge smiles. Harry stuck his head out the side window as the first soldier, a very youthful sergeant, ran to his window and looked up at Harry.

"Hey sergeant," called out Harry, "I hope you're expecting me. I've got a planeload of gas I'd like to get rid of lickety-split if you know what I mean."

"That's swell lieutenant! By the way, the name's Bridewell, but everyone calls me Sarge."

"Ok, Sarge." Harry glanced around the field and didn't notice anyone else in the area. "It's just the five of you?"

A Messerschmitt 262, the "Swallow", in summer camouflage similar to the aircraft Harry encountered on the ground. Harry recalls it was the left engine (not the right engine as shown above) that appeared to have been undergoing repairs.

"Not quite Sir. We've got a couple of half-tracks tucked up against the backside of that hangar." He advised Harry each half-track had two men in the cabs, and with the help of Harry's crew, they'd get the plane unloaded pronto.

Harry told him it sounded like a good plan, and then he could get the hell out of there. He expressed the fact he didn't want to get caught on the ground, to which Sarge responded they'd heard planes flying around all day, but he really couldn't tell the difference between "Kraut" plane engines and ours, unless it was "one of them screaming jets".

"I just lay flat and wait till they're gone." His inability to identify various types of aircraft was, he confessed, the reason he waited so long before coming over, and he'd intentionally failed to set up any signal flares in the event that it caught the attention of the Luftwaffe. Sarge said he thought Harry may have been a planeload of "Krauts" flying in so they could grab the jet and that he "wasn't taking no chances". At the sound of truck engines coming to life, Sarge turned and looked toward the far side of the hangar where the first of what would prove to be two half-tracks was appearing from around the corner.

"Where's everyone else? I thought there were tanks around here." Harry asked.

"They've hunkered down about a mile that away," Sarge said as he pointed west.

He explained everyone else was dug in a few hundred yards back, and he and his squad were the only ones around. He beckoned for Harry to come on down, so he could explain the tactical situation.

Harry swiveled around in his seat to face Al and Chief. "I think we'd better chip-in as the man says." No sooner were the words out of his mouth then the skies opened up, and it began to rain with a punishing force, reducing visibility to near-zero. The deluge was accompanied by an unsettling series of nearby lightning strikes, and the thunder was deafening to the point it drowned out the clatter of the still-idling engines. Harry found himself shouting to be heard above the racket as the rain pounded against the metal skin of the plane: "Cut the engines and pray that lightning doesn't blow us to Kingdom come!"

"Right, brakes on, engines off!" Al replied.

Harry quickly worked his way through the narrow opening between the floor-to-ceiling stacks of 5-gallon Jerry cans. Chief opened the hatch for Harry who, without even looking, jumped to the ground, landing directly in the center of a puddle of muddy water.

"Damn! Every time I come to France it rains!" Harry was talking to himself, but Sarge heard him and laughed.

"Sorry lieutenant, they tell me the weather's going to get worse as the day wears on."

Harry watched the half-tracks back up as close as they could to the open hatch. The infantrymen proceeded to quickly form a pair of lines leading from the open hatch to the first half-track while Chief and Harry's radioman, "Sparky", began handing-down Jerry cans, which were passed from man to man for fast loading.

Al, having completed his duties, joined Harry and Sarge, who asked them to take a short walk with him. He said they needed to be apprised of the tactical situation they had flown themselves into. Harry grew concerned when he heard the words "tactical situation", despite the fact the sergeant's body language was relaxed, and his tone of voice was nonchalant.

"Lead the way," Harry said as he pulled his cap down over his brow in an attempt to shield his eyes from the relentless downpour.

Sarge led Harry and Al about 100 yards beyond the hangar where, without saying a word, he dropped to his right knee. They were on the crest of a small knoll that was covered by 4 to 5 feet high stands of willowy grass. Harry and Al, despite the ongoing deluge, followed suit as each man took a knee. Sarge pointed in the direction of a heavily wooded area a few hundred yards distant.

"See that?" He asked.

"Yeah, what of it? Those trees aren't even in my flight path," replied Harry.

He chuckled as if what Harry had just said was laughable, annoying both Harry and Al.

"What's so funny?" Al asked.

"Well, I'll tell you. There's seven German tanks in those woods, and they're backed-up by at least 800 infantry. They've got themselves half-tracks, some artillery, and God only knows what else." He paused to let the information sink in. Harry looked at him, wondering if Sarge was yanking his chain. Before Harry could decide whether Sarge was bullshitting them, the sergeant said:

"Right now those Krauts are probably hunkered down for the night, all warm and cozy in them woods. But come daybreak, you can be damned certain they're going to make a dash for this road and high-tail it east just as fast as they can. You ought to be happy they aren't SS." Sarge paused and, with a sly smile, said, "At least I don't *think* they're SS."

The road to which he referred was not more than 50 yards from where they knelt.

"What? Are you kidding me? 800 Germans, and they've got tanks?" Harry paused to take a breath and said: "Well, if that ain't the kiss-off, I don't know what is."

Harry could barely contain himself as a vision of Colonel Donalson screaming at him when learning his plane had been destroyed by German tanks danced through his mind. The intensity of the downpour was increasing almost as quickly as Harry's discomfort level. Sarge, apparently realizing he may have over-stated the facts said:

"Relax lieutenant. Those Krauts ain't looking for a fight, they just want to get back to their lines 'cause they're cut-off. They probably don't know we're out of fuel here or they might've broken out already. Who knows, maybe they're short of fuel too, which is why I parked the trucks between your plane and the woods so they can't see what the hell we're unloading."

"What do you mean they're cut off? G-2 said nothing about them. And why should I relax?" Harry's voice fully reflected his anxiety.

"Lieutenant, we've got 'em covered on three sides of that forest, but we don't have the tanks we need to flush 'em out because they're out of gas. That's why you're here and not at some cozy pub back in England enjoying some warm English brews with a couple of English dames on each arm. I gotta say, you flyboys have it made. And as for G-2, those guys aren't even going to get their boots muddy, so I wouldn't pay them no heed."

Harry didn't bother to respond as he and Al were staring at the forest. To Harry, all seemed calm enough. There were absolutely no signs of any Germans out there or anything else for that matter.

"It looks quiet enough to me." Al said.

"Well, if you don't believe me…" Sarge didn't finish the thought because Harry cut him off.

"We believe you, but we'll be out of here in short order, so what's it to us?"

Sarge glanced at the sky, looked around the airfield, noticed they were rapidly becoming fogged-in, and visibility was growing tenuous. Large puddles of water were forming on the surface of what had become a water-logged runway, to the point where distinguishing between a puddle and a shell crater filled with water was no longer possible.

"It seems to me like you ought to start thinking about staying the night."

"Stay the night? Are you nuts?" Harry nervously glanced in the direction of the forest. Satisfied all still appeared calm, he realized he'd been so focused on the supposedly German-occupied forest he'd completely failed to recognize how much the weather conditions had deteriorated.

"Right, I see your point. We can bed down in the plane and fly out at first light."

"I wouldn't do that if I were you. If anything goes wrong and it turns into a shooting match, you can be damned certain your plane will be a helluva tempting target for some trigger-happy Kraut."

"So what do you suggest we do? Bed down in the hangar?" Harry nervously glanced at the forest, now just barely visible in the continuing torrential downpour and the onset of an ever-thickening fog. The thunder and lightning combined to create something of a surreal aspect to the situation, causing Harry to experience ever-increasing discomfort. He looked at Al and noticed he had a soggy cigarette hanging from between his lips, telegraphing the fact he was very nervous.

They were accustomed to dodging flak and the occasional German fighter plane, but this was an entirely different situation, a situation he had only a limited ability to control. In the back of his mind he was sincerely hoping Sarge was joking about the Germans, but he certainly appeared to be sincere. Harry decided he had to plan for a worst-case scenario.

Sarge explained the hangar wouldn't be a good place to bivouac either. He told them should the Krauts spot the Messerschmitt in there they'd likely lob a few shells at it. He explained when they received notice to expect a planeload of fuel, they had attempted to close those "damned" doors, but they were too damaged, so there was no way to hide what the Luftwaffe had left behind. He advised Harry he didn't think he had a lot of choices about where to bed down for the night.

"What d'ya mean? What are we going to do?" Al asked.

Making no attempt to hide a broad smile, the sergeant said:

"I'll round-up some shovels for you boys." He then explained Harry and his crew could dig themselves a couple of "nice, cozy foxholes". Sarge indicated they should follow him, and he'd show them a good spot where they could dig in. He warned them: "And by the way, no Boy Scout campfires, it'll draw their attention."

He directed Harry and Al to an area of tall grass and bushes a hundred yards from the plane, but not particularly far removed from the road, the same route the Germans were expected to use in the morning.

"This would be a good spot." He paused and looked around. "You've got yourselves a pretty good field of vision from here. You can see your plane, the hangar, the road and, come dawn, the Germans." Harry noticed Sarge was again making no effort to suppress a wide grin as we he was enjoying the prospect of watching "flyboys" hunkering down in the mud and rain.

"I suggest you gather up your crew while I fetch those shovels for ya." He paused a moment then said: "Hey, lieutenant, I almost forgot. There's a case of French champagne waiting for you on your flight deck, so it's not all bad. Puzzled, Harry asked him where it came from. The sergeant told him it was courtesy of "General George S. Patton himself."

Without waiting for a response, Sarge jogged away in the direction of the hangar while Harry and Al hurried back to the plane where they found Chief and Sparky huddled inside, the unloading accomplished. As they clambered into the cabin, Chief said:

"Please don't tell me we're going to take-off in this muck."

Harry recognized the stress in his voice as he ducked far enough into the cabin to dodge the rain pouring through the open hatch. The fog had cleared, at least for the time being, but had been replaced by high winds driving the rain with ever-increasing force. He couldn't help but notice the cabin reeked of gasoline so they wouldn't have been cooking in there that night, even without the German army camped nearby.

"Hell no, we're not going to attempt a take-off tonight, but let me tell you the alternative is no piece of cake either."

"What do you mean?" Chief asked, his voice revealing more anxiety than usual for him. Sparky, standing alongside Chief, was busy bandaging a small cut on his wrist.

Harry proceeded to fill them in on the situation, and as he pointed towards the forest, Chief and Sparky poked their heads out the hatch and took a long stare at the not-so-distant tree line. Recalling the Orly incident, Harry decided to radio the base and advise them of the situation. The four men then slogged out to where Sarge suggested they dig a foxhole and found him patiently waiting for them, four shovels lying in a heap at his feet.

"Hey, what's the pea shooter for?" Sarge pointed to the rifle slung over Al's shoulder.

"If the Krauts get close enough, I intend to plug a few of 'em." Al replied. "I might never get another chance!"

Sarge disapprovingly shook his head from side to side. "If you take a pot-shot at the Krauts when all they're trying to do is get the hell away from here, they'll likely take that as an invitation to stand and fight. You've got to understand those guys have at least seven tanks, maybe 800 men and some armored half-tracks. Just what do ya think might happen if they figured they had to fight their way out?" He stared at Al for a moment and didn't wait for an answer. "Let me tell you what'd happen. They'd blast your foxholes, your plane, that hangar, and everything else in sight. Then they'd still run east, but some of you wouldn't be leaving here, not ever."

"Don't worry Sarge, nobody's going to even think about taking any pot-shots." Harry placed his hand on his holstered pistol and said, "And this baby is staying where she is, you can count on it."

"Great," he said , "just be smart and stay low. Now I think it's time to leave you to your first-class accommodations."

"Wait!" Exclaimed Al. "How deep should we dig the holes?"

Sarge smiled, "It's never too deep, or deep enough." He glanced at the dark grey and purple sky, rain plummeting across his face as he did so, shrugged his shoulders and said, "I'll see you boys in the morning!" He trotted away and quickly disappeared. The wind had suddenly decreased considerably, replaced by thick fog.

Despite the fact Harry harbored some doubts about Sarge's story, he ordered his crew to start digging as it wasn't going to stay light forever.

After about an hour of continuous excavation, Chief was complaining that the more they dug, the more the water poured in. Though he was not even waist deep in the foxhole he and Sparky had been digging, Chief exclaimed they had dug about as deep as they could. He said the water was piling up faster than they could dig, so it made no sense to continue. He threw his shovel off to the side as if it were an exclamation point.

Harry and Al had made only slightly better headway with their foxhole. One of the problems they faced, regardless of the depth of their accommodation, was the fact none of them could sit down, let alone lie down because of all the (as Al put it) "God awful water!"

By the time darkness set in, the men were cold, wet, and thoroughly miserable. A dinner consisting of cold C-Rations didn't help their morale. Al suggested they make a little fire in the plane's cabin so he could brew some coffee, but Sparky reminded him that some of the Jerry cans had been leaking, so it would definitely not be a good idea.

For Harry, just the thought of having a hot cup of anything was enough to warm him up a little as the men took turns voicing their particular gripes. Eventually, Harry felt it necessary to squash all further talk of making a fire in either the plane or the hangar by telling them any movement they make could bring the Germans down on them.

When Sparky complained he couldn't get comfortable, Harry's response was: "We're just going to have to learn to sleep while we squat. If we lie down in this water and muck, we'll all wake up with pneumonia. Instead of complaining, just think about how good the champagne's going to taste when we get back." Harry squatted to demonstrate the technique. "Just make the best of it because it can't rain forever."

The four men proceeded to crouch in their respective, water-logged foxholes, a steady stream of rain assuring them of a thoroughly uncomfortable overnight bivouac. The rain stopped around 0200 hours, and occasional breaks in the clouds and fog allowed Harry to stargaze.

Stooping, knee-deep in water, soaked from the hours-long downpour, and feeling utterly miserable, his thoughts drifted to whether there was any such almighty entity as God. He couldn't suppress a smile when he remembered Golden Lang told him he was convinced he'd seen God sitting in the instructor's cockpit during his first solo flight.

Then he considered a recent incident when he narrowly escaped taking a direct hit from German Flak because he "had a sudden feeling" he should change altitude. He thought God may have been whispering into his ear, telling him to drop the nose, for moments after he did so, there was a shell burst just above them, precisely where they would have been. As he stared at the stars, he decided to write himself a "Letter to God" when he returned to base. Finishing the thought, he whispered aloud, "God willing." Suddenly, the stars disappeared, swallowed up by a new blanket of fog. He closed his eyes and did his best to get some shut-eye.

The first traces of sunrise were finally making themselves evident when a consistent breeze kicked in and began to dissipate the fog. It was good news overhead too, the pre-dawn sunlight was revealing partially broken cloud cover. The runway was still heavily puddled but was looking more encouraging by the minute.

All of them were shivering, soaking wet and hungry when the distinctive roar of tank engines warming up demanded their immediate attention. They carefully peeked over the top of the mounds of dirt in front of their foxholes. But there were no tanks, or Germans, to be seen.

Harry hoped Patton's refueled tanks, bivouacked somewhere to their west, would show up, and that they were responsible for making the racket, not the Germans. The clamor of engines warming up was coming from the enemy-infested woods, but it quickly became apparent that the refueled tanks weren't interested in an early morning fight with a group of desperate Germans.

For the moment, nothing was moving anywhere within their view as they remained crouched in the foxholes, facing the forest, waiting for the Germans. Making a run to the plane and attempting a take-off seemed like a potentially good idea, but Sarge's warning from the previous day kept them in place. Harry anticipated a quick and quiet enemy withdrawal and hoped the Germans would proceed in the manner Sarge had predicted. He also knew they couldn't just switch on the plane's engines and fly away. They'd need to warm them up first, which would make a lot of noise and could draw unwanted attention.

Al asked Harry whether he thought the Krauts would come towards them, his voice cracking from the cold, damp conditions, amplified by the fact he was scared.

"Here they come!" Chief shouted as he pointed towards the middle of the forest where the barrel of a German Mark IV tank was breaking through the tree line. Soon it was followed by six more tanks, one of which had a fixed turret, something Harry had not seen before. There were also several armored half-tracks, one towing a Nebelwerfer, a much-feared German rocket launcher. There was even a twin-barreled anti-aircraft battery mounted on, what looked to Harry to be, a modified tank.

Harry breathed a sigh of relief when he noticed an absence of the dreaded Tiger tanks. He heard they were equipped with an uncannily accurate and

The above scene is not all that different from what unfolded only yards away from where Harry and his flight crew were dug in. A German tracked vehicle is towing a Nebelwerfer rocket launcher. Harry recalls seeing something very similar to the above that early morning in France.

long-range 88-millimeter cannon. He learned a great deal about them from D-Day glider pilots and had no desire to ever see one that wasn't knocked out of commission.

As the Germans progressed toward the road, Harry observed each tank was carrying at least nine or ten infantrymen who were hanging onto the tops of the turrets as they bounced over the uneven terrain. When the tanks completely cleared the forest they fanned-out, forming a horizontal line, and slowly worked their way across the meadow lying between the forest and the road; the road that would take them east to their companions.

For Harry, watching the Germans advance directly towards him was as scary as anything he'd ever experienced. There was no guarantee they'd turn onto the road and go east. They could just as easily proceed to roll-over Harry's position and blast Colonel Donalson's C-47, the hangar, and anything else they decided to blow apart.

The first tank reached the side of the road, pulled up onto it, made a partial left-turn, and came to a complete stop. Harry was wondering what the tank commander was planning when its turret began circling towards them. He gulped and found himself momentarily spellbound as the tank's turret continued turning until it faced directly down the road, to the west. For a brief moment, Harry had found himself staring directly into the barrel, a moment when he unconsciously held his breath. With the gun barrel safely facing westward, the tank let loose a shot that shook the ground and reverberated through Harry's chest. It remained stationary for not more than ten seconds before the turret slowly swung back to the forward position, and the tank began to slowly rumble away to the east.

Additional infantry was jogging close behind each tank. None of whom so much as glanced in Harry's direction; they were looking straight ahead, at the back-end of their respective tanks. Al picked up his rifle and took aim at one of the soldiers riding atop the last of the tanks. Just in time, Harry noticed and knocked the rifle away from him as hard as he could.

"Are you nuts? You want to get us all killed?" Harry's voice was nowhere near as commanding as he intended, the result of many hours of enforced silence in the cold, however, his anger was evident enough as Al meekly lowered his head and said nothing. He looked down at his rifle, mostly obscured by the muddy water accumulated in the bottom of the foxhole, and mumbled something about needing to clean it. He made no further effort to fire at the retreating Germans.

They spent the next thirty minutes observing the German's withdrawal until the last infantryman was safely out of sight. Harry stood, stretched

A German Heavy Tank Destroyer emerges from a forest. Harry recalls seeing a similar tank among the retreating Germans.

his legs for a few moments, and began walking to the plane. Without saying a word, Al, Chief, and Sparky fell in behind him. Harry made a quick inspection of the ground conditions so he could be reasonably sure he wouldn't sink the colonel's plane into a muddy quagmire. Satisfied the conditions, though marginal, were acceptable, he conducted his pre-flight check and made ready to "get the Sam Hill out of there."

Twenty minutes later, they were lifting-off and steering a course back to England, the sun burning brightly. They didn't see Sarge or anyone else before leaving and wondered if they had withdrawn during the night, just in case they were wrong about the German's intentions. All four of them were still sopping wet but were so happy to be in the air again that nobody voiced even the smallest complaint. About thirty minutes into the return flight Harry said, "Well, I guess this turned out to be just another dull supply run." He smiled as he looked at Al, adjusted his course, and kept "pouring on the coal".

"Yeah, these milk-runs are getting a bit boring," Al replied. He flashed a big smile before returning his attention to the matters at hand, his muddy rifle stowed alongside his seat, a reminder of their hair-raising experience.

Chapter 2

Courtney, Pennsylvania
December 1932

Two days before Christmas Olga Watson, hands firmly placed on each hip, was slowly shaking her head back and forth as she stood in the kitchen of her 50-year-old two-story frame residence. Her once jet-black hair was forced into a tight bun, and a bright red scarf helped keep her warm in the chilly house. Olga's still-youthful face was furrowed into a deep frown as she took stock of the rapidly dwindling and critical household coal supply.

Several empty, tall black buckets sat alongside the kitchen stove, along with another that was only half full. For the Watson family, their stove was more than a cooking appliance. It was the sole provider of heat for the entire first level of the home. It was also the source of the wondrous aromas of simmering stews and home-baked bread that greeted Mr Watson when he returned home from working in the coal mine each wintry evening.

Realizing there was only enough fuel to last one more day, at best, she called for her 10-year-old son Harry Junior. In a matter of moments, he was standing before her, smiling as usual. She asked him to go and fetch the sled from the shed out back and all the buckets he could fit atop it and get dressed because they were headin' out. She didn't need to tell him where they were going; this wasn't the first time during that particularly nasty winter she'd made such a request.

Blond-haired, blue-eyed Harry Junior was short for his age, slender built, but exceptionally strong. He was the second of seven children and the oldest boy. As he prepared to pull on his winter clothing he didn't bother to remove his shoes and instead firmly shoved his feet into the boots. They were worn-out hand-me-downs from an uncle and several sizes too large. Not removing his shoes resulted in a near-perfect fit. After grabbing his only winter coat, a pair of gloves, and a hat missing one of its ear warmers, he raced out to the shed.

As he opened the unpainted, worse-for-wear wooden door, he paused and checked the weather conditions. The snow had been falling for hours and appeared to be developing into a full-fledged snowstorm with steadily increasing winds. He noticed there were already several inches of fresh snow on top of roughly 1 foot of prior accumulation. Harry liked snow and snowstorms, but the thought of pulling a sled loaded with coal across fresh snow put a slight damper on his enthusiasm.

The shed was windowless, the sole source of lighting being the open door. Unfortunately, the sled was secured on a nearby wall, a full foot above Harry's head. Undeterred, Harry stood on his toes and, using both hands, carefully guided it to the ground. He set it just inside the doorway. Always the thinker, he also grabbed a wood-handled garden pick and tossed it into the sled.

His father had constructed an enclosure around the entire sled by cutting off the front part of a large corrugated tin tub. Thus modified, they could put the sled to use for hauling groceries and supplies from the local general store, 2 miles distant. Harry would occasionally allow some of his younger siblings to crawl onto the sled, and he'd then pull them around the yard as fast as he could. But on that particular day there'd be no time for fun as it was already pushing half-past one in the afternoon. Nearing the winter equinox, the sky grew dark early in southwestern Pennsylvania, and he knew he had no time to waste.

Harry grabbed six beat-up, semi-rusted 5-gallon buckets and loaded them into the sled upside down to keep the snow out. He took the rope attached to the front of the sled and slipped it over his head. Then he slid it under his arms and around his chest as if he was a horse pulling a sleigh. Harry dragged the sled to the front of the house where his mom was waiting, an ancient kerosene lantern in her right hand.

She told him they were going to old shaft number nine to fetch us some coal. Old shaft number nine had been closed for decades and nearly sealed tight by a partial collapse. However, she'd calculated there was enough room for Harry to wiggle across the top of the heap of rubble and crawl into the coal mine where he could fill the buckets with as much coal as he could scrounge. Their destination was nearly 2 miles from their home. They didn't dilly-dally around, and immediately set out.

The storm quickly intensified, and Harry found himself pressing a hand over his exposed ear in an attempt to keep it warm as they purposefully trekked forward, directly into a blisteringly frosty wind. By the time they reached the mine shaft, the snow had been whipped into an imposing drift, burying the entire entry. The small opening at the top of the shaft Olga had been counting on was a sheet of white. Nary a hint of the mine's entry remained. Olga paused and considered whether her memory of an opening large enough for Harry to wiggle through was correct.

Harry pulled the old sled as close as he could to the snow-covered pile of stone and dirt blocking the mine opening, dropped the rope, grabbed the pick and one bucket. He said, "Don't worry, mum."

He clawed forward a few feet, slipped back a couple of feet, over and over, until he finally reached the top of the shaft. Harry poked his hands around until he brushed enough snow away, revealing a narrow opening into the dark mine shaft. He looked at his mom and watched as she cupped her hands around a matchstick, struck it, and lit the lantern.

She tossed him the pick which he used to snare the lantern. With the lantern perilously perched on the business-end of the pick, he carefully lowered it into the shaft. She tossed him one of the buckets, which he pushed through the opening, before deciding to slide in himself. He was halfway through the narrow opening when he realized he was stuck, at which time he panicked.

Olga couldn't hear his screams over the steady roar of the storm, complicated by the fact he was screaming into the mine shaft. It was only the fact he was vigorously shaking his feet up and down that caused her to finally realize he was trapped.

A partially blocked coal mine not unlike the shaft into which Harry ventured.

As she frantically crawled up the slope, she found herself fighting against a fresh layer of slick snow. Olga's boots were even older than Harry's, and the worn soles caused her to slide back several times before finally making it to the top of the rubble where Harry, still stuck, continued to howl and wildly kick his feet into the air.

"Quit yer complaining!" Olga called, and told him to hold his legs as straight as he could. She began pushing him by the bottoms of his boots until he finally fell into the mine. In a few moments she breathed a sigh of relief when he poked his head through the narrow opening and said "Fetch me them other buckets mum."

Harry lined the buckets at the base of the entry and was quite pleased with himself when he discovered a large nail protruding from an overhead wood beam, from which he hung the lantern. With the lamp in place above, he proceeded to fill the first bucket with chunks of loose coal he discovered near the entry.

Rather than venture further into the mine shaft as he had done in the past at other mines, Harry reckoned he'd determine how difficult it might

Harry's family home. Young Harry is the first boy from the left.

be to chisel some coal from the walls with his pick. The sides of the shaft appeared to be solid black coal. Ever the optimist, he thought he might be able to mine enough coal near the entrance to fill the buckets without going too deep inside of the long-abandoned shaft.

He chose a spot in a wall where there appeared to be a large crevice at the extreme upper end of his reach. Harry drew the pick backward as far as he could and drove it forward with all his strength, directly into the center of the crevice. He was shocked when a chunk of coal about 4 feet wide splintered from the wall forcing him to quickly jump back as it fell to the ground with what he considered to be an unusually soft thud.

Much to his delight, the coal split into several pieces. He proceeded to break them into small chunks with his pick and quickly filled two more buckets. Harry was very pleased with himself for in the space of about 15 minutes, he'd filled three of the six buckets.

Despite his initial success, it was almost an hour later when he passed the six buckets bristling with coal to his mother and quickly scampered down to join her. In the late afternoon darkness they each grabbed the rope and began pulling the sled home together.

While they labored through the wind and blowing snow, Harry couldn't help but wonder why his father and his uncles always complained about how hard it was to mine coal for a living. He found it to be relatively easy and a bit of fun. In a few years he'd experience life in a working coal mine first hand and change his mind.

Chapter 3

Growing up

Three miles north of the town of Monongahela, which is home to the only high school in the area, sits Courtney, Pennsylvania. The Monongahela River, a major waterway, runs alongside the town and provides a source of recreation. With a population of only 382, there wasn't much to Courtney in the 1930s other than a church and a small general store. Pittsburgh, which by then had earned the dubious title of "The Dark City" because of its severe air pollution, was about 22 miles north and easily the largest city in the state, outside of Philadelphia.

Coal mining, upon which the steel mills of Pittsburgh relied, had been the nearly single source of income for the population of Courtney and the surrounding towns since long before the Civil War. As a result, the regional economy was not at all diversified. Instead, a very limited job market, utterly dependent upon the coal industry, developed. As long as coal was in high demand, the local economy boomed.

The Roaring Twenties had ushered in an era of slackening demand for Pennsylvania coal and a concomitant drop in coal prices. The result was a startling loss of coal mining jobs and severe reductions in wages paid to the miners lucky enough to retain their positions. To the local population, it appeared as if the entire Pennsylvania coal mining industry was on the verge of collapse. While most of the country was flourishing, the Pennsylvania coal mining towns, including Courtney, languished in poverty.

The Great Depression further aggravated what had already become a dire economic situation. At times some of Harry's family members worked in the coal mines, not for money, but for coal to heat their homes and to cook food in their coal-fired stoves. In their desperation, they considered themselves lucky to have any work at all, for getting paid in coal also gave them a product they could barter. Harry was still too young to fully appreciate what was transpiring all around him.

Harry's parents met under particularly unique circumstances. One summer day in 1916, Olga, who lived in Coal Center, Pennsylvania, wrote her name and address on a piece of newspaper, along with a little information about herself, placed the note into a bottle, sealed it, and threw the bottle into the nearby Monongahela River. She was 16 years old.

About 30 miles downstream, Harry's father-to-be – also named Harry – was swimming in the Monongahela when his head struck something hard. It was the bottle containing Olga's note. He was quite taken by what she'd written and, being too far away to visit, chose to write her a letter.

His initial letter quickly developed into a weekly exchange. Over time they became intimately interested in each other, though they had yet to meet. A full year passed before they managed to get together in person, and it didn't take long before they knew they'd spend the rest of their lives together.

Olga and Harry were wed in 1920, following an honorable discharge from his service as a bugler in the United States Army during World War I. In 1921 they had a daughter, Ethel, and Harry Junior was born about eighteen months later in 1922.

The Watson family stuck together no matter how bad the economy might have been, and each night the entire family sat down to eat dinner, no matter how basic it might be. Harry's parents made a point of eating and praying as a family unit, though Harry admits he pretended to be praying when he was, more likely, kicking one of his siblings under the table.

Harry had a handful of chores to perform, mostly to do with keeping the stove stoked in the winter. His father taught him how to "bank down" the

Harry's father (first row-center) was an army bugler in WW I deployed to France.

burning coals each night so they wouldn't burn out before morning. Harry was also charged with scavenging the requisite newspaper and kindling to start the fires in the second-story fireplace. He had an additional menial but necessary chore: fetching water into the house from the well, without regard to the weather, as the house lacked indoor plumbing.

The chores, though simple, provided Harry with a sense of self-worth. He took pride in performing them and viewed the tasks as a way he could make a difference for his family and leave his parents with a little extra, and precious, free time.

His responsibilities didn't consume much of his day, leaving him with plenty of opportunities to venture outside and have fun with his best friend, Kenny. Though Kenny attended the local Catholic school, he was "a bit of a devil" and led them into some dangerous explorations.

Sometimes they hitched rides in empty boxcars, then caught a return train to get home. Harry fondly recalls they always made sure to know where the "Cinder Dicks" were hiding out, looking for hobos catching illegal rides. They'd both heard stories about how extremely violent the "Cinder Dicks" could be when they found someone riding on one of their trains; the two boys had no intention of experiencing having their guts kicked out and steered clear of them.

In the summertime, they enjoyed skinny-dipping in the Monongahela River whenever the mood struck, which was often. Their favorite adventure was to grab hold of a passing barge and climb aboard for a ride. Up-river or down-river, it didn't matter. The tugboat pilots would wave at them and swear they were going to teach them a lesson, but they were helpless to do much about it. Harry and Kenny considered aggravating the tugboat pilots as part of the fun. The only problem with grabbing onto barges was that, in the process of latching onto a ride, they would become caked in oil. It was tough for them to wash off and proved problematic for Harry when attempting to explain to his mother how he came to be in such an oily state.

The fact he was putting himself in danger each time he climbed onto a barge, or a train, never occurred to him. When a neighbor told his father he'd seen young Harry and a friend hitching a ride on a river barge, his father scolded him and ordered him never to do it again. Harry, however, was a bit incorrigible and proceeded to engage in the newly prohibited activity the very next day. When he looks back now, he marvels at how he managed to avoid severe injury or death. Harry never experienced an aversion to risk-taking, a trait that would bring him near a court-martial later in life.

GROWING UP

As long as he was healthy, the lack of money didn't really mean very much to young Harry. However, when he was 12 years old, he learned a hard lesson about money and what it could mean to his quality of life.

Harry was suffering badly from an infected tooth. It was swelling and distorting the entire left side of his face, giving him a rather frightening appearance. His parents whisked him to the nearest dentist in the neighboring town of Monongahela, who examined young Harry and pronounced that the tooth had to come out.

The dentist explained it would cost "four bits" (50 cents) for him to pull the tooth. He went on to tell his parents if they didn't want Harry to suffer more than necessary, he'd need to be paid an additional four bits. For a total of one dollar, he would inject an anesthetic before pulling the tooth, and Harry would experience no pain.

Harry's dad yanked the pockets of his overalls inside out, revealing two quarters. The dentist took the money, stuffed it into one of his own pockets,

The Courtney baseball team posed before a game on June 11, 1939. 16-year-old Harry is in the second row, the second from the right.

reached for some "really scary-looking pliers", ordered Harry's dad to grab hold of Harry's shoulders, and promptly pulled the tooth. To this day, Harry remembers how much it hurt and how badly he wished he had the extra four bits.

Before the tooth-pulling episode, Harry had never paid much heed to his family's tough economic times. The lack of money was just a fact of life, and there was nothing he could do about it. Nobody among his friends came from a family economically any better off than his. But the lack of four bits for an injection of pain killer did begin to instill in Harry a desire to do better for himself.

Harry's attitude regarding their economic straits permanently changed in June 1940, following his graduation from high school. In previous summers, Harry had managed to make a little extra money for the family by performing odd jobs here and there whenever someone might need a hand and was willing to pay for it. That summer, however, he took a job in one of the coal mines; his family had become particularly hard-pressed, and he desperately wanted to help.

He knew what the inside of an abandoned coal mine looked like but was not prepared for the shock of an active, large-scale coal mining operation. Witnessing the men coming off the shift ahead of his, covered in black soot, and looking exhausted was appalling and made him seriously consider whether he had made the right decision.

Making matters worse, the only way he could land the job in the first place was to work in exchange for coal rather than for money. But he knew his mom was desperate, and he was anxious to uphold his role within the household, so he did it. All summer long, he sweated day by day deep inside a coal mine. It wasn't long before he decided there was no way in hell he'd spend his life earning a living the way his dad, granddad, great-granddad and all of his uncles had done.

When his summer stint in the coal mine was over, he made himself a solemn vow never to step into a coal mine again. His problem was trying to figure a way to escape the coal mines, something nobody in his family had yet to accomplish. It appeared to be an impossible undertaking.

One night he confessed to his mom he couldn't face a lifetime in the coal mines and needed to figure a way out. The two of them sat on the living room sofa and thought about it for a little while when his mom suddenly blurted out, "Harry, there ain't but one way out of here and that's the military!"

It was as if someone lifted the weight of the world from his shoulders. He'd long admired the men who flew airplanes in World War I and had seen the exciting Douglas Fairbanks Jr. movie *The Dawn Patrol*, which was a matinee mainstay at the nearby movie theatre on numerous occasions. Until that moment, sitting on the sofa with his mom, he'd never considered the possibility he might become a pilot, because the cost of lessons was entirely beyond his financial resources.

Harry realized the military would not only train him to fly, but they'd also pay him to do so. Once resolved to his new future, his family's poverty-stricken situation became a little easier to endure. As they sat together that fateful night, he made his mom a promise. He said no matter what, he'd send her part of his earnings every payday for the rest of his life. And he did.

It was early August 1940, and Harry would be turning 18 years of age in October. He needed to bide his time until his 18th birthday as returning to the coal mine was, in his opinion, not an option. Following up on his mom's advice, he did some library research, which made him all the more dead-set on becoming an Army Aviator.

Harry decided to circle his birthday on the large Pennsylvania Railroad calendar his mom hung on a wall in their kitchen as a constant reminder of his new life-career goal. But when he looked at the calendar, he realized his birthday, the 20th, fell on a Sunday. He circled Monday, October 21 1940, instead, because the recruiting station was closed on Sundays. Harry figured there was no time to lose and began planning how he would get himself to the United States Army Air Corps recruiting station in Pittsburgh, more than 20 miles away.

Early on the morning of October 21, he used some of the precious money he had saved up since high school graduation and boarded the trolley to Pittsburgh, the location of the nearest army recruiting office. His excitement was thoroughly dashed when the recruiting sergeant advised him the army had no openings at the time, but he'd let him know just as soon as something opened up. He gave Harry the impression it would be just a matter of a few weeks, at most, and proceeded to direct Harry to take a seat and complete the necessary paperwork. Knowing he had officially commenced the enlistment process was little consolation to a very disappointed Harry as he rode the trolley back home. He didn't look forward to conveying the bad news to his mom.

Harry returned to the recruiting office for a second time in November only to be told there were still no openings. He was advised it was only a matter of a couple more weeks. He returned, yet again, just before Christmas. The sergeant scolded him to "hold onto your britches", because the army doesn't move at any speed other than "army speed." Harry returned home.

It wasn't as if he'd been sitting around the house all day, wasting time. He set a series of trapping lines to catch possums, weasels, skunks, and muskrats, the generic term for the mammals being "polecats". The polecats fetched him 15 cents per hide. He used the money to cover the cost of his round-trips to the recruiting office and help purchase groceries.

He also managed to land a job in a local junkyard paying him 30 cents an hour. His first paycheck, following a full forty-hour-long work week, netted him $11.88; 12 cents had been deducted for Social Security taxes.

He took $5.00 from his first paycheck and sought a dentist for some repair work he needed. Unlike when he was 12, he had the additional money for the use of a pain killer. He still gets chills when recalling that the drill the dentist used was foot-powered and would speed up or slow down depending upon how fast the dentist pumped his foot. At the time, it felt to him as if the dentist was drilling for hours, though he thinks it was only a few minutes.

First thing on the morning of Friday, January 10 1941, Harry, accompanied by his mother, made yet another visit to the recruiting station. The cost of the disappointing round trips was taking a toll on his resources, and his mother had "plum run out of patience" with the Army Air Corps. When the sergeant he'd seen in earlier visits began to give her the same answer he'd been handing her son, she cut him off in mid-sentence, instructed Harry to "sit down in that chair", and proceeded to take up a position in the seat alongside his. She announced they weren't "going nowhere" until he gave them a "solid date" when they'd accept her son into the Air Corps. She scolded the sergeant: "It had better be real soon!"

It wasn't long before the sergeant realized she wasn't kidding. He left the room for a little while, and when he returned, handed her a piece of paper bearing Harry's reporting date, time, and location.

Friday morning, January 17 1941, Harry was standing at the streetcar stop to take him to Pittsburgh, where he was to report for active duty. His mom handed him two dollars, which was all the money she had. The two dollars, along with the clothes on his back, represented the sum-total of Harry's possessions. She planted a kiss on his right cheek, bid him farewell, and told him in no uncertain terms that he'd better not forget their home address as she expected Harry to write home "a lot".

He was sworn into the service at the Pittsburgh recruiting office and placed onto a train bound for Denver, Colorado, later the same day. It was the first time he'd ever left the state and certainly had no idea he would one day be routinely circling the world at the controls of a four-engine plane, though he certainly did dream of the possibility.

The train had a flock of recruits aboard, including three other young men from the general vicinity of Courtney. Harry quickly befriended them and found some comfort in the fact he wasn't the only person traveling from their little corner of Pennsylvania for the first time.

Chapter 4

"You're in the Army Air Corps Now"

Before Harry was sworn into the Army Air Corps at the Pittsburgh recruiting station, he was handed a test and directed to take a seat. He was given a lead pencil, told to take his time and do his best. Nobody had ever said a word about taking a test, so he was surprised, yet he didn't ask any questions. After he returned the completed test sheets, he was ushered into a room with a few other recruits for the official Swearing-In Ceremony. No explanation about the need for the test was offered, nor did he even think to ask.

The train ride to Denver immediately followed. After he'd been traveling about an hour he learned from another recruit that the test he had taken back at the recruiting station was to determine his "level of intelligence". He'd always been a good student, so he didn't worry about it. He would soon forget about the test entirely. Harry was not the worrying type and was more of a forward-looking individual than most people from his town. He was looking ahead to flying planes rather than the pending boot camp.

They made numerous stops along the way to Colorado as they picked up additional recruits, along with civilian passengers. Harry enjoyed the food and scenery, especially when the flat corn and wheat fields began to change to rolling hills and eventually gave way to mountains. As he looked through the windows, he thought about his future and considered the train trip to represent the actual beginning point of his life's adventure. Harry and his three new friends were very excited when they finally arrived at the Denver train station. As they stood in line to exit the railcar, he could hardly control his breathing as he'd never been quite so excited in his life. He said he was more exhilarated than when he'd hitched a ride on a boxcar.

Harry and a few dozen additional recruits disembarked onto the platform and were immediately confronted by three uniformed men. The youngest of the three, a corporal, ordered the recruits to form up, two-deep, with their backs facing the train. It took the recruits a little while to comply, but after a couple of minutes shuffling around, they were ready for an impromptu inspection.

The uniformed men positioned themselves in front of the loosely assembled recruits. One of the three stepped forward and introduced himself as being their lieutenant. He proceeded to introduce a sergeant and the sergeant's corporal. The lieutenant took a step back and motioned toward the sergeant, who was the tallest of the three, and immediately took over the proceedings.

Harry considered him to be old enough to have participated in World War I. He also noticed the chevron on the sergeant's shirt sleeves had extra stripes connecting the top of the chevron to the bottom but was one stripe short of being a perfect connection. He would soon learn the patch meant he was a sergeant, first class, and a person to be reckoned with. For the moment, all he knew was the man appeared to be "hard-boiled" and in a bad mood, sort of like his dad following a particularly hard day in the mine, only worse. The sergeant stood in front of the group as he quietly looked up and down the rows, slowly shaking his head back and forth in disapproval.

He came to a halt, stood straight as an arrow, and belted out, "You tramps look like a bunch of Okies standing around looking for a hand-out." He paused, but only for a moment as he stared at the group as a whole, a menacing scowl on his face. "Stand at attention! You're in the Army Air Corps now, so act like it!"

Harry recalls being so startled he jumped backward, nearly pushing the man behind him off the train platform and onto the tracks. All of them quietly stood at attention for what, to Harry, seemed like half an hour. The sergeant strolled up and down, taking just enough time to look each man in the eye, if only for an uncomfortable second or two. Sometimes he made comments about a particular recruit's appearance, forcing Harry to hold back a laugh, while other times, the sergeant simply stared, which is what he did when he looked down at Harry.

After what to Harry felt like an eternity, the sergeant backed off a step and ordered them to "Right face!" He proceeded to march them to a waiting bus, which took them to Lowry Airfield. Upon arriving at the airbase, the group was marched to a barracks building. Harry gave the barracks the once over and decided it appeared to be "brand, spankin' new".

The barracks could accommodate more than 3,000 men, and Harry was astonished by its size. He thought to himself there must be "a trainload more recruits coming soon", because the place was half-empty. He quickly discovered his new surroundings were just about as comfortable as being back home, only a whole lot newer, and there was a lot of work required to make sure things were always "spanking clean and neat".

MIDNIGHT FLIGHT TO NUREMBERG

In the years before 1938, Lowry Field had been barely more than a small, sleepy airstrip. The facility began to change in 1938 when the dirt runway was extended and paved, signaling a period of ever-expanding aerial operations. There was an old, out-of-use sanatorium complex located on the grounds which had been converted to serve as the army post's new headquarters. At the same time modernization work was progressing on the sanatorium, the army began construction of an expansive barracks building, which is where Harry was bunked. The barracks had been completed only months before Harry's arrival and explained the reason for it being more than half-empty.

Most of his contemporaries used their free time in Denver. Harry had a different itinerary, he spent his spare time making friends with the aircraft mechanics who, in turn, gave him practical lessons in the nuts and bolts of an aircraft. Without realizing it, he was giving himself a head-start on the U.S. Army Air Corps Ground School.

The ground crews were friendly and eagerly demonstrated how the flaps, rudder, and ailerons worked, what moving them in different directions would do while in flight, and their relationships with the stick and the pedals. Harry would spend time in his bunk, lying on his back, eyes closed as he imagined sitting in front of a plane's controls and taking imaginary flights under all manner of flying conditions. The practice became part of his nighttime routine.

Harry, along with every other recruit, had to first make it through boot camp which, in 1940, lasted about eight weeks. The thin, mile-high air never bothered Harry very much, though he witnessed quite a few of his pals "heaving out their breakfasts", following the forced marches that were part of the morning regimen.

Boot Camp included instruction in military discipline, close-order drills, learning rudimentary first aid techniques for battlefield applications, a great deal of physical training, military tactics, and the use and care of all manner of weapons. Harry appreciated the breadth of the training regimen but believed too much time was being devoted to physical conditioning drills.

He had been the star of his high school track team, so conditioning wasn't an issue and he felt bored with it. In letters to his mother, he complained he'd joined the army to gain a chance to fly. Running laps, in his opinion, wasn't getting him any closer to his goal of earning his pilot wings. Harry, however, kept his displeasure to himself, the last thing he desired was to do anything that might rile-up the sergeant. In fact, just the thought of getting him upset caused Harry to consciously reign in some of his risk-taking instincts.

Harry was transferred to Barksdale Field outside Shreveport, Louisiana, in 1941, after he tested very well in a series of vocational testing and scored an IQ of 161. He was assigned to the 383rd School Squadron, where, based on his test results, he was assigned to a specialty and educated in advanced statistical data while continuing with the usual army training regimen.

When he arrived at Barksdale, the airstrip was still under construction and wasn't completed until the middle of 1941. On December 7 1941, Harry was performing kitchen police duty in the officer's mess when news spread of the Japanese surprise attack at Pearl Harbor. He remembers thinking, "Here I am with my elbows buried in soap suds while the Japs are bombing the heck out of us over in Hawaii."

The slow progress he'd experienced in his efforts to become a pilot was even more difficult for him to accept, given the dramatic events in the Pacific. There would soon be a flood of newspaper and radio reports supplemented by newsreels projected in the base theatre describing how both the Japanese and Germans were making devastating use of airpower.

He grew "antsier by the day" as he accomplished every task he was asked to do while he patiently awaited reassignment. There was little in the way of entertainment, so, just as he did at Lowry, he spent his spare moments hanging around the airplane mechanics and learning how critical they were in keeping the planes in tip-top condition. He admired them for their tireless dedication. Once in the European Theatre he continued the practice; his mechanics could be the difference between life and death and he made a point of befriending them.

In March 1941, Congress announced a goal of training as many as 30,000 pilots annually representing a dramatic increase in the number of army pilots at the time. To achieve this, The Army Aviation Cadet Act, Public Law 97, was signed by President Roosevelt on June 3 1941. The program created a grade of "Aviation Cadet". It stated, "Male citizens of the United States may enlist as aviation cadets," and included men already enlisted in the U.S. Army. The new law was a perfect vehicle for Harry to, literally, get his aviation career off the ground.

He quickly applied for inclusion in the cadet program, specifically, as an "Aviation Cadet (pilot and bombardier)." It was a program where raw recruits with the requisite talent and brains would be trained to be officer/ pilots. The tests he'd taken at the recruiting station back in Pittsburgh, again at Lowry and yet again at Barksdale, clearly indicated he had the requisite aptitude. His application was promptly brought under consideration.

Back home in Courtney, his mother gathered the various written recommendations the army requested. They sought endorsements from his grade and high school teachers, as well as local businessmen who had come to know him. She forwarded the documentation to the army, completing the requirements of his application over which Harry had control. In addition, the FBI conducted an extensive background check on him as part of the standard requirements for entry into the accelerated training program.

Upon graduation from the cadet program, Harry would automatically become a full-fledged second lieutenant in the U.S. Army Air Force. Harry and his mom considered the time spent complying with the background confirmations to be well worth it. He admits to having been just a bit nervous as his application slowly made its way through the army's red tape. Eventually, word soon filtered back to his mom that the FBI was interviewing their neighbors in Courtney. All Harry could do was go about his routine and wait, and he was never much for waiting.

As part of the process, Harry endured yet another battery of testing. Failing any one part meant washing out as a cadet candidate and transfer to a rifle brigade or, perhaps, airplane mechanics school. After passing a rigorous physical examination with flying colors, he sat for the Aviation Cadet Qualifying Exam. The exam measured his comprehension skills, judgment, math aptitude, leadership qualities, and even his mechanical ability. The army used a "psychomotor" to measure eye-hand coordination, his reflexes, his ability to perform under pressure, and his visual acuity. The final piece of the testing regimen was an interview with a trained army psychologist.

In August 1942, having passed all the tests with exceptional scores, Harry was accepted into Cadet Class 43E. The class designation meant he would graduate in May 1943.

Initially, he was transferred into the 383rd School Squadron at Kirtland Army Air Base outside of Albuquerque, New Mexico. Once settled in, he learned he'd be there for just a little while because he and the balance of Cadet Class 43E were waiting for the current Cadet Class to progress forward in the instruction regimen. However, before he could settle into his new surroundings, he was shipped off to Santa Ana Army Air Base in Orange County, California. There he would begin pre-flight instruction and, of course, further conditioning and military indoctrination.

He received no advance notice of the transfer to Santa Ana. One morning he was summoned to his lieutenant's office and was told to pack up "pronto!" because he was shipping out that afternoon. Harry was aware the army must

New cadet Harry
Watson, a couple
of days before
transfer to the
383rd School
Squadron at
Kirtland Army
Air Force
Base near
Albuquerque,
New Mexico, in
1942.

have known the day he arrived at Kirtland when he'd be shipping out again,
but he'd discovered life in the army was reactionary and learned to always
be prepared for the unexpected.

At Santa Ana practically every other day involved taking tests to review
the most recent lessons. The frequent testing kept everyone on their toes.
Harry soon concluded the Cadet program was keen to root out anyone who
wasn't fully committed to becoming a pilot as he couldn't figure out any
other reason why the tests were coming so fast and furious.

In addition to a vigorous pre-flight training regimen, all candidates were subjected to daily military drills, including strenuous work-outs and extended-length marches. In some ways, Harry considered it to be a repeat of basic training, but more brutal.

Each day men disappeared without a trace as if they'd never been there. Later, he'd learn the same practice applied when a pilot was killed. The number of wash-outs was, in Harry's opinion, a bit alarming. With so many men failing to make the grade, Harry was always on edge and deeply concerned he could be next to disappear. Looking back, he wonders how he managed to avoid giving himself a stomach ulcer.

Harry had been excellent in the shorter track events in high school and particularly excelled in the one-quarter and one-half mile sprints. His slender, 5 foot 7 inches, 145-pound frame was well suited to the shorter distance events. Upon completion of all the qualifying tests, and before proceeding to the next section of pilot training, the instructors presented the candidates with a final hurdle: a one-mile sprint. Why they thought running a one-mile sprint would be a fitting conclusion to pre-flight training was, as Harry said at the time, anyone's guess.

A sergeant, known for taking delight in watching men vomit their guts out after enduring intensive physical drills, went about the task of matching pairs of runners for the sprint. Harry found himself paired with a fellow by the name of Golden Lang. Lang was over 6 feet tall, ruggedly handsome with thick, dark hair, and built as if he were made to play football as a quarterback.

The two men sized each other up, and the moment their sergeant blew his whistle, they took off running. The track was a quarter-mile in length, making it a four-lap race. Harry had a good lead after one lap and a small lead after two. However, that's when his stamina began to "plum peter out". By the end of the third lap, he was no longer in the lead, though he was still within a few feet of Lang.

It appeared to Harry as if Lang was simply cruising along while Harry was sweating profusely. Despite Harry's attempt to "pour it on" as if he was "shoveling coal into our old stove", Lang began to steadily pull away from him throughout the fourth and final lap. When they were about a quarter away from the finish line, Harry gave it one last effort, and when Lang sensed Harry was gaining on him, he quickly pulled further ahead, leaving Harry in the dust.

When the race was finished, Harry was bent over, struggling to regain his breath. Sweat was pouring from his face and dripping onto the turf.

Lang walked over, put his hand on his left shoulder, and said: "Don't worry, you did good, I was state champ in the mile back in Utah, so you've got nothing to be ashamed of."

From that moment forward, the two men became close friends and stuck together right through Transition Pilot Training many months later.

Following the Japanese attack on Pearl Harbor, the army had quickly dropped the requirement for all pilot, navigator, and bombardier cadets to possess up to four years of formal college experience. The change in the standards lopped off at least two years from the original training program by eliminating the need to attend college classes. Before lowering the educational standards, Harry had been facing an accelerated college curriculum, but the Japanese surprise attack shortened his path to becoming an officer.

Harry is striking a pose during a rare break from the training routine at Santa Ana around August 1942. He intended to send the photo home.

There were still classes to attend regarding military theory and protocols as an essential element of officer training. The most crucial classroom instruction, to date, was the requirement each cadet pass the absolutely critical and comprehensive Ground School. It was a mandatory requirement to continue in the cadet program. Failing Ground School meant an immediate transfer to an army rifle company, and Harry's dream of becoming an airline pilot after the war would be forever lost.

The U.S. Army Air Force Ground School at Santa Ana, California, addressed every aspect of what a pilot needed to know about flying, except the actual act of flying. Learning to fly would come following successful graduation from Ground School. Navigation, weather, the various parts of a plane, how they worked, and what they did, along with information about the weight of fuel, water, and oil, were all elements of the intensive schooling.

He learned it was critical to know the weight of fuel, oil, and water in the calculation of the amount of flight time remaining until the fuel tanks went empty. Harry and Lang would spend about two hours each evening quizzing each other on the day's lessons while also prepping for the next day's material. The two men stuck with their nightly regimen, no matter how exhausted they might be.

They worked exceptionally hard on the course sections addressing weather and navigation as they formed strong personal beliefs it was impossible to learn enough about either discipline. Harry, in particular, had a gut feeling that the two-courses could prove critical in practical wartime applications, above all other courses.

When Ground School was nearing completion, the cadets faced a series of fifteen final exams. Harry demonstrated a high aptitude in mathematics and finished number one in the Class of 43E, having achieved a score of 100 percent in fourteen of the fifteen separate final exams. In the 15th exam, he was in a hurry to finish and put a decimal point in the wrong place on the last question, resulting in a score of only 98 percent. To this day, he regrets not taking his time to figure out the correct placement of the decimal point and never rushed through a test again for the rest of his life.

Regardless of the 98 percentile score, he considered finishing number one in the testing to be a noteworthy accomplishment for himself, particularly when taking into account his impoverished background and the fact that as a kid, he wasn't exactly in love with school. With the Ground School section of the program successfully behind him, he was transferred to basic flight instruction. He was about as excited as he'd ever been in his life when he boarded the train bound for Ryan Field, outside of Hemet, California.

Chapter 5

God was his co-pilot
Aviation Cadet Class 43-E

With Ground School behind him and bolstered by his classroom successes, Harry could hardly wait to commence Primary Pilot Training. To say he was feeling confident would be an understatement.

In November 1942, the army was still heavily relying on private flight schools to train the majority of incoming pilots. Hemet Field was home to a civilian pilot training school operated by the Ryan School of Aeronautics,

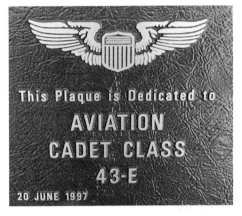

Photo courtesy of HMdb.org. The Historical Marker Database.

which also manufactured its own trainer aircraft, mostly the Ryan PT-22, "Recruit" two-seat trainer, along with a handful of similar PT-21s. Both the PT-21s and 22s were designed to absorb a great deal of stress. Whether they were also excellent aircraft for first-time flyers remains a subject for debate.

Ryan personnel were heavily supplemented with army officers. Ryan instructors were required to attend a U.S. Army training protocol program where they were taught army terminology, procedures, and operations. Although most of the instructors at the time Harry was at Hemet were civilians, it didn't lessen the military climate. It was, first and foremost, an Army Air Force facility, and that fact was driven home, especially by the sergeants, each and every day of the week.

Harry and Lang managed to arrange for adjoining bunk beds as their friendship continued to grow. Golden, at 6 feet 1 inch, was about 6 inches taller than Harry, though it never seemed to matter to either of them. Both men spoke incessantly of their mutual desire to fly fighter planes, but were well aware they'd be flying whatever aircraft the army deemed to be in highest priority at any given time. As they spoke of their respective childhoods, it didn't take long for the two men to discover they were both life-long risk-takers. As they learned more about each other, the bond of friendship grew tight.

On November 4 1942, both men were handed their respective Pilot Log Book and commenced what would be about sixty hours of in-flight training on the way to completing the first of four distinct courses in army aviation. Each of the four pilot training courses ran a few months in length.

Primary Pilot Training was a four-month phase and taught cadets how to fly, utilizing two-seat trainer aircraft.

Basic Pilot Training, approximately three months long, taught cadets how to fly in formation, navigation techniques and to become accustomed to flying long distances.

Advanced Pilot Training required a training period of up to six months. Successful completion would result in graduation and the award of the new pilot's "Wings". Cadets would focus on either single-engine or multiple-engine airplanes during this course of instruction. The army dictated the type of plane in which the cadets would train, leaving the cadets with no input in the decision-making process.

The fourth phase, Transition Pilot Training, was sixty hours, in total. Pilots who had previously focused on single-engine planes would proceed to formal fighter plane training. While pilots who'd focused on multi-engine aircraft would, generally, train in various types of transports and bombers. Following graduation, new pilots would be transferred to combat duty.

During the war, time devoted to each of the above sections grew shorter as the demand for more pilots became almost desperate.

Harry, Lang, and three other cadets met their civilian instructor, Mr Reed Kinert, at the designated aircraft hangar to finally begin their flight training. It was anticipated that following about eight to twelve hours of in-the-air training with an instructor at the controls, each cadet would thereafter fly solo. The first order of business had more to do with what happens when something goes wrong while in flight; they were given a demonstration on how to correctly put on a parachute.

Harry watched with interest and concluded it appeared to be a relatively easy task. When it was his turn to slip into the "parachute contraption", he lost track of which foot went where and, to the amusement of the other cadets, found himself hopelessly tangled up, causing him to lose his footing and awkwardly tumble to the ground. He wasn't alone, for in short order

DATE 1942	AIRCRAFT IDENT. MARK	MAKE — MODEL AND HORSEPOWER OF AIRCRAFT	FROM	TO		CLASS OR TYPE		DUAL or LINK
		ARMY						Dual
11-4-42	PT-22	RYAN PT-22 KINNER-165	RYAN FIELD Hemet, Calif	Local		Se-L		00:35
11-5-42	"	"	"	"		"		00:40
11-6-42	"	"	"	"		"		00:20
11-9-42	"	"	"	"		"		00:30
11-10-42	"	"	"	"		"		00:35
11-12-42	"	"	"	"		"		00:35
11-16-42	"	"	"	"		"		00:40
11-17-42	"	"	"	"		"		00:50
11-18-42	"	"	"	"		"		00:30
11-19-42	"	"	"	"		"		01:05
		CARRY TOTALS FORWARD TO TOP OF NEXT PAGE						06:30

Pages from Harry's Pilot Log Book. Flight theory training was intermixed with actual flight time.

DUAL or LINK	SOLO FLIGHT TIME			Total	Time	REMARKS: Each maneuver and the time spent thereon, attested to by the instructor is to be entered in this column for all instruction received. Any serious damage to the aircraft MUST be entered here also.
	Day	Night	Instrument			
Dual						
00:35				00:35		ORIENTATION FLIGHT - St ½ Level
00:40				01:15		90° turns - climbs - glides
00:20				01:45		S across road - gliding turns - Pattern
00:30				02:15		360° turns - steepbanks - Pattern
00:35				02:50		Power stalls - 360° turns
00:35				03:25		Stall Sequence - Elimentary 8's
00:40				04:05		Stalls - Spins - Landings
00:50				04:55		Landings - S across road - 8's
00:30				05:25		Spins - Coordination excerises
01:05				06:30		Landings - Take offs
06:30				06:30		PILOT'S SIGNATURE Harry E. Matson Jr

most of the men discovered for themselves getting into a parachute wasn't as easy as they thought it'd be.

Afterward, Kinert took them for a walk to the flight line where a bright blue and yellow, two-seat training plane, a Ryan PT-22 Recruit Trainer, awaited them. Kinert arranged for a ladder to be brought up alongside the plane, allowing more than one student at a time to observe him as he identified each of the controls in the rear cockpit. He made a point that the front cockpit was his seat, and they weren't allowed to use it. He made it abundantly clear the cadets, even when flying solo, were relegated to the rear cockpit.

Before their initial meeting with Kinert, they'd all experienced sitting in a mock-up of the plane, but this was their first opportunity to view and touch a real, working aircraft. One of the men asked Kinert: "What are those rubber hose-things for?" Harry remembers his reply.

"They're called gosports, you dodo. You're supposed to follow my instructions through those, get it?" Kinert's voice signaled he wasn't a patient man. The unfortunate cadet decided to follow up his question with another, "Well, how do I talk to you?"

Kinert's caustic response came without hesitation. "Listen to me, dodo. When we're up there," Kinert pointed to the sky, "I'm going to be telling you what the hell you're screwing up. You don't need to tell me anything. What you do need to do is follow my instructions, so you don't crash this crate with me in it!" Kinert proceeded to have the unfortunate man take a lap around the entire airfield.

The first plane Harry flew during Primary Pilot Training was, as it turned out, the Ryan PT-22 Recruit Trainer. It had been designed and developed by the founder of the flight school, T. Claude Ryan, in the early 1930s and was originally intended to serve as an aerobatic sports trainer, which explains why it was initially designated as the "Ryan STA-Sports Trainer, Aerobatic". The Ryan STA was lauded as an excellent plane, easy to fly, with few bad characteristics. It was Ryan's primary trainer at its civilian air schools and earned a reputation as being a very safe and predictable aircraft.

In the years leading up to World War II, the army dictated numerous changes be made to the Ryan STA to better suit army pilot training for aerial combat situations. In response to the army's required alterations, the plane was fitted with a larger, more powerful, military-style radial engine in place of the original Monesco engine, which was an in-line, four-cylinder, air-cooled, inverted engine and not mainly designed for power. The Monesco-equipped plane was only suitable for civilian use as it lacked the horsepower required by the army. The army was fixated on power, and Ryan had no choice but to comply.

The army also mandated Ryan add thicker aluminum skin and significantly beef-up the landing gear. Complying with all the army's requirements increased the plane's weight, changed the center of gravity, and forced Ryan to sweep the wings back by about four degrees to partially compensate for the weight increase.

Due to the crisis of the era, there was inadequate time for testing the final product, which proved to be a fatal oversight for many cadets. The resulting plane, renamed the PT-21/22 Recruit, had a laundry list of bad habits and tendencies, allegedly giving it the narrowest margin of safety of any trainer of the era. As an aside, the actor Harrison Ford was flying a PT-22 when he crash-landed onto a golf course in 2015. He survived the crash, unlike numerous cadets during World War II.

The vast majority of the Ryan trainers built during World War II were the PT-22 variant. The distinctive, heavily protected landing gear of the PT-21 was the easiest way to distinguish between the two aircraft. All the cadets flew with an instructor for approximately twenty hours before ever

Harry also trained in the similar Ryan PT-21, shown above. The front seat was strictly reserved for the instructor. The student always flew in the second seat, even when flying solo. Note the radial engine and reinforced landing gear. Photo courtesy of Harry E. Watson.

experiencing a solo flight. As long as they were flying with an instructor, they were relatively isolated from the plane's faults.

Harry and his fellow cadets, for reasons unknown to Harry, were not schooled in the plane's handling deficiencies. Harry would never learn whether the training oversight was intentional, but it was likely a contributing factor why Harry's first solo flight in a Ryan PT-22 was almost his last.

First thing in the morning on November 18 1942, the Hemet airfield was crowded with PT-21s and 22s being readied by the flight crews for the day's adventures in flying. Kinert informed Harry he wanted him to begin flying solo that day and handed him a list of maneuvers he was to practice once airborne and told him to be "damn certain" he performed each and every one of them.

As Kinert turned to leave, he paused and mentioned something to Harry about the plane tending to pull to the left when the pilot powers up, and to compensate Harry should "just keep your foot on the right rudder." He didn't advise Harry just how much pedal pressure he would need to exert. Instead, and despite Harry's attempt to question him, he quickly walked away.

Before he could begin his first solo flight he was required to trek over to Supply and check-out a mandatory parachute rig. Once he managed to squeeze himself into the parachute "contraption", he ventured onto the tarmac in search of his PT-22. Once he located his aircraft, he climbed into the cockpit and made himself comfortable. He glanced around the airfield and, for the first time in his experience, noticed the control tower was conducting "two at a time".

With more than a little trepidation, he realized he'd be sharing the runway with another plane at take-off. He spent a few minutes observing as the tower was directing one aircraft to take up a position on the left side of the runway while a second plane was being directed to the right side. The airfield lacked a sufficient number of runways to accommodate all of the cadets. Apparently, someone had determined that it was as good a time as any for the trainees to grow accustomed to sharing a runway, even those embarking on their first solo flights.

Harry's crew cranked the engine, and after two attempts, it roared to life. The tower directed him to taxi into position towards the right side of the runway while another plane lined itself up on the opposite side. He was cleared for take-off the moment both pilots signaled the tower they were ready. According to Harry, "That's when the shit hit the fan."

Bearing in mind Kinert's instructions, Harry "poured on the coal" while keeping a lot of pressure on the right rudder pedal. He found himself rapidly accelerating into a full-right turn because he was applying much more pressure on the right rudder than was needed to offset the engine's torque-pull to the left.

Panicking because he was about to run out of paved runway, he fully released the right rudder pedal and slammed his left foot down on the left rudder pedal instead. As a consequence, his plane made an abrupt 180-degree turn. He immediately realized he was on a collision course with the control tower, or possibly the rows of planes parked on the tarmac in front of the tower, or both.

In a fraction of a second, Harry found himself completely shocked out of his mind. He knew if he didn't act fast there could be a catastrophe, and was horrified at the prospect of his first solo flight ending in a fiery disaster.

He decided he needed to deal with one problem at a time, and the most immediate challenge was to avoid striking the planes lined-up in front of him. He desperately attempted to bring the rudder back to the right but was only partially successful as the engine was relentlessly pulling hard to the left. The throttle was wide open as a thousand things went through his mind. Harry felt as if everything was happening in slow motion, and yet at full speed. It was a sensation he'd experience again during the war, but it was new to him at the time.

He calculated he was still moving too slowly to effect a take-off and was traveling too fast to stop in time to avoid, at a minimum, hitting the planes sitting on the tarmac. He made the split-second decision to fly above the parked aircraft because failing that, he'd undoubtedly crash into them. He gently put backward pressure on the elevators and managed to get the tail up, then the nose came up, and for a brief moment, he was in the air.

It was at that moment he realized there was a fighting chance he could actually fly himself out of the situation, and that's exactly what happened. The aircraft lifted from the runway and just missed crashing into the line of aircraft on the tarmac. He discovered, however, that he was flying directly towards the center of the control tower.

He noticed there were three men in the tower desperately waving at him. Then, just like that, they ducked out-of-sight. Harry knew he had to execute a turn, but there was precious little leeway for maneuvering. His reflexes kicked in, and he lowered the nose a little to increase his airspeed, which is exactly how the plane responded. With the increased speed, he then pulled back on the stick and commenced a right turn. He had generated just enough additional airspeed to pull off the maneuver.

As he roared past the control tower, he noticed the men inside were, by then, diving into the bunker alongside the tower, and the ground personnel in the vicinity were running for the hills. He had come within 15 feet, or less, of crashing into the tower and only by the grace of God continued to gain airspeed and ultimately full control of the aircraft. The entire adventure lasted a matter of seconds.

His confidence returned once he realized he was free and clear of disaster, and the plane was properly responding to his inputs. He decided since he was safely in the air, he'd go ahead and practice the various maneuvers Kinert had ordered him to perform. About thirty or forty minutes later, after executing numerous lazy-eights, stalls, spins, loops, chandelles, and more, he entered the landing pattern and brought the plane home without further incident.

Harry was making his way to the hangar where Kinert had told him to meet him when he returned from his first solo flight. The parachute he was lugging was both heavy and awkward. It was capturing most of his attention when he suddenly realized he was about to walk directly into Kinert and Captain Simpson, the base commander. Harry stopped in his tracks, dropped the parachute, and saluted. Captain Simpson didn't return the salute, so Harry held his salute in place while both Kinert and Simpson silently stared at him.

After what felt to Harry to have been thirty or forty seconds, Simpson walked to within a foot of him; his arms fell to his sides as they suddenly went limp, as he looked up at the 6-foot tall Simpson. The two men locked eyes, and Harry began to fear the worst. Finally, after what felt to be an eternity, Simpson blurted out:

"Watson, you've got nerves of steel, but someday they're going to send you home in a pine box." Without saying another word, Simpson turned around and walked away, shaking his head back and forth. Kinert was also shaking his head, as if silently agreeing, then turned to catch up with Simpson. Harry had just dodged being "washed out" following his first solo flight.

At mess hall that night, Lang told Harry he'd witnessed his stunt. Then he turned serious and said, "Harry, I seriously affirm I saw God sitting in Kinert's cockpit with you this morning. There's no other way to describe it." Golden then explained how Kinert had a few words with Captain Simpson before the three of them met up and, whatever Kinert had said to Simpson, it apparently mitigated the circumstances for Harry. That's when Harry learned just how close Simpson had been to washing him out.

Harry considered Lang as being a person who wasn't somebody prone to telling tall stories and pondered whether he hadn't been alone in his plane. He asked himself why Kinert would stick his nose out to plead his case? It made no sense because Kinert was always keen to wash out would-be pilots. He was immediately covered with goosebumps as the possibility that God had been with him struck home.

At that moment, several cadets who'd been present when Harry took-off that morning came over to tell him they'd never seen such flying and took turns to heartily congratulate him. Harry, for his part, didn't let on to the fact the whole episode was a near-disaster, and he'd barely escaped with his life. He jokingly told them he'd had God as his Co-pilot that morning, which brought more than one "Amen" response.

Harry had no further incidents over the balance of his Primary Pilot Training except for the fact Mr Kinert traded him for another student after the near catastrophe. Every now and then, he'd run into Kinert, but Kinert always managed to be looking the other way. If Kinert had passed on anything negative about Harry to his new instructor, it never showed. He fully indulged Harry's never-ending questions concerning everything from how to restart a stalled engine to how he should deal with a sudden, unexpected deterioration in visual flight conditions.

For the record, Harry did not record the details of his harrowing first solo take-off in his Pilot Log Book and merely noted he had taken an "orientation flight-St. & Level". From time to time they were required to turn their logbooks in for review, so he just figured he'd leave well-enough alone. Later in his military career, there were times he would be directed not to record the actual destination and/or mission purpose, but rather, insert destinations of approximately the same amount of flight time and be non-specific as to the purpose. The altered records would coincide with missions he would later conclude to have been "a bit out of the ordinary".

On December 30 1942, Harry logged his 60th hour of flight time. It was also the third consecutive day of performing various acrobatics while his instructor observed him from the ground. Harry understood the instructor's

Harry at Ryan School of Aeronautics, Hemet Field, California, a few days following his harrowing first-solo take-off.

MAKE — MODEL HORSEPOWER OF AIRCRAFT	FROM	TO	CLASS OR TYPE	DUAL TIME	SOLO FLIGHT TIME Day	Night	Instrument	Total Time	Time	REMARKS: Each maneuver and the time spent thereon, attested to by the instructor is to be entered in this column for all instruction received. Any serious damage to the aircraft MUST be entered here also.
N PT-22 UNER 165	RYAN FIELD HEMET, CALIF	LOCAL	SE-L	21:48	21:24			43:12		
"	"	"	"	00:37	02:21			46:10		POWER STALLS - SLOW, SNAP, HALF ROLL - LAZY 8 + CHANDELLES
"	"	"	"	00:52	01:30			48:32		Chandelles - LAZY 8's - STALLS - SPINS - SNAPROLLS - SLOW ROLLS
"	"	"	"	00:35	02:00			51:07		60 hr. Check - ACROBATICS
"	"	"	"	00:43	02:00			53:50		ACROBATICS - FRONT SEAT RIDE
"	"	"	"		03:00			56:50		ACROBATICS
"	"	"	"	00:45	02:25			60:00		ACROBATICS - FINISHED COURSE
				ALL TIME LOGGED IS CERTIFIED TO BE CORRECT. COMPLETED U.S.						
				ARMY PRIMARY STAGE Reed Kinert CIVILIAN INSTRUCTOR						
				COMMERCIAL LICENSE + RE-RATED INSTRUCTOR No. 27006.						
CARRY TOTALS FORWARD TO TOP OF NEXT PAGE				25:20	34:40			60:00		PILOT'S SIGNATURE Harry E. Hatton Jr.

Harry's Pilot Logbook Entries.

presence meant he was nearing the completion of the training regimen, and the instructor was confirming for himself Harry could competently perform all the required maneuvers.

But on the 30th there was a notable change. Kinert, who had not attended any of Harry's flights for about a month, made an appearance. After only ten minutes of flight time, Kinert hand-signaled him to land immediately. Harry felt a pang of worry, and his stomach rolled over a couple of times. He wasted no time landing. By the time he'd disembarked from the plane, Kinert had walked over and was waiting for him. Before Harry could say a word Kinert said in a monotone voice:

"You passed." He turned around and walked off. That was the sum-total of the conversation, but Harry considered it was all he needed to hear and found himself relieved to watch Kinert walk away for the last time. Later that day, Kinert sought him out so he could sign-off in his Pilot Log Book.

Chapter 6

Basic Pilot Training

Primary Pilot Training seemingly flew by as Harry became proficient with the PT-22 and graded-out at the top of his class. Harry and Lang, who graded right behind him, were shipped off to Gardner Army Airfield outside of Taft, California, to undertake the next phase of training: Basic Pilot Training.

Harry was required to master several challenging techniques, which included multiple plane formation flying, the intricacies of instrument flight, and extended overnight excursions with numerous airport destinations, often landing and taking off on unlighted runways. The next eight or nine weeks would convert them into what the instructors deemed "real pilots". Failure likely meant an immediate transfer to a rifle brigade.

Gardner was a sprawling air base with three state-of-the-art runways running north/south, east/west, and northwest/southeast, allowing for take-offs and landings under all manner of wind conditions. In addition to the main field, Gardner operated six nearby auxiliary airfields enabling the army to train large numbers of recruits from a centralized location.

Cadets on review at Gardner Army Airfield about the time when Harry and Lang were flying BT-13's there.

Harry looked around the base and concluded that the whole place looked like it was temporary, and nothing seemed as if it were built to last. Most of the buildings at Gardner were hastily constructed with plywood and tarpaper put to extended use.

The base also included a hospital, always a busy place, underscored by the fact at least twenty-six cadets and eleven of the training officers flying with them over the course of the war would die in flying-related accidents. Many more would be injured and require hospital services.

Gardner would be Harry's home for about two months, during which time he was expected to accumulate seventy hours of flight time in his new aircraft, the Vultee BT-13, nicknamed "the Vibrator". Harry had overheard the nickname used in joking terms before, but nobody he knew had ever flown one, so the source of the moniker was a mystery to him.

Harry's first hands-on experience with the BT-13 was on January 7, 1943. As soon as the engine screamed to life, he recognized the BT-13 was going to be a great deal faster than the Ryan PT-22. The construction of his new plane was also significantly more massive, which was necessary to support the more authoritative engine. The Vibrator was powered by a Pratt & Whitney nine-cylinder, air-cooled, radial unit producing a robust 450 horsepower and allowing the plane to achieve a top speed of 180mph. It was roughly three times more powerful than anything Harry had flown before.

His instructor made a comparison of the BT-13 with the German Messerschmitt 109(e) on the first day of instruction because he wanted to impress upon the cadets the fact they still had a long way to go in their training. Harry recalls the instructor joked, "y'all think you're a bunch of big-shot aviators", flying a 450 horsepower plane. He scolded them when he said they still had "a hell of a lot of training" ahead of them before they'd stand a chance of going up against the 1,455 horsepower Messerschmitt with a top speed around 400mph and armed with a cannon, twin machine guns, and rockets. Harry found the comparison very sobering.

Along with a new plane to master was an abundance of unfamiliar cockpit equipment. Rather than a one-way set of rubber ear tubes, there was a state-of-the-art two-way radio communications system as well as landing flaps and a two-position, controllable pitch propeller. Learning to best use the new propeller would assist the pilot in maximizing efficiency by literally changing the pitch of the propeller to improve the performance of the aircraft across varying speeds, in part by reducing drag. The controllable pitch propeller also improved overall performance and saved fuel. The plane, however, lacked hydraulics; therefore, like the PT-21/22, the Vibrator lacked retractable landing gear.

The absence of a hydraulic system also meant the wing flaps were controlled by a crank-and-cable system, requiring more effort by the pilot. It was among several new features he needed to thoroughly master. It was essential the use of the additional controls, gauges, levers, and switches become instinctive, which meant practicing as much as possible. Harry and Lang would set aside time each day to conduct their own private version of ground school, during which time they focused on the BT-13 Vibrator and took turns quizzing each other, as Harry recalls, "over and over again until we got sick of each other."

When Harry switched-on the engine to commence his first instructional flight, he immediately experienced an emotional rush from the powerful engine. When the wheels left the runway, he felt like he was flying a tank. It was so much larger and heavier than the PT-21/22 trainers had been. He immediately loved the plane, but following his initial solo flight, he realized there were numerous quirks to contend with.

Aerial practice included the art of forcing the plane into a stall and learning to recover from it. The first time he practiced the maneuver, just as he approached stall speed, the BT-13 began to violently vibrate to the point he was genuinely concerned the plane was going to break apart. Just when Harry was convinced the aircraft was going to break, it suddenly stopped vibrating. Though there was an audible stall warning signal, the designers apparently believed a physical input was also necessary, thus the vibrations. His instructor assured him the plane would not break up unless he actually went into a stall and failed to recover. He assured Harry in the event that he didn't recover from the stall, then the subsequent crash would cause the plane to break apart, with Harry in it. Harry didn't appreciate the joke.

In later years Harry would look back and consider the merits of the BT-13. He questioned whether the stall-speed vibration really had been intentionally designed into the plane, for it was the only plane he ever flew that exhibited such a characteristic. He realized the time constraints caused by the war likely resulted in some design flaws to go unaddressed and concluded the vibrating was probably one of the defects.

When he practiced the more acrobatic defensive maneuvers, the canopy vibrated, again leading Harry to believe it might break off, though it never did. He reasoned, right or wrong, it must have been another design quirk.

An additional unsettling characteristic he discovered had to do with the two-position propeller. When it was in "high pitch" mode, it vibrated the plane in what he considered to be an unnatural manner, yet nothing ever broke away, and the aircraft performed as it should have. In fact, the plane had such a multitude of vibration quirks, it was little wonder it had been dubbed, "the Vibrator".

In addition to dealing with a myriad of vibration quirks, he also considered the BT-13 to be a somewhat unforgiving plane to fly. His instructor attempted to justify the characteristics that made it unforgiving as the real strengths of the aircraft as a trainer. Harry, for his part, rationalized that if the plane was easy to fly, then he wouldn't be learning anything. He didn't take any comfort with his theory and looked ahead to his next phase of training.

Throughout the instructional process, he and Lang pushed their planes hard, and both men were becoming well known as risk-takers. Following each day of flying, they'd compare notes and discuss their findings as they strove to discover the plane's ultimate limitations, without crashing. Despite the Vibrator's many drawbacks, which Harry and Lang probed at will, the aircraft was also quite agile, ultimately making it an excellent transition vehicle before graduating to the final phase of the Cadet course: Advanced Pilot Training.

One night the two friends were discussing the air war in Europe as compared with the air war in the Pacific. After reviewing the pros and cons of flying in either theatre, they decided they'd prefer to find themselves in the European Theatre of Operations. However, neither would decline the opportunity to avenge Pearl Harbor and fly against the Japanese. It was during one of their almost nightly discussions Lang mentioned he intended to get married and leave a legacy behind after they graduated Cadet School.

"Harry, you're like me." He explained. "We take risks when we're up there, and that's part of why I don't think I'll make it through this war alive. I don't ever get the feeling I've got someone with me like you did at Hemet and I want someone to carry on my family legacy. I don't know how much time I have left to do it."

Harry took his statement to heart and began to think maybe he should be looking to leave a legacy himself. Unlike Lang, who had a continuing relationship with Lillie, his high school sweetheart, Harry had no girlfriend, let alone a potential wife. He had long ago realized he was a risk-taker himself, and he thought it was part of the reason the two men got along so well. But Lang's remarks caused Harry to feel a bit alone.

He'd never had a genuine girlfriend, and now, thanks to Lang, he realized there were long-term considerations which he had ignored. He found himself thinking about how to go about acquiring a girlfriend and maybe planning for the future. He changed the way he approached the future; it was not going to be as though he'd continue going it alone. He began thinking about getting married, starting a family, and doing it all before he was deployed to a war zone. For the first time in his life, he felt there wasn't enough time to accomplish what he needed to do. Time had been limitless, but now he had goals and time was short.

About halfway through their regimen, Harry, Lang, and Rick Hayward, who went by the well-deserved nickname of "Wayward", were assigned a flight plan taking them on a circuitous, nearly four-hour-long route. Harry remembers it was a Thursday, and the weather was great.

The training excursion began with a late afternoon take-off and ended near 1900 hours. Harry still fondly remembers he had complete confidence in Lang, but both of them had some serious reservations concerning Wayward.

Harry felt particularly unlucky when he was assigned to lead the three-plane squadron with Wayward as his wingman. On the one hand, he knew he'd be looking at Wayward off his right wing-tip for the entire flight, but

A critical element of Basic Pilot Training was learning to fly in formation. Formation flying was practiced under multiple weather conditions, night and day.

on the other, he wasn't looking forward to getting a kink in his neck from continually checking on Wayward's position. To complicate matters a bit more, the proposed flight included many abrupt course changes. Lang would be positioned off to Harry's left, but he had no concerns about Lang's flying skills.

On February 11, 1943, formation flying was still a relatively novel concept for them. Harry found himself to be especially on edge whenever a course correction called for any type of bank to the left because he knew he'd lose sight of Wayward flying behind his right-wing. Should Wayward cut over too soon or too sharply, he might plow into Harry's plane and could even send Harry into Lang and take down all three of them. Later in the war, while flying in England, Harry would witness exactly such a mid-air disaster, with many more lives on the line than the three of them.

Harry considered himself lucky when he reviewed the flight plan and recognized the initial course correction of the day would require a 45 degree turn to the right, keeping Wayward safely within his view. Neither Harry nor Lang trusted Wayward, and Harry conducted himself accordingly.

When the time came for the first right-turn course correction, Harry was under the impression he'd successfully communicated the pending course change to both Lang and Wayward. After he sent the agreed-upon radio signal, Wayward turned towards Harry and gave him the "thumbs up" sign, which Harry took to mean Wayward comprehended the instructions. He would later learn Wayward considered a "thumbs up" to say that everything was okay, but not necessarily confirming he understood a message or signal.

Per the plan, Harry verbally counted down to three over the radio before starting the course correction. When Harry finished the count-down, Wayward didn't change course and instead, maintained the original heading and speed. Harry was upset. He could have crashed into Wayward, and Lang could have crashed into him. But both Harry and Lang hesitated before starting their course change as they wanted to be certain Wayward was making the turn according to plan. Harry, realizing Wayward failed to execute the maneuver, glanced over at Lang, who put up both of his hands as if to say "no surprise".

Anticipating there'd be some issues with Wayward, Harry and Lang had huddled together beforehand and decided that before making any course corrections towards Wayward, Lang would slightly delay until he was certain Wayward had started to make the necessary bank-right, thereby avoiding any potential collision. Their discussion likely saved the lives of at least one of the three men.

Harry re-communicated the course change to Wayward and ordered him to repeat the instructions on the radio. After what Harry considered to be an overly long pause, Wayward finally acknowledged and repeated the directions. While Wayward didn't miss any further course changes that day, Harry could never be sure where Wayward's plane was. Sometimes Harry would look to his right, and Wayward was where he was supposed to be flying. Other times he might be flying behind him, or too low or too high. When they landed shortly before 1900 hours, Harry was just about "fit to be tied" and was feeling lucky to be alive. The stress of flying with Wayward left him with the sensation he'd been flying all week.

Once safely on the ground, they reported to their instructor. Lang and Harry separately gave him an earful about the day's experiences then bee-lined for the bunkhouse. When they arrived, they noticed Wayward was quite a bit behind them as they hadn't bothered to wait for him. When they reached the front door, rather than proceeding directly in, they skirted-off to the side of the building and quickly walked behind it where they made themselves comfortable on the back stairway because they needed to spend some time for their tempers to cool off.

Harry remembers mentioning he might be tempted to take up smoking if he ever had to fly with Wayward again. Lang burst out laughing; it took him a minute to regain his composure, then Lang said: "I'd rather hit my head with a hammer than fly with that dodo bird ever again." They decided to hang around a bit to make sure they'd not see Wayward again that day. After a couple of minutes of keeping their thoughts to themselves, Harry broke the silence.

"If they assign that idiot as my wingman again, just shoot me," Harry said without making any effort to disguise his frustrations.

"Harry, if I shot you every time you told me never to let you do this or do that or whatever else you might do again, you'd look like a piece of Swiss cheese by now." Lang laughed and then offered up a thought:

"Tomorrow, let's make sure we're on the USO truck. We're going to put this trip out of our minds."

"Amen to that! Harry replied.

After they waited what they considered to be more than a sufficient time for Wayward to have showered and hit the sack, they went inside, cleaned themselves up, and called it a day. There was no extra studying that night as they were tuckered out.

The primary source of recreation for the cadets, and just about everyone else stationed at Gardner, was the USO club located about 9 miles away in Taft, California. Every Friday and Saturday night, a truck would shuttle base personnel to and from the USO club. The last vehicle to take the men to the base each night left promptly at 2300 hours, and if anyone were to miss the truck, they'd find themselves breaking the 2330 hours base curfew.

The curfew was strictly imposed, and anyone caught in violation would be put on Report. Kitchen Police duty, or worse, awaited anyone caught out of their barracks after curfew. Several sergeants took particular delight in apprehending someone, especially cadets, wandering around the base after 2330 hours. As it was, it didn't take much in the way of a transgression to earn KP duty, so Harry was always one of the first to board the last truck returning to the base.

The next day, Friday, February 12 1943, didn't require any formation flying with Wayward. It was a day of studying instrumentation and practicing airwork and, particularly, acrobatics. Harry and Lang made sure they were among the first to board the lead truck to the USO that evening, just as they promised themselves the day prior.

Lang didn't drink alcohol or coffee, though Harry might imbibe in an occasional beer. At that point in his life he didn't enjoy alcohol all that much. Once he'd been deployed to the European theatre for a month or two, he did learn to appreciate English pubs and English brews along with an occasional Scotch.

The USO was an excellent way to escape the strict atmosphere on the base, kick back, and relax. It was the only time they could enjoy the camaraderie of just sitting around with a bunch of the guys for a few hours without someone looking over their shoulders.

Fortunately for Harry and Lang, their flight instructor, Mr MacKenzie, preferred rotating the pilots within each formation, and neither of them had to ever again endure the experience of flying with Wayward. They would joke among themselves that Wayward could probably cause both of his wingmen to crash if only given enough time.

To their amazement, Wayward actually made it through Basic Pilot Training and progressed forward into Transition Pilot Training. Rumor had it he was going to be training in fighter planes. If true, it was an enviable posting. Just about everyone wanted to be a fighter pilot, except Harry. Harry changed his mind about flying fighter planes because he figured his best chance for postwar advancement as an airline pilot would be if he flew multiple-engine aircraft in the army. His wish was granted when he was assigned to master the art of flying transports. Transports could be equipped with as many as four engines and could provide a sound basis for his civilian transition to piloting an airliner.

BASIC PILOT TRAINING

The specialized assignments for Advanced Pilot Training were based on anticipated wartime needs, and the Army Air Corps was expecting a need for a great deal more transport pilots as the war progressed, and especially after the Allies opened a front in France. Though the D-Day invasion was more than a year away, the Army Air Force was already planning how many planes of each type would be required to accomplish the tasks ahead. The number of trained pilots was carefully calculated to match the anticipated wartime needs.

They graduated from Basic Pilot Training on Thursday, March 4 1943. The two friends had nothing to do the next day, a Friday, so they hopped a ride on the first truck going to the USO in Taft. On the trip over Lang shared with Harry the fact he intended to bring Lillie, who was living back home in Utah, to their Class 43E graduation ceremony. Harry was amazed when he announced they were planning to get married immediately following the service.

Lang again mentioned he had a gut feeling he wouldn't survive the war and reconfirmed his desire to leave a legacy. He and Lillie had corresponded a great deal, but Lang admitted he never expressed his feelings of mortality to her. Lang again referenced Harry's first solo flight and told him, based upon what he'd witnessed, Harry had got nothing to worry about. Harry let the topic drop, at least for the time being, as they fell into silent contemplation.

Harry spent the balance of the drive reflecting on Lang's earlier comments about the two of them being risk-takers and how Lang believed he wouldn't make it through the war alive. He realized Lang was dead serious and determined never to bring the topic up again as he found it very unsettling.

When they arrived at the USO, the two men split off, Lang to spend the night shooting the breeze with other pilots while Harry danced the entire night with a young lady, immensely enjoying himself. They just barely caught the 2300 hours bus back to the base, but not before Harry got the young woman's mailing address.

Harry couldn't chase Lang's comments about not making it through the war, and his desire to leave a legacy behind, out of his mind. It didn't take him long to decide he'd ask June, the girl from the USO, to marry him. He did so in the first letter he wrote to her. She mailed back her acceptance, and they set the wedding date to coincide with his graduation from Cadet Class 43E on Thursday, May 20 1943. As a consequence, graduation became an even more life-changing event for the two men. But they still were facing about eight weeks of Advance Pilot Training before graduation, and it required they first move to a new base to complete their course-work.

Chapter 7

Advanced Pilot Training

Advanced Pilot training required transferring Harry, Lang, and about 200 additional cadets to Stockton Army Airfield, located about 3 miles south of Stockton, California. Both Harry and Lang had been designated for instruction on learning to pilot multiple-engine aircraft. Lang was destined to command a B-24 bomber, but the army had some different ideas for Harry. First, however, both men were required to master the twin-engine, high-performance Curtiss-Wright AT-9. They would be spending about seventy hours of flight time, over eight weeks, learning to master the plane.

The new plane was also their first exposure to retractable landing gear, something neither had ever experienced. After a couple of weeks, Harry was surprised at how many trainees would forget they needed to lower their landing gear as it was no longer a static apparatus. Harry could hear the control tower staff cussing at an unwitting trainee coming in without the landing gear lowered and ordering him to immediately abort the landing and try again.

There was more to learn about the retractable landing gear than merely raising them after take-off and lowering them before landing. Harry discovered he could reduce his airspeed by lowering the landing gear without cutting back on the engine. It was a technique he practiced for certain maneuvers and was something he'd call into play more than once when he was deployed to the European Theatre during 1944–45.

The AT-9 featured twin Lycoming R-680-9 nine-cylinder air-cooled radial engines producing 295 horsepower each and a top speed of just under 200mph. Though much heavier and larger than the BT-13, it was somewhat faster and was intended to perform like the twin-engine bombers and fighter planes of the time.

Harry recalls being very impressed the first time he climbed into the two-man cockpit. It was the first time in his life sitting in a cabin where both sets of pilot controls were contained in the same space, rather than fore and aft. He described it as a feeling of "being at home, as if I was always supposed to be there".

The army initially took control of the airfield at Stockton in August 1940. At the time, it was severely lacking in amenities, not the least of which was a control tower. The airport lacked a tower until late 1941.

With the onset of the war, the airbase was quickly expanded as thousands of Cadets and trainees poured in. Five additional auxillary airfields were established nearby to address the need to train as many pilots, navigators, and bombardiers as quickly as feasible. By the time Harry and Lang arrived at Stockton, there were approximately ten barracks' buildings dedicated to the cadets along with a single, vast mess hall. Three newly constructed 800-foot wide by 4,600-foot long runways had been added and could comfortably accommodate large, multiple engine aircraft. Harry remembers Lang taking a look at the runways for the first time and, with a smile on his face, asking Harry: "Think they're wide enough for you?" Harry remained quiet, he had no defense.

The Curtiss-Wright AT-9 "Jeep" twin-engine trainer entered service in 1942. The Curtiss-Wright designers made it purposefully tricky to land and operate in preparation for assignment to larger, more sophisticated aircraft the cadets would be flying in combat. The plane was so tricky to fly that post-war sales of the AT-9 to civilians was banned.

The base featured a library, theatre, cleaners, and an expansive depot offering discounts on a wide range of goods. Of particular importance was most of the items offered for sale, including shoes, which were otherwise hard to come by, were not subject to ration stamps.

Indications that the airfield had been constructed in a hurry were obvious. The runways were not concrete but instead were paved with blacktop. When the temperatures climbed into the 80s, it was easy to skid when applying the brakes as the runway surfaces would soften and grow slick from oil that would rise to the surface.

The buildings were constructed from wood or metal, never brick or stone, again creating a feeling in Harry that the whole place was temporary. Harry and Lang quickly grew accustomed to the frenzied activity they faced at Stockton as planes were landing and taking off at all hours, and classroom study was piled on high. For reasons neither man could figure out it was soon apparent to them the army appeared intent on booting out anyone who didn't meet every single one of the high standards the Army Air Force was setting. Though pilots were sorely needed, the failure rate was high.

Military protocol was strictly followed, and officers always expected a salute, though many didn't bother to return one. One day, for no apparent reason, the entire cadet class was ordered to form-up in front of the operations shack. A second lieutenant, who he recalls had been nicknamed "Eyeballs", was followed by an enlisted man grasping a clipboard and trailing one step behind him. Eyeballs ordered the assembled cadets to remain at attention.

He proceeded to casually stroll across the entire assembly. When he reached the far end of the assembled men, he reversed course and took up a position at the center of the group. He had yet to say a word. Following a brief pause he began what appeared to be nothing more than a routine inspection, which was nothing out of the ordinary.

Eyeballs would stop and face each cadet, staring him in the eyes. Sometimes he'd instruct the enlisted man following behind him to write the cadet's name on his list. Other times he would stare at the cadet and move on without saying a word. When he reached Harry, he found it necessary to glance down a little as he was about 5 inches taller than him; Harry stared right back at Eyeballs, never so much as blinking. Without revealing any expression Eyeballs remained silent for a few moments then proceeded to the next cadet.

When the inspection was finished, Eyeballs announced all the men whose names he had called out were to follow the enlisted man carrying the clipboard. He dismissed the remaining cadets and walked away in the opposite direction of the group he'd dispatched. Harry was immediately devastated as he believed he and the remaining men were being washed-out. He wondered how Eyeballs knew who to choose and felt seriously short-shrifted.

Later the same evening, he discovered the men who'd been singled out earlier that day had been deemed unfit as officer material and were being immediately reassigned to either bombardier or navigator school. The apparent randomness of the selection process didn't do Harry's self-confidence much good. He and Lang discussed the day's event and decided they would redouble their efforts to make sure they would attract the right kind of attention and never be summarily washed out.

Both men concurred they learned faster and more efficiently with the presence of an instructor sitting beside them in the cockpit rather than in the fore and aft positions as had been their prior training experiences. The two men were among the first in their class to fly their own solo flights in the AT-9, and they took full advantage of the new freedom. Whenever they weren't perfecting formation flying, they'd be up there practicing on their own.

On their solo flights, they each explored the limits of the twin-engine plane's performance envelope. Harry would sometimes imagine he was in a P-38 and attack an imaginary foe, opening the throttles all the way, the term being "to pour on the coal". He experienced a thrill unlike any other when he'd push the plane into a tight turn, throttles wide open, feeling the engines vibrate and the fuselage shake. He said hitching rides on trains and river barges didn't come close to the thrill of opening the throttles and diving on an imaginary target.

Needless to say, Harry had a great deal of fun flying the new plane. With the AT-9, everything was faster, as if time somehow sped up while he pressed the aircraft through the drills. He was flying faster than he ever had before and was loving every moment in the air.

In Harry's opinion, the AT-9 absolutely demanded immediate reactions from the pilot. He discovered it was a finicky plane that allowed minimal leeway for errors or delayed pilot reactions. A simple wrong move could easily prove fatal, and it added to his excitement.

Despite the plane's idiosyncrasies, he cherished the opportunities to explore the plane's performance limits and experience how it responded under all manner of conditions. His penchant for scrutinizing the aircraft at the extremes of its designed performance parameters didn't go unnoticed, as he would discover after he commenced the next leg of his training journey, Transition Pilot Training.

Harry loved the opportunities to take an AT-6 "Texan" out for gunnery training. The AT-6 was a single-engine, 2-seat aircraft with a Pratt & Whitney R-1340-AN-1 Wasp radial engine, producing a robust 600 horsepower. In the AT-6, Harry could quickly accelerate to speeds over 200mph; diving onto a target was great fun. And fun was something Harry experienced on each and every flight.

As part of the extensive training regimen, Harry also flew the BT-13/15 "Valiant", the difference between it and the Texan being the manufacturer of the engine. He preferred the additional power of the AT-6 over that of the Valiant. The two planes prepared him to begin flying larger multi-engine aircraft, and he was looking forward to mastering bombing techniques in the next plane he'd be required to master, the Cessna "Bobcat". He'd heard a lot of scuttlebutt about the "Bobcat" and some of it was not good. In all events, he knew he was about to learn the Bobcat's pros and cons first-hand.

Above: The Cessna "Bobcat" was dubbed by the Air Corps as the "Bamboo Bomber."

Left: 50 Canadian built Avro Anson 652s were redubbed the AT-20 for the U.S. Army Air Force.

ADVANCED PILOT TRAINING

Just about every pilot of a twin-engine plane would, sooner or later, find themselves in a Cessna "Bobcat", except Harry. To his dismay, he was designated to train in a similarly constructed twin-engine plane employed by both the Royal Air Force and the Royal Canadian Air Force as a trainer. The aircraft had been banned from wartime service as it was deemed unsuitable for such duty, if not outright dangerous.

Because of the extensive use of wood and fabric in the AT-20's construction, it was similar in many ways to the "Bamboo Bomber". Yet it was a very different plane. Harry would not become a fan of the Canadian manufactured Avro Anson 652 a/k/s AT-20 and considered himself lucky to have survived it.

It was Harry's opinion the AT-20's engines were prone to icing-up if there was so much as a hint of moisture in the air and the temperature was anywhere close to 32 degrees Fahrenheit. Air tends to grow colder as a plane gains altitude, so icing-up was something he needed to be on the watch for. Harry also believed the brakes were next to useless and, all-in-all, considered the AT-20 to be the least desirable plane he'd experienced to date. Looking back after the war, he would rate it as absolutely the most unreliable and dangerous plane he'd ever flown.

On March 23 1943, he was scheduled to fly an AT-20 and take a co-pilot cadet/trainee with him to practice bombing runs. They had performed all the necessary pre-flight checklist items, and everything appeared to be as it should. Harry strapped himself into the pilot's seat while the cadet/trainee did the same in the co-pilot's seat to Harry's right. Once the engines warmed up, Harry was given guidance from the tower to proceed to the runway, and, once in place, he was cleared for take-off. Harry recalls that this was about the time "things would go wrong, very, very wrong, in a big hurry."

He pushed the throttles full-open and the plane quickly began to gain speed. He was just about halfway down the runway and almost to the point of lift-off when the right engine started coughing. He immediately concluded the engine had iced-up. Without any hesitation, he executed every one of the accepted techniques for dislodging ice.

Too far down the runway to abort the take-off, matters quickly grew worse. The second engine began sputtering, and, at that moment, he knew he was in really deep trouble. Both engines were sputtering and sounded to him as if they were starving for fuel. Rather than gaining speed, the plane was slowing down.

Harry knew he had no choice but to abort the take-off. He immediately cut the engines and applied the brakes as hard as he could. However, it felt as if the plane was actually speeding up. He always had little confidence in the AT-20's brakes, so he wasn't particularly surprised when they failed, though he was seriously disappointed.

In a matter of seconds, he consumed the balance of the runway as both engines finally conked out; 30 yards of grass was all that remained between him and a small lake situated at the end of the runway. At an estimated ground speed of at least 40mph, the short stretch of grass was crossed in an instant, and the plane sped directly into the lake.

When the landing gear struck the water, the plane's momentum caused it to immediately flip forward, nose-down, leaving Harry and his co-pilot hanging from their seats. Incredibly, neither of them was injured, and after a brief struggle, each man was able to climb out of the plane, just as several rescue vehicles were pulling up on the nearby shore. Harry was soaking wet, disgusted, and worried. Graduation was not all that far off, and a crash on take-off certainly wasn't going to look good on his record.

After the rescue workers determined neither man had been injured, they were whisked to the Operations hut and placed into separate rooms for debriefing. Harry described everything he'd experienced, which matched exactly with what his co-pilot had explained to his own team of three interrogators. The two sets of investigators had asked each of them the same questions from various points of view, but the truth was the truth. And, of course, the interrogators were pilots themselves and aware of the plane's propensity for engine icing. The separate interviews lasted about thirty minutes each.

Once the interrogations were complete, they were taken to the squadron commander's office. By the time they arrived, the commander had already conferred with the interviewers. Harry doesn't recall his name, but he remembers he was a colonel and appeared genuinely concerned for the physical and mental well-being of his two young pilots. He spoke with Harry and his fellow cadet for a couple of minutes and then asked each of them if they desired to continue with their training. Both men enthusiastically responded that they most certainly wanted to do so. The colonel then turned to a captain sitting next to him and said: "Make it happen."

Harry recently checked his official record and discovered the accident recited above remains a part of his record. However, it only refers to there having been an accident and contains no details. Harry says: "At least it didn't wash me out or kill me!"

Harry and his co-pilot were driven out to the tarmac, where they were assigned another AT-20. They went aboard and proceeded to complete their bombing run practice drills without any further hitches. Harry, however, did allow the engines in his replacement plane to warm up an extra few minutes and revved them at length before proceeding to take-off. As the plane lifted from the runway, they flew directly over the AT-20 they'd just dunked into the lake. Looking back at the nose-in-the-water plane caused Harry to wish one of them had brought a camera along.

He enjoyed bombing runs, making a practice of flying as low as feasible to achieve maximum accuracy. He pressed his replacement plane particularly hard and recalls feeling compelled to force the aircraft to its absolute limits as if he were daring it to resist him a second time. His co-pilot never said a word, and when Harry glanced at him while pulling out of a bombing run, he noticed he had a big smile on his face. As they returned to base and were taxiing to the tarmac, Harry concluded he'd rather fly the AT-9.

By the time they disembarked, the crashed AT-20 had been plucked from the lake and moved to a hangar. He walked over to take a look at it and was surprised at the absence of visual damage.

Graduation day was Thursday, May 20 1943. Early that morning, Harry needed to enlist a driver and a Jeep to take him over to the Stockton train station where he would meet his bride-to-be and her mother. He was an outstanding pilot at that point but had never learned how to drive a car.

A striking visual comparison of an AT-9 sitting beneath the wing of a twin engine, Curtiss C-76 "Commando" transport plane. Mastering the AT-9 paved the way for learning to fly the C-76 and C-47, among other multi-engine aircraft. Photo courtesy of the Library of Congress and military.wikia.com.

His parents didn't own one, and he could almost count on one hand the number of times he'd even been in a car while growing up in Courtney.

Through an almost daily exchange of correspondence, Harry discovered June's father always called her "Wee Junie" because she had been such a tiny baby. Harry adopted the moniker and addressed his letters to her as "Dear Wee Junie". He would eventually name his plane, "Wee Junie". The nickname would stay with June throughout her life.

His memory of the night they spent dancing at the USO was somewhat fuzzy. It had been relatively dark in the dance hall, and the weeks since then had been packed with flying. He was experiencing a certain amount of trepidation as he stood on the train platform, waiting for his future mother-in-law and bride. He couldn't even be sure he would recognize Wee Junie.

He'd always been a risk-taker, but what he was about to do meant risking more than his future as he knew he was about to alter the course of Wee Junie's life as well as his own. For the first time, he was feeling a demand to be responsible because whatever he did no longer affected just him. He would struggle a bit with the concept throughout the war as testified in a letter he would write her, which is reprinted in the final chapter of this book.

Lang's fiancée Lillian, aka "Lillie", had arrived earlier from Salt Lake City, and the couple was to meet up with Harry's group back at the base. The passenger train pulled in about ten minutes late and proved to be very crowded. Harry watched intently as scores of both civilians and service personnel disembarked, cluttering the station platform with passengers and luggage. After a few minutes, the platform was rapidly clearing, and there were only a handful of people standing around. Harry was beginning to wonder if they'd missed the train when he spotted a little grey-haired lady. Following close behind her was a young woman who turned out to be the 18-year-old "wee Junie". Harry was 20 years old at the time.

He confidently strode up to the two ladies and politely introduced himself. Suddenly he realized he didn't recognize his bride to be. He'd never seen her in proper lighting as it had been pretty dark that distant night in the USO dance hall.

Harry politely inquired whether he was the person the two ladies were seeking. Her mom smiled and told him how excited she was to finally meet him "in the real person". He shook hands with her mother and then turned to face Junie. Immediately the clarity and sparkle of her blue Irish eyes impressed him, and any thoughts of bailing out that he may have been harboring vanished. They shook hands because Harry didn't want to appear to be anything less than an officer and a gentleman, per the Army Air Force oath. He noticed her hand felt very soft as she flashed a big smile at him. He recalls he and Junie slowly, and gently, shook hands. Harry proceeded to gather their luggage and then sought a cab for the ride to the base.

Following the graduation ceremony, Harry and Lang, both newly sworn-in second lieutenants, sought out their respective fiancées and, along with Wee Junie's mom, departed for the chapel. A Mormon bishop presided over the Lang ceremony while a Catholic priest presided over Harry and Junie's nuptials.

The freshly married couples, including Harry's new mother-in-law, went into downtown Stockton, enjoyed lunch at a little place called Cedar's Fountain, stopped for ice cream sodas, and eventually spent the night at the grand Hotel Stockton. Both men and their brides would enjoy two days of honeymoon in Stockton, after which they'd all travel together to a new base where Harry and Lang would commence the final phase of their training: Transition Pilot Training.

Harry's mother-in-law caught an early train back home on May 21st. The couples made the most of the remaining two days. Harry remembers they spent most of one afternoon watching an exciting Henry Fonda movie, *The Ox-Bow Incident*. On Sunday morning, May 23 1943, they boarded a train for Austin, Texas, where Harry's army career would continue, and the two relative strangers would begin their sudden transition to married life. They didn't waste any of Harry's off-duty time and promptly set about the pleasant task of discovering everything there was to know about one another.

The "Grand" Hotel Stockton. Photo courtesy: Michael Aivaliotis – Own work, CC BY-SA 3.0, https://commons.wikimedia.org/w/index.php?curid=21844171

Harry and his bride, "Wee Junie", enjoying a rare weekend pass outside of Austin, Texas.

Harry's next posting, and the couple's first home, was at Bergstrom Army Air Base near Austin, Texas. The facility had been designated by the army as a troop carrier training field, so Harry had reason to believe he was destined to fly transports unless some intervening event occurred. To Harry, it no longer mattered what type of plane he flew, his priority was to finish training and get himself into the war.

Chapter 8

Bergstrom Army Airfield

Lang was ordered to report for bomber training while Harry transitioned into transport training, which could be anything from a two-engine to a four-engine plane. Both men had about two months of intensive, hands-on flight and classroom instruction awaiting them. Following successful completion, they anticipated being transferred into a combat zone. The two friends decided should they be deployed to England, they'd try to get together whenever possible.

Harry didn't know it, but he'd find himself at Bergstrom longer than he'd spend at any other single airbase throughout the war. It was time for him to begin mastering the model of aircraft the army needed most and, in its opinion, would be the best position for Harry. While Harry knew he'd most likely be learning to fly transport aircraft, the risk-taker within him still held out a slight hope it might be the twin-engine P-38 Lightning fighter plane.

Harry, proudly displaying his Flight Instructor's pin, posing in front of the Texas State Capitol building in Austin, Texas, a few hours after promotion to Flight Instructor in 1943.

However, the new responsibility of being married forced him to look beyond the war, which meant flying whatever was best-suited to land him a post-war job piloting passenger planes.

Lang soon found himself flying the B-24 Liberator, a four-engine heavy bomber. While he had no idea whether he'd be operating in the Pacific or European theatre of operations, at least Lang knew the type of aircraft he'd be piloting. He telephoned Harry to tell him about the B-24, and, as Harry recalls, he sounded genuinely excited.

For Harry's part, he was keenly aware that should he find himself flying transports, then he might be assigned to the Far East. If he was sent there, he could be flying supply missions over the treacherous "Hump" in Burma. If sent to the European theatre, he could be flying throughout the Mediterranean. He was hoping to be based in England, which had come to be his preference based on the "scuttlebutt" he'd been privy to. What he didn't desire at all was an assignment piloting trans-Atlantic cargo flights because that meant he would never be close to any action. What he did not foresee, however, was to find himself facing a completely unexpected quandary.

One late afternoon in July 1943, he was summoned to appear before his commanding officer; he had no clue why he was being sought. He sat across the desk from his colonel and waited to hear what was up. The colonel advised Harry he was facing a situation unlike he'd ever seen before, while also confirming that he had Harry's application to transfer into a transport group in the field, he also had three additional requests pending. Harry was confused and explained all he knew was he had requested transfer into a combat transport group.

The colonel picked up a sheet of paper and advised him he was looking at a recommendation from an instructor to send Harry to Bombardier School. He put the paper down and picked up another sheet and said he had a second recommendation to send Harry to Navigator School. Both were based on solid performance reviews and numerous first-class test results.

Harry didn't know how he should react and remained quiet for a few seconds. He certainly didn't want to offend his colonel and carefully began to explain that he had no desire for either of the two courses of specialized instruction for which he'd been recommended. The colonel told him he wasn't finished yet as there was a third, "very impressive" recommendation. Harry was staring at the colonel seeking a clue from his facial expression when suddenly the colonel smiled. Harry wasn't accustomed to that.

The colonel proceeded to explain that the commander of his Advance Pilot Training School class had put Harry up for an appointment to the United States Military Academy at West Point. Harry was stunned. West Point! A kid from the coal mines going to West Point was just about unheard of. It took him a few moments to get a handle on everything the colonel had just told him. His mind was racing, and he found himself blabbering everything he could think of, and then some.

He remembers explaining he was already a second lieutenant. If he were to attend West Point, the war could be over by the time he graduated, even though he'd be facing a war-abbreviated two-year course of study rather than the standard four years. After all, he argued, it was the middle of 1943, and time was moving along. Harry emphatically stated: "I don't want to miss out on the war," and reiterated his request for assignment to a combat-zone based transport group. But the colonel had yet one more proposal to throw at him.

He told Harry to bear with him and asked him to immediately sit for a series of tests. Upon completion, they'd meet again to hammer everything out. Harry complied, and a week later he was back sitting in front of the colonel who had the test results spread out before him. The longer he spent looking over the results, the larger the grin on the colonel's face, which didn't necessarily put Harry at ease. His first flight instructor, Mr Kinert, loved to put on a big smile just before reaming him out, something he never forgot. Harry was uncomfortable and wiggling around in his seat as he watched his colonel review the test results.

Harry can't remember how much time passed, but it felt like hours. Eventually, the colonel pushed his chair back a few inches, looked Harry square in the eyes and said: "Watson, these scores are truly exemplary. I am pleased to announce you're being promoted to Flight Instructor, with a concomitant pay increase, effective immediately. Congratulations!"

At first, Harry didn't know what to say. It sounded great, but what about the war? If he was an instructor, he'd be stateside, at least for the foreseeable future. He had enough common sense, however, not to argue, and before he could formulate a response, the colonel added: "And by the way, you're the youngest instructor on the field." Harry smiled, thanked him, and took off to find his wife and convey the news. The additional pay was something the young couple very sorely needed, and they immediately celebrated their good fortune in private. Junie was particularly delighted as the promotion meant he wouldn't be going into the war yet, if ever.

MIDNIGHT FLIGHT TO NUREMBERG

One morning in early August 1943, Harry had just finished a classroom session explaining navigation techniques to a class of about twenty pilots. As he walked out of the classroom building, he noticed a Jeep was parked out front, but nobody was in it. He had been aware a couple of officers were not far behind him when suddenly he heard one of them call out:

"Hey, lieutenant!" Harry stopped, swiveled around, and discovered he was facing a colonel and a captain, both men standing about 10 feet away. The colonel motioned with his right hand, indicating he wanted Harry to come over. After looking around to make sure the colonel was calling him and not someone else nearby, Harry quickly approached the two senior officers.

"Lieutenant, I'd like you to drive us down to the control tower." He paused when he noticed Harry's instructor insignia, then continued: "Unless, of course, you're due to conduct a flying lesson."

Harry was utterly taken aback and advised the colonel he was finished with his duties until 1400 hours. The colonel pointed to the Jeep and ordered him to give them a ride over to the control tower, which was approximately 1 mile away. Harry briefly thought he should mention he'd never driven a car before in his life but decided to stay quiet. He was too embarrassed to admit it, especially since he was a flight instructor. The three men climbed aboard the Jeep, the colonel to his right while the captain sat behind the colonel.

Harry wasn't sure how to start the Jeep when he recalled he once heard someone say something about putting the clutch down before turning the key, which he did. Except the Jeep didn't start when he turned the key. Making a second attempt to start the engine, Harry pressed the clutch pedal into the floor as hard as possible, resulting in the Jeep roaring to life. He let off the clutch, pushed the gas, and the Jeep immediately lunged forward, throwing both of his passengers back in their seats.

As he drove along, searching for the gears, he managed to kill the engine more than once. He was just starting to get a handle on how to work the clutch when they finally reached the tower. It had been a bumpy and unusually long 1-mile ride. He was praying the officers didn't intend to ask him to wait for them as he planned to immediately walk back and leave the Jeep where it was.

The three men disembarked, and as Harry began to walk away, the colonel called out to him, forcing him to stop and reverse course. He feared they were going to ask him to wait and perhaps even drive them somewhere else.

"Lieutenant," the colonel was slowly shaking his head back and forth, "I sure as hell hope you can fly better than you drive." The two men proceeded into the tower without saying another word. Harry decided it was best to remain silent and get the heck out of there as fast as he could.

In February 1944, Junie suspected she was pregnant. After a visit to the doctor, her pregnancy was confirmed, and the fact that she knew Harry would likely be staying in Texas, instructing new pilots, was a comfort for her. Many of her married friends had found it necessary to return to their parents' homes when their husbands were transferred overseas. She'd been absolutely delighted when Harry was promoted to instructor instead of being shipped to a battle posting. At the time, she told him she was counting her blessings.

With the pregnancy, Junie appeared to be wearing a perpetual smile. Harry was pretty excited himself and did occasionally reflect how Lang didn't think he'd survive the war, though he kept such thoughts to himself. He was still not comfortable with Lang's assertion that Harry wasn't alone when he took his maiden flight, but was incredibly happy his wife would be giving birth to their child before he left for the "shooting war". He didn't care if it was a boy or girl, just so long as the baby and Wee Junie were "A-OK".

Time was passing rapidly, Junie's pregnancy was coming along well, and the young couple were very excited at the prospect of having a baby girl or boy. In May 1944, when she was about four months pregnant, Junie complained about unusual pains in the side of her stomach. Harry had never heard her complain about anything before and took immediate notice. She wanted to give it a day or two before seeking out the base medical staff. When Harry returned from his duties on the second day, he found her nearly passed-out on the sofa. He checked her pulse, realized she was drenched in sweat, and immediately summoned an ambulance.

It didn't take long for the medical staff to determine she was suffering from a severely infected kidney. She was immediately hospitalized, and they began to treat her condition. The infection, however, was not responding to treatment. A decision had to be made quickly, or both Junie and her unborn child would soon be in dire jeopardy.

After discussing the situation with Junie, Harry granted the requisite consent, and the medical decision was made to remove the kidney, which was successfully accomplished without causing any harm to either Junie or the baby. However, she needed an extended period of complete rest, and the doctors recommended she travel by train to her mom's home in Taft, California, for the remainder of the pregnancy.

With great reluctance and a flood of tears, they mutually agreed they must follow the doctors' orders. She told Harry, sooner or later, she knew they'd be separated, but never anticipated she'd be the one leaving, and Harry would be the one left behind. Her mother was ecstatic at the prospect of Junie re-joining her and wasted no time seeking an appropriate hospital for the delivery.

With Junie safely home with her mom, Harry was at a loss over what to do with all his newly discovered free time. He considered his various options regarding what might serve him best once he was in the war. After conferring with his base commander, Harry decided he'd spend virtually all of his spare time perfecting his instrument flying skills. In short order, he became a fixture in the Instrument Flight Rules, "IFR", hut.

He was reasonably sure he'd eventually be piloting C-47s or similar transports. It dawned on him that if he were to be dropping paratroopers and towing gliders, then he should know, first-hand, what the paratroopers and glider pilots experienced. He reasoned if he practiced what it took to be a paratrooper or a glider pilot, then he'd be a better transport pilot for it.

Over the next two weeks Harry made many convincing arguments to his colonel, who finally relented and drafted the order allowing Harry to commence glider pilot training. After making five solo glider flights, he received his certification as a glider pilot.

Harry was keenly aware of the fact he had not needed to leave the base to achieve his new glider pilot certification and calculated that fact likely weighed on the colonel's favorable decision. During his glider pilot training regimen, he managed to conduct classroom sessions and the occasional

One of the 255-foot tall parachute practice towers at the Parachute School in Fort Benning, Georgia.

flight training, so it wasn't as if the colonel lost all of his services. He feared his next request might prove to be a bit more taxing on the colonel, and he was correct.

For about six weeks, Harry stubbornly and repeatedly argued he should be sent to the Parachute School at Fort Benning on a short-term assignment to earn his parachute certification. He stressed that as a C-47 pilot dropping paratroopers behind enemy lines, he should possess first-hand knowledge about what parachuting entailed so he could more intuitively guide his plane. He could, in turn, incorporate what he learned into his instruction of new pilots.

Every few days, he'd make a point of seeking out the colonel. Sometimes he'd catch him out and about on the grounds, one time at the mess hall, but mostly at his office. The colonel was much more hesitant to grant Harry's new request because it meant losing an instructor for about a month. If Harry were to suffer a serious mishap while parachuting, he might lose him permanently. Eventually, he could no longer resist Harry's consistent haranguing and approved the temporary reassignment. He shipped Harry off to Fort Benning, Georgia, home of the U.S. Army's Parachute School.

Harry was one of a small handful of pilots in his parachute class. The training included what he felt was the most challenging aspect of the entire regimen: learning to pack a parachute. He was anxious to move forward but had to endure what he considered mundane stuff, like jumping from a simulated C-47 hatchway onto a hangar floor.

He fondly recalls having a whale of a good time when he found himself strapped into a twin-seat lift-chair with another paratrooper candidate and dropped from the top of one of the parachute towers, while attached to a bungee cord. No carnival he'd ever attended offered a ride anywhere near the thrill of bottoming out on a bungee cord drop from a more than the 250-foot tall tower. After making his requisite five parachute jumps from planes, he received his diploma and parachute badge.

Once he completed Parachute School, he requested a short leave. He was already in Georgia and decided he'd like to make a trip home for a visit with his parents. He hadn't seen them since the summer of 1941, and it was already around May 1944.

When he arrived home, the neighbors put together a "Welcome Home" barbeque where he regaled them with tall stories. Many of them spoke with him about what he'd be doing after the war. He sometimes found himself biting his tongue because he wasn't sure he'd survive the war and didn't want his parents and neighbors to learn of his fear. Time flew past quickly, and in short order, he was back at Bergstrom, which was bathed in the heat of an unrelenting Texas summer.

The first thing he did upon his return to Bergstrom was check-out an AT-6 and take her up for an open-cockpit joy ride. He made sure to bring along a training pilot so both could log some hours while cooling off from the sweltering Texas heat a little at the same time. Logging hours was an essential part of being an army pilot, and he never missed the chance to log a few more.

The conversations in the Officers' Club were almost always about the war in Europe. The pilots followed the air tactics surrounding every aspect of the Normandy invasion and speculated they'd soon be sent over there to join the "fracas". Harry, having been in the service longer than everyone around him, was particularly antsy to get into the action. He began making

queries with his colonel about being transferred to England. Some of them were subtle and others less so, always resulting in the colonel responding: "In due time, lieutenant, in due time."

Shortly after June 6 1944, the colonel summoned Harry to his office. As Harry strolled in, he noticed the colonel, well known for his scowls, was wearing a broad smile. When Harry approached his desk, the colonel stood and offered a salute. Harry was quite taken aback as the usual protocol overlooked salutes.

Harry, with his parents following graduation from Parachute School at Fort Benning in 1944.

A "V-Mail" letter from Junie.

He quickly recovered, stood at attention, and returned the greeting as smartly as he could. The colonel then said:

"Harry, here are your orders." He handed him a small stack of papers. "You're off for Europe, lieutenant!"

He told Harry there was a brand-spanking-new C-47 sitting on a tarmac at Baer Field, just waiting for him. He proceeded to explain Harry was joining the 438th Troop Carrier Group. The Group had only recently formed at Baer Field near Fort Wayne, Indiana, and was in the process of relocating to England. He explained Harry didn't need to worry about anything except getting himself to Baer on time. He said an aircrew, including his co-pilot, was already in the process of being assigned to Baer from which he'd fly his new plane all the way to Greenham Common, an airbase in England.

He told Harry Greenham Common was going to be his new station and wished he was going there himself. The colonel also confided he had actually "gotten something of a kick" from Harry each time Harry made a plea for transfer to combat, and he was going to miss him. He also said the boys in the Link Trainer (IFR) shack were probably going to be a lot less busy with him gone.

He extended his right hand and said, "Congratulations!" Harry quickly took his hand and shook it hard. He didn't know what to say and blurted out: "That's really swell Sir!"

Harry felt almost dizzy with excitement. He grabbed the orders, started to leave, but paused to ask if there was anything else the colonel needed. The colonel laughed and advised Harry to get himself to Indiana, "lickety-split".

Harry made a beeline for a telephone to call Junie, but had to make a stop first so he could learn where Greenham Common was located so he could better explain his destination to her. Junie had been expecting he'd be transferred to a combat posting sooner or later and took the news in her stride. They talked for at least half an hour until the base operator cut in and advised them to end the conversation as the line was needed. Harry told Junie he'd call again when he knew his travel plans. His mind was racing, and even to this day, he says the sequence of events that whisked him from Texas to England happened so quickly they are as much of a blur now as they were in 1944.

Chapter 9

The Northern Route

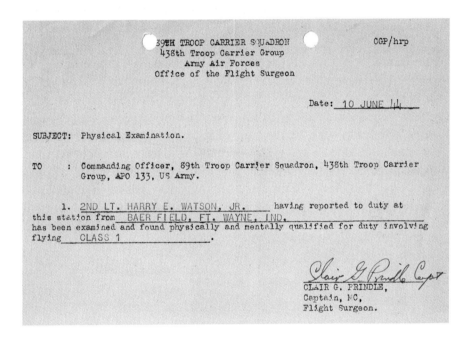

On Monday, June 26 1944, Harry and his new crew gathered around a freshly delivered Douglas C-47 "Skytrain" sitting on a tarmac at Baer Field, just outside Fort Wayne, Indiana. Harry, at 21 years old, was the youngest among them. However, he'd been in the army longer than any of his crew. His youthfulness didn't have any negative impact concerning how he was regarded by the men. When his crew chief spotted Harry's flight instructor pin, he told Harry, "I've been with a lot of kooky pilots in the last year and was afraid I'd wind up with someone who'd get me killed. I'm proud to be with you, lieutenant."

Harry and his crew took their time inspecting the exterior of their new plane and taking photos. His crew chief, who proved to be something of a camera buff, consumed an entire roll of film.

Once Harry was satisfied everything was in proper order, he was the first to climb into the cabin. As he stepped through the hatch, he was greeted by the sight of four, 200-gallon plywood fuel tanks. They were located just before the flight deck with a narrow aisle between them. The tanks were full of aviation fuel, and the additional 800-gallon capacity would allow him to make each leg of the pending trans-Atlantic flight without the need to land for refueling.

The additional gasoline did come with a couple of caveats, for it weighed a little over 4,800lbs and also meant there'd be no smoking. The extra weight would take a measurable toll on the plane's anticipated range and slightly modify its flight characteristics, something Harry figured he'd need to grow accustomed to.

Harry could direct the engine's fuel source from either the built-in tanks located within the wings or the additional containers, without leaving his pilot's seat. He made a point to always draw-down from the extra fuel tanks first because he wasn't comfortable with the idea of carrying so much fuel between the flight deck and the sole exit point of the aircraft, a single hatch in the rear of the cabin.

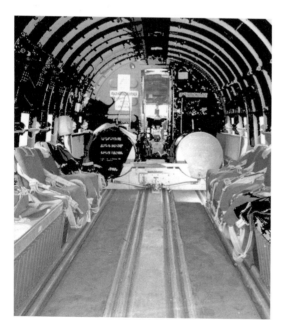

A C-47 equipped with a pair of temporary fuel tanks. The photo depicts a plane configured to transport "VIPs", per First Lieutenant Harry Watson.

84

They wasted little time taking the new plane for a one-hour flight check which did reveal a handful of small issues the ground crew would address the following day. Later the same day, Harry and his co-pilot, Al, were examining the proposed flight path they'd follow to their ultimate destination, the airbase at Greenham Common, England, via the "Northern Route." They pieced together about three maps and, using a ruler and a pencil, drew a sketch of the entire route. They posted it inside the cabin, which provided their crew chief ("Chief") and radio operator ("Sparky") something to reference as they made their way to England.

Harry's orders stated he, along with his plane and crew, were to report to Greenham Common, England. How he went about getting there was left for Harry to determine. They would not be part of a formation and were strictly flying on their own.

At first light on Wednesday, June 28 1944, Harry and his crew ate some "hot chow" before starting the first leg of their journey to Grenier Army Airfield, located near the town of Manchester, New Hampshire. They were facing about a 900-mile flight, which was a good 200 miles further than Harry had ever flown in a single day.

After an aggressive day of flying, they made it to Grenier in about five hours, leaving the new C-47 in the hands of a pair of mechanics who were aware it had been the plane's maiden long-distance flight. The ground crew conferred with Harry and Al, asking them various questions about their experiences on the trip. The chief mechanic told them not to worry about anything except the business of flying because they were going to "check the whole shebang" and make sure there was not one thing out of order.

The support services at Grenier made them feel right at home. Harry and his crew enjoyed an exceptional dinner after which they were set up in a Quonset hut, took showers, and hit the sack. Before bedding down for the night, Harry pulled Al aside and reviewed the next day's flight plan one last time, just to be certain.

At first light the following morning, Harry filed his flight plan and was assigned a take-off slot. He met with the mechanics who confirmed they'd thoroughly inspected the plane, and everything was in first-class working order. Later in the morning, they took off for Goose Bay, Labrador, which was a distance of approximately 900 miles and would take them across vast expanses of incredibly dense forest.

It was the first time in his life Harry had left the United States. In fact, none of the crew had ever been outside the States, and they were all pretty excited. They spoke about the fact they were embarking on a great adventure

At least 2,000 Douglas C-47 aircraft were sent to England under the Lend-Lease program. The English gave the plane their own nickname, the "Dakota". Note the open side hatch indicating it may be returning from a paratroop drop. The windows appeared to be covered, a possible clue the plane had been transporting paratroopers.

and were anticipating what England might be like. Each man made it clear he was more than ready to become personally involved in the war. Nobody mentioned the potential dangers they'd likely face soon.

Flying conditions were good, matching the mood of Harry and his crew. They didn't observe so much as a single plane during the trip. Al mentioned that if they had to crash-land, they might not ever be found; Harry told him not to think about things like that. Harry had already considered the possibility and felt voicing something so negative could be bad luck.

Eventually, Harry believed he was close enough to Goose Bay to initiate contact with the control tower, which proceeded to direct him to a runway. Visibility was almost unlimited, and when the runway came into view, as Harry recalls, "I was in the slot and on the numbers." He was soon on the ground in Labrador and taxing behind a "Follow Me" Jeep.

Harry was stunned at the size of the Royal Canadian Air Force airfield. As it turned out, it was the largest airfield in the entire western hemisphere. Because it was the final North American stop for planes making the flight to Europe, the U.S. Army had constructed its own facilities on the base. They included expansive sleeping quarters, a mess hall, a HQ building that really wasn't much larger than a shack, and repair facilities with hangars.

The Jeep guided him to tarmac alongside one of the American hangars. They were soon met by a few other pilots and taken on an abbreviated tour of the sprawling base by a very pleasant and cordial Canadian corporal.

Harry and his crew were impressed not just by the size of the base, but the extent of the seemingly well-coordinated activity and the frequent landings and take-offs of twin and four-engine aircraft of every manner. Harry had never before seen some of the planes that were present at Labrador and found it to be a learning experience.

The following morning their departure was delayed. The weather was miserable but was expected to improve later in the morning. The weather forecast was correct, and by late morning they were on their way to Meeks Field in Iceland. Harry had never flown across a body of water larger than a lake and was impressed by the horizon-to-horizon stretches of ocean. He recalled the experience helped him better appreciate what anti-submarine patrol pilots and crews had to cope with and wondered how they could ever spot a submarine from up there.

He discovered daylight hours were greatly extended due to how far north they were operating. There was no worrying about whether they'd need to make a night landing once they reached Iceland. Thanks to the on-board fuel tanks, they were able to make the non-stop 1,500-mile journey to Meeks Field situated on the far south-western tip of Iceland in about eight hours. Meeks had been purposefully constructed on the first piece of landfall on the route to Europe, minimizing the duration of the flight from Canada.

Meeks Field, Iceland, served not only as a critical refueling post but also as a significant base for flying anti-submarine patrols. The weather, however, could be severe.

Despite the fact that it was June, Harry had expected to see a landscape covered in ice. Instead, he was taken aback by how green and beautiful Iceland appeared to be. In later years he'd fly to Greenland as the pilot of a commercial airliner and wonder to himself why Iceland and Greenland had never swapped names.

Due to an extended period of inclement weather, he would spend five long and tedious nights at Meeks. He does recall the base happened to have a pretty nifty Officers' Club where he and Al caught up with all the recent scuttlebutt about the war.

Pilots on long-term stations at Meeks regaled them with stories of extended air patrols seeking out German U-boats, and at least one pilot claimed to have sunk one. Harry was envious of their adventures, and the longer the bad weather persisted, the ever more antsy he became. He didn't take much solace in the fact that at least forty or fifty other aircraft were also stuck at Meeks. He wanted to get himself and his crew into the action, and sitting around in rain and fog wasn't sitting well with any of them.

As the days dragged on, Harry met quite a few characters, one of whom was a Royal Canadian Air Force Pilot who went by the name of "Moose". He was a large man, causing Harry to wonder how he even managed to fit into a cockpit. Moose was loud, could out-drink just about anyone, and very much enjoyed talking about flying his "Digby" on anti-submarine patrols. Harry never heard of a "Digby", so after listening to Moose carry on about diving on unsuspecting U-boats in his "marvelous Digby", he walked over to him because he just had to ask: "What the hell is a Digby?"

Moose appeared astonished at the question. He stood up from his chair, which was at a table with other Royal Canadian Air Force pilots, all of whom were snickering, and sauntered up to Harry. He pretty much towered over Harry, who figured Moose must have 8 inches in height on him and at least 150lb, if not more. He noticed some of the buttons on the lower part of Moose's shirt appeared to be straining to remain in place.

Moose switched his beer mug from his right hand to his left, put his right hand on Harry's shoulder, and smiled. He finished off his beer and proceeded to explain that the Digby was a Douglas B-18, twin-engine bomber, converted by the Royal Canadian Air Force into a "first-class sub-hunter" and the pride of the air fleet at Meeks.

Harry decided the best course of action was to appease Moose. He thanked him for the new knowledge and bought him and the pilots at Moose's table a round of beers. He fought off the desire to enlighten Moose and his friends to the fact the plane was actually the B-18 "Bolo". Harry knew the Digby to be a very outdated design and was generally considered to be unfit for front-line duty, but kept quiet because he didn't want to rattle Moose's cage.

The next evening Moose was nowhere to be seen. Harry knew there'd been a break in the Icelandic weather that morning, but the weather over Scotland was not expected to clear for another twenty-four hours, forcing Harry to stay an additional day. Moose had embarked on an anti-submarine patrol, along with several other planes during the break in the weather. Someone mentioned Moose was several hours overdue from a patrol mission; as it developed, Harry would never see Moose again. Later on, he'd inquire about Moose but was never able to ascertain whether Moose or any of his crew ever returned.

Five days after arriving at Meeks, the weather improved considerably, both there and at his next destination in Scotland. On the morning of Wednesday, July 5 1944, Harry set out for Prestwick Air Base near Glasgow, Scotland, glad to be rid of Meeks and its lousy weather. It was a relatively easy 850-mile flight in what proved to be pretty decent flying conditions.

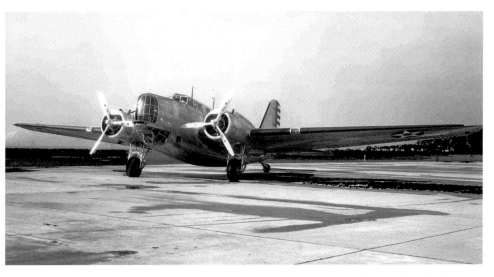

The Douglas B-18 bomber carried a six-man crew. Dubbed the "Bolo" by the USAAF, the Canadian version was officially referred to as the Douglas Digby Mark I, "Digby" for short.

Harry landed at Prestwick in the early afternoon and was immediately greeted by a Royal Air Force lieutenant who had been in the front passenger seat of the Follow Me Jeep. He motioned for Harry to join him, and once Harry was satisfied all was fine with the plane he hopped into the back of the Jeep and was whisked to Operations.

The Operations hut proved to be a busy and crowded place. Harry was introduced to an RAF sergeant who looked old enough to be Harry's dad. The sergeant was very familiar with Harry's entire route, from Indiana to Greenham Common, having made the round-trip himself. He also suggested a flight plan for Harry for the final leg of his journey, taking him to Greenham Common. Harry thanked him, looked the plan over, and smiled.

He considered the English to be "rather thoughtful folks", but then the sergeant told him it would likely be a day or two before he could embark on the final leg, sending Harry into a bit of a sullen mood. The sergeant explained Greenham Common was in a fog bank, and they were expecting the weather at Prestwick to quickly deteriorate, so either way, he'd be staying on for a wee bit. The sergeant showed Harry where he and his co-pilot would be bunking and suggested he try out the Officers' Club and to have themselves a "nice afternoon tea". He also explained that a couple dozen "Yank pilots" were already at the club and had grown fond of the afternoon tea themselves. From the grin on the sergeant's face, Harry wasn't sure if he was serious or pulling his leg.

Harry returned to his aircraft, where he discovered Chief was conferring with a couple members of the airbase ground crew. When the conversation was over, Chief reported the ground crew was going to prep the plane to adequately protect it from the incoming inclement weather. Harry glanced towards the cockpit and noticed two men were already in the process of stretching a canvas shield across the cockpit's glass. That's when Chief told him they were anticipating some hail in the forecast. Harry remembers fighting back the desire to yell at the sky, but thought the better of it and kept his cool. He'd never encountered so much bad weather in such a short time since joining the army and was feeling helpless.

Satisfied his crew knew where to report for their respective quarters' assignments, Harry and Al went to the Officers' Club, where they drank Black English Tea and listened to veteran pilots talking about engagements with the Luftwaffe and German rocket glider/bombs. It turned out the sergeant was correct about there being many American pilots already there, so Harry and his co-pilot fit right in.

THE NORTHERN ROUTE

Since his arrival in Iceland, Harry had been encountering weather conditions very unlike those he experienced in California and Texas. Looking out the windows of the Officers' Club, he hoped the scores of hours he'd spent practicing instrument flight training would prove to be good enough to at least get him to Greenham Common. It was at that moment he resolved to spend as much of his spare time as feasible to further refine his instrument flight skills because it appeared to him he'd be needing them. First, however, he had to get himself and his crew to Greenham Common as per his orders. Thanks to the weather, he'd be stuck in Prestwick six long nights with nothing much to do except wait for the skies to clear.

Chapter 10

Greenham Common, England

It was mid-morning on Tuesday, July 11 1944, when he filed his flight plan and took off for Greenham Common, England. It was the shortest leg of what had become a marathon fourteen-day journey, and the last thing he wanted to do was lose any more time. Fed up with climate-related delays, he didn't dare risk the English weather suddenly stopping him in at Prestwick. He'd been advised the weather in England was considered to be iffy, and the Greenham Common airbase could be shut down with little warning. He told Al they needed to get going, while the going was still good. Al simply shook his head in agreement as the two men jogged to their waiting aircraft.

He arrived at Greenham Common by mid-afternoon and was quickly sought out by his squadron's number two man, Captain Beard. Beard introduced himself, shook hands with Harry and Al, and stated they should report to him at 1000 hours the following morning. Beard had been accompanied by a staff sergeant who proceeded to whisk Harry and Al to their new sleeping quarters.

Harry was excited to finally be in England and wrote letters to both his wife and his mom that very first night. He'd hardly settled in when the news came he'd been promoted to the rank of first lieutenant, so he found it necessary to write a second set of letters. Harry had no idea he was being considered for promotion and was elated with the new rank. He recognized the extra money would certainly make things easier for Junie back home, as well as for his mom; he was true to his word and sent her money each month without fail and would do so for the remainder of her life.

In addition to the Army Air Force spouse stipend sent directly to Junie each month, Harry also sent her whatever money he could spare. He didn't smoke or even own a camera, so what he might otherwise have spent on cigarettes, film, and developing left more money available that he could divert to Junie. She would prove to be very smart when it came to creative ways of saving money and, unbeknownst to Harry, was building a nest egg of cash for when he returned home from the war.

Lang beat him to England by a few months and was flying bombing missions as the pilot of a B-24J Liberator. He was stationed at Old Buckenham, an army airbase roughly 30 miles from Greenham Common. He'd been following Harry's progress and left a greeting card for him. This didn't surprise Harry, Golden always had a knack for knowing more of what was going on than he did.

On July 28 1944, Lang showed up, unannounced, at Harry's doorstep with a surprise. He'd borrowed a P-47 fighter plane, stripped of its weapons and being utilized as a trainer. He told an ecstatic Harry he could take her for a spin.

Harry flew the plane for a little more than an hour and described the experience as the greatest joy ride of his life. Afterward, he and Lang hung out at the Officers' Club for the balance of the afternoon. When Lang needed to return to his base, he told him he'd stop in again on a day when he knew they both wouldn't be flying. Harry didn't ask him how he came to possess such information and simply said he was looking forward to it.

Because of his relative seniority, Harry was frequently flying the lead plane in what typically were three to five plane formations. He might fly missions as many as seventeen days in a row before enjoying a day-off. Sometimes the weather would provide him with a few no-fly days, but in the summer of 1944, bad weather days were relatively rare. Consequently, Harry wasn't able to spend significant time in the flight instrument training shack, so he compromised his off-duty time. On days when he flew a mission no longer than three hours, he'd dedicate at least one hour in the instrument flight training shack.

Harry was already painfully aware of the potential for frequent rainy and foggy weather conditions in England. He justifiably believed he'd need to call upon an ability to fly strictly by instruments on a routine basis. Unbeknownst to Harry, Colonel Donalson, the squadron commander, had taken notice of the young instructor/pilot and had made a mental note to himself to remember Harry when inclement weather conditions might come into play.

When he wasn't running supplies over to the troops in Normandy, the balance of his routine would include engaging in practice runs where they'd drop live paratroopers at locations all across England. There was also extensive glider-towing practice, which required flying at very slow speeds and at even lower altitudes than when dropping paratroopers.

Chief had to learn how, and when, to disengage the tow cable leading from the C-47 to the towed glider. The C-47 pilot was, as a rule, in direct contact with the glider pilot via a phone cable as coordination between the two pilots was critical. The glider pilot could also release from the C-47 on his own.

Timing of the glider release was crucial, for even at reduced airspeeds of 95 to perhaps 110mph, they would be over the prime landing zone for a very short time. Missing the target by as little as half a mile could have disastrous consequences for the glider as the terrain might alter dramatically over short distances. Not only could the landscape quickly change, but which army controlled the territory, German or Allied, could also come into play.

Something happened one morning that, to this day, Harry continues to occasionally re-live when he finds his mind wandering back to his days at Greenham Common. The squadron was engaged in a practice paratroop drop and flying in V-shaped, three-plane formations. Each plane held about twenty paratroopers, and each paratrooper was packing about 80lbs of gear. As the formations approached their target area, it was necessary to make a final course correction to properly align the planes with the targeted landing zone.

C-47s flying in a typical nine-plane formation. Note some pilots are more adept at close formation flying than are others. In the practice accident, it was the far-left formation depicted above that experienced the collision.

Colonel De Broefy was at the controls of the lead plane in the first formation. Harry had his group a little behind him and to the right. The position provided him a perfect view of a tragedy unfolding in front of him.

There was a three-plane group flying to the colonel's left. As the group began to execute a course correction to the left, the pilot of the plane flying as the right-side wingman started to fly too low and too slow. Harry watched in alarm as he immediately recognized the pilot was rapidly losing control of his plane.

Harry grabbed his microphone as he intended to call out a warning, but before he could do so, the plane suddenly flipped over on its left-wing and crashed into the wingman flying on the opposite side of the three plane formation. Both aircraft plummeted into the ground, killing the crews and all of the paratroopers aboard. Already committed to the paratroop drop, the mission continued. The paratroopers in the remaining planes jumped without further mishap. Harry assumed most of them were unaware of the disaster.

When the squadron landed at Greenham Common, all the pilots were immediately summoned into the briefing hut. Colonel DeBroefy was already on the stage, waiting for them. He appeared to be furious as he rapidly-paced back and forth at least a dozen times, from one end of the elevated stage to the other, without saying a word or looking at his audience.

After what felt like fifteen minutes to Harry, but was probably not more than a minute or two, DeBroefy took up a position at center stage and stared at the assembled pilots and co-pilots. Harry remembers thinking to himself the colonel resembled a man gone mad. DeBroefy inhaled a long, deep breath, then fairly well shouted what was on his mind. Harry remembers it well:

"The next one of you who kills any of my guys." He paused as if he were looking for the right words, then, while still shouting, said: "I'll kill you!"

He very quickly left the building from a side exit without saying so much as another word. The loud slam from the door was an appropriate exclamation point for his abbreviated speech.

There were no flight operations scheduled for the next day, providing everyone the chance to put the disaster behind them. Harry and a couple of friends decided to go into London for the afternoon after he first spent an hour or two in the instrument flight shack. The three men intended to enjoy an ale or two and perhaps catch a movie.

While they were crossing a London street on their way to a movie house, they heard a loud explosion that wasn't more than four or five blocks away. They immediately looked skywards, but other than some mild cloud-cover, nothing appeared amiss. There had been no air-raid sirens, so they knew they weren't about to be bombed when suddenly many ambulances came screaming from around the corner, racing in the direction of the explosion.

Harry flagged down an air-raid warden who explained to the men the explosion they heard had been from a German "buzz" bomb. The men looked at each other. Without saying a word, they turned around and went in search of a pub. They decided to die with a mug of ale in their hand was more appealing than the thought of dying while sitting inside a movie house.

After that they made less frequent forays into London. Despite the reduction in London-bound excursions, he was still there often enough to hear, and feel, two more of the German V-1 buzz bombs strike London. Each time he considered himself lucky, it was apparent to him he quickly could have become a victim of the German vengeance weapon. His experiences with the V-1s served to reinforce his secret uneasiness about not making it through the war. But then he'd consider how close he had been to disaster so far, and yet he was fine.

A German V-1 "Buzz" Rocket-Bomb running out of fuel and beginning its deadly fall to earth.

Harry remembers from time to time encountering glider pilot veterans of the Normandy invasion, be it on trips into London or at local pubs. He was impressed by their seemingly unquenchable thirst for warm English beer and sex.

One day an RAF captain was sitting alongside Harry and Al in a cozy little pub, pretty much keeping to himself. After a little time passed, Harry noticed he was staring at a rather loud gathering of glider pilots behaving, as the captain quietly pointed out, boorishly. He laughs when he remembers the captain then referred to the pilots as "over-paid, over-sexed and over here". There had been an emphasis on the word "here". He proceeded to gulp down the remainder of his pint and quietly, though swiftly, exited the pub. Harry never did run into him again but had to agree with his observations, a phrase he would hear many more times.

The quaint English market town of Newbury was next door to Greenham Common. If the mood struck him, Harry might hop a ride in a Jeep with a couple other pilots and spend two or three hours exploring the markets, and of course, the pubs.

Upon his first visit to Newbury, Harry was surprised and shocked at the discovery of extensive bomb damage, smack in the center of town. One of the locals explained what had happened. In early 1943 a lone German bomber had appeared overhead late one afternoon. There had been no air-raid sirens or any manner of warning. He said, from out of the blue bombs were dropping all around him. He was forced to take shelter under a table in the pub where he'd been enjoying his favorite draught and was lucky to survive, unscathed.

He explained to Harry that after the bombing the local air warden learned the lone German had followed a set of railroad tracks right into the town. The German pilot didn't even hit the nearby airbase. Instead, he managed to demolish a church, various public buildings, and more than 200 residences. Harry remembers being angry at the German pilot who, in his opinion, intentionally targeted civilians rather than risk attacking the Greenham Common airfield, which he concluded was plainly visible to him. He felt pity for the man telling him the story and bought him a pint.

About a week or so later, it was Harry's first day-off after several successive days of flying supply missions. He looked at himself in the mirror that morning and promptly decided he was overdue for a haircut. After breakfast, he decided his next stop would be to visit the base barber. Afterward, he intended to spend two or three hours in the Instrument Flight Simulator practicing IFR flying techniques.

The barber was located, literally, under the base's control tower. While the barber was trimming his hair, he found himself in the perfect position to observe C-47s practicing glider tow take-offs.

As a general rule, glider tow practice was conducted with live paratroopers on board the gliders, which would allow the glider pilots to gain experience flying fully-loaded aircraft. Not only did the glider pilots need to understand how their gliders performed when fully loaded, but the C-47 pilots also were required to have the same experience.

Towing a glider with two people on board differed from pulling one loaded with fully equipped paratroopers, each packing 70 to 80lbs of equipment. Both paratroop and glider practice runs were carefully planned to duplicate combat zone conditions as closely as possible. Practice flights would be conducted at locations all across England, over many different landscapes and at varying altitudes.

He was watching with interest as a C-47, towing a British Airspeed Horsa glider, was about to take-off. He'd piloted his share of similar practice runs and was curious to observe the operation from the ground, without the distraction of flying his plane. Harry initially focused on the C-47 because he wanted to see how the aircraft physically responded when the slack in the tow rope to the Horsa disappeared and became taught as the C-47 gained ground speed.

The C-47 effortlessly rose from the ground and began to climb above a lightly forested area situated just a little beyond the end of the runway.

The British Airspeed Horsa Glider was 67 feet long with a wingspan of 88 feet. It could carry up to twenty-five fully-equipped paratroopers.

The Horsa was obediently following behind, a little lower than the C-47, and slightly off-center to the right. Suddenly Harry jumped up from his seat, shocking the barber who instinctively pulled his arms away from him and stepped back, likely thinking he'd somehow scratched Harry's scalp. Harry found himself speechless. All he could do was silently point towards the end of the airstrip with his right hand, which was still cloaked with the barber's towel.

As the Horsa was about to clear the tree line, its tail suddenly broke away. Harry watched in horror as a couple of dozen paratroopers tumbled from the suddenly near-vertical cabin and were falling to their death. The quick-thinking crew chief aboard the C-47 immediately released the Horsa, the balance of which plummeted into the trees, killing the remaining men on board. The C-47 flew away, undamaged.

Harry was sick to his stomach and had a bad feeling regarding what could have caused such a catastrophe. He had just witnessed as many as twenty-seven men perish and realized it could have been him piloting the C-47 and towing the doomed Horsa. The alert C-47 crew chief had apparently been watching the glider from the open hatch. If he'd hesitated in releasing the remaining portion of the glider, the suddenly dead weight from the front three-fourths of the stricken aircraft would have doomed his own plane to the same fate.

A subsequent incident review proved the event was caused by covert action. A close inspection of the tail section indicated a saboteur, probably using a hand-drill to keep noise to a minimum, had drilled holes into the plywood frame of the Horsa, entirely encircling the tail assembly. Whoever committed the treacherous act then back-filled the drill-holes with putty. No one noticed the irregularities.

Harry mused the damage may have been over-looked because the tail was designed so it could be split away from the main cabin once on the ground to facilitate quick unloading. Until then, Harry assumed the ground crews were trained to look for deadly modifications. He had made a wrong assumption.

When Harry learned the cause of the disaster, he thought to himself it was already bad enough he had to worry about German sympathizers pouring sugar in the gas tanks. Still, it appeared to him the clandestine operatives had risen to an entirely new level of sophistication and cunning. He rationalized the existence of saboteurs was just one more piece of stress to deal with, and there was little he could do about it. That night he noticed his first grey hairs.

Realizing the airbase ground crews and security details had failed to diligently seek out signs of malicious tinkering with the aircraft, he ordered his aircrew to be extra vigilant. He also instructed them to check the ground around the fuel fillers for indications of sugar, or anything odd or otherwise out of the ordinary that might indicate what he termed, "chicanery".

He also ordered the hatch was to be kept closed when the plane wasn't in use, and he further directed Chief to leave a discrete marker in the hatch door to alert him if anyone had opened it. Even with the extra precautions, the possibility of sabotage held a firm place in the recesses of his mind. Harry rationalized that during wartime, there were lots of ways to die, and if he had to perish, let it be while on a combat mission.

He knew full-well if there was sugar in the gas lines at the point of lift-off, which was the moment when the engines would have grown hot enough to solidify the sugar and block the carburetors, then both engines would quit, and the plane would almost certainly crash. Unlike the freezing carburetors on the AT-20, sugar-sabotaged engines would not stall until the aircraft was already in the act off lifting-off and fatally vulnerable to a sudden loss of power. With sugar in the fuel, there would be no advance warning anything was amiss. The engines would suddenly die from fuel starvation, and all power would be irrecoverably lost.

In mid-August 1944, as the Allies continued their break-out from the beachheads at Normandy and streamed across France, the Germans found themselves being compacted into an ever-smaller pocket near the French town of Falaise. The Germans had overly procrastinated before executing a retreat and had found themselves surrounded on three sides by the British, Canadians, and Americans.

When the Germans finally began to withdraw, the only escape route was via a very narrow and unshielded dirt road. Allied airpower pummeled the fleeing Germans who, according to Harry, were crammed like sardines onto the road as they attempted to escape through what came to be called the "Falaise Gap". The resulting carnage of men, animals, and equipment was gruesome in its scale.

The battle of the Falaise Gap ended on August 21 1944. Harry immediately began flying low-level supply drops, which took him on a route directly over the Falaise Gap battle scene. Flying at an altitude a little above 300 feet to assure accurate drops and with the cockpit windows open, per his habit, Harry and Al were met by the most appalling stench they'd ever experienced. In fact, to this day, Harry claims it was the most unpleasant smell he's ever suffered through, far and away more potent than anything he'd encountered, "even in Pittsburgh". He recalls his eyes teared, and the tears burned.

Fortunately, he was only required to conduct a couple of round-trip flights over the carnage, for they were soon put on alert for a new paratroop operation. It was anticipated his group would be dropping elements of the 82nd Airborne outside of Paris, France, in an attempt to secure the city before the Germans could put it to the torch or blow it up.

Rumors were flying. Scuttlebutt spread that Hitler issued orders to the commandant of the Paris region to destroy the city. The Allies weren't going to take any chances and decided to seize the city with a parachute assault. Just in the nick of time, Patton's Third Army arrived and liberated Paris on August 25 1944. The airborne landings were called off.

The consequences of being left with only a narrow road for the evacuation of several German armies without air support to cover their retreat, or tree lines to shield them from aerial surveillance.

Chapter 11

Blood Run to Orly

Just before dawn on August 26 1944, the Mission Briefing hut located at the U.S. Army Air Station at Greenham Common, was packed with more than 250 pilots. There was a loud buzz in the well-lighted, corrugated steel-walled hall as the men were anxious to learn why 126 C-47 troop transports were going to be sent on a short notice, maximum effort mission.

Harry, sitting alongside Al, was very excited. He'd been chomping at the bit to get more involved in the war. The risk-taker in him was causing Harry to feel more antsy than usual, and the general excitement in the air certainly didn't do much to mollify his desire to feel as if he was an active participant in the action.

An elevated stage at the front of the otherwise undecorated room was dominated by a large map of Europe. Greenham Common and Orly Field, newly renamed "A-47", just outside of Paris, were both circled in red. Harry, like the balance of his fellow pilots, assumed he was heading for Paris and began to anticipate an opportunity to see the famous city first hand. He recalls the briefing was very close to how it is retold here:

As Colonel John M. Donalson appeared from a doorway to the right of the stage, a staff sergeant forcefully called out:

"Gentlemen, attention!"

There was an immediate racket of shuffling feet and chairs scraping the floor. Slowly the room grew silent as each man came to attention. After a few moments, allowing Donalson time to climb onto the stage, the staff sergeant called out:

"At ease," which signaled the men to take their seats.

The charismatic Donalson, his leather flight jacket wide open and a pistol poking out from beneath, disdained podiums and pointers. He purposefully walked to the center of the stage, stopped, and looked around the room for a few moments as he made occasional eye contact. Not until he was good and ready did he begin the briefing.

"Gentlemen, as you know, Third Army's been running flat-out across France at a pace our supply columns simply can't sustain. It's a long way from the beachheads in Normandy to the front line, and it's been damn-near impossible for the supply trucks to keep up. The fuel, ammo, and supply shortages have kept us scrambling to make sure our front line units are timely supplied and equipped. Still, at this moment it's the lack of medical supplies, especially whole blood, that's become a top priority. Today's mission will help alleviate that critical shortage."

He walked over to the map and pointed towards Paris with his right hand.

"Our Combat Engineers have been working like the devil to repair Orly Field, and as of this morning I'm pleased to report Orly is fit for service and the medical folks there are anxious for our arrival. Right now, your planes are being loaded with either desperately needed whole blood, medical supplies, or both. But at least as important is the fact that each plane will also be carrying human cargo." He paused for effect.

"Each of you will have two nurses aboard who will, in turn, relieve nurses in field hospitals at Orly. Quite a few of our nurses have been in our forward field hospitals since just after we came ashore at Normandy, and many of them are in bad need of some R&R." Gazing at the map, he paused just long enough to gather his thoughts.

"As you know, our planes can handle about eighteen litters of wounded.* You'll be flying back the most desperately injured men along with two nurses to attend to them during the flight. Gentlemen, this mission is more than about delivering blood to save lives. It's also about bringing home our severely wounded boys and getting them into fully equipped hospitals where they can receive the full-time care they most urgently require and deserve."

Donalson paused again as he took a deep breath.

"Men, you all recall the horrific 'aroma' we encountered during our low-level supply flights over the Falaise Pocket." Donalson was forced to pause as an undercurrent of hushed voices spread through the audience.

"Now I'm not saying some of the wounded you bring back will remind you of Falaise, but there are many burn victims still in the field who are in bad need of hospitalization back here in England. So brace yourselves and remember, whatever discomfort you might face will not come anywhere near what your passengers and their nurses have, and will most likely continue to endure."

"Take-off is planned for 0900 hours, so we should reach Orly by late morning. Good luck."

The assembled officers stood as Donalson exited the stage, and the staff sergeant simultaneously called out: "Dismissed."

Harry and Al fell in with the group of pilots as they made their way to the scores of waiting Jeeps. As they climbed into their Jeep, Al in the back seat, said, "Just the mention of 'Falaise' brought chills down my spine." Harry replied he hoped he'd never again see such carnage and mockingly thanked Al for reminding him about it.

Harry was shaking his head side-to-side and complaining he must be in Donalson's dog house for the reason the colonel has him as the lead plane in the very last formation. Harry remembers grimacing at the thought of a long delay in landing at Orly as he waited for 123 planes to land ahead of him. Al was upbeat about it and told him: "Think of it this way, we'll log more hours."

Harry smiled as they climbed aboard a Jeep that whisked them to their C-47 where Chief and Sparky awaited news of their mission. Both men began to quickly walk towards Harry as his Jeep approached. Before he could jump out of the still-moving Jeep, the always quizzical Sparky was immediately on him: "Skipper, where are we heading?"

"Paris, but don't get your hopes up because we might be coming right back."

Sparky appeared to be very disappointed and moped around a little until he realized there'd be nurses on board. Wearing a sly grin, he abruptly sprung up the stairs and disappeared into the cabin.

"Plane's all loaded, and we're good to go," reported Chief.

"That's swell. Time to get everyone aboard while I take care of the pre-flight," said Harry.

Harry, clipboard in hand, performed his pre-flight inspection. Once satisfied all was well with his aircraft, recently christened "Wee Junie" in honor of his wife, he climbed aboard.

As he strode past the nurses while on his way to the flight deck, Harry paused long enough to say, "Ladies, we'll have you on the ground at Orly in a jiffy." The nurses smiled, which caused his face to turn a little red as the 21-year-old Harry had always been shy around females. If it hadn't been so dark that night in the USO at Taft, California, Harry might not have had the nerve to ask Junie for a dance, let alone dance for hours.

As Harry navigated his way around the cases of firmly secured cargo, stacked to the ceiling, Al turned over the engines. When Harry popped into the cabin and belted himself into his seat, the first planes were already lifting-off. In short order, all of the aircraft were flying in one large, extended configuration.

The colonel's group was in the lead as they flew in small group configurations of three planes each, nine planes to each grouping. Harry's plane had the lead spot in the very last of the formations. From his position, he couldn't even see Donalson's plane as it was too far in the distance.

Greenham Common was fewer than 60 miles from London, and in a short time, Harry was flying over the English Channel. The weather cooperated beautifully until the French coast became visible on the horizon. It looked like a solid curtain of pure white/grey smoke. The smoke was fog, the unpredictable and single most significant inhibiter of American airpower at that stage of the war.

The radio suddenly spurted to life, and the voice of Colonel Donalson came through the headsets: "Abort! I repeat: abort the mission and return to base."

Harry looked troubled and continued on the original course while 125 planes, including the two planes flying with Harry, reversed their respective flight paths and headed home for England. Al, puzzled, stared at him and asked,

"Harry, did you hear that? The mission's aborted. It's gotta be the fog."

Harry looked at him for a few seconds before responding: "Al, get everyone up here so I can talk to them."

"What?"

"Just do it, Al."

A typical formation of C-47 "Dakotas" in the European Theatre.

Al unbuckled his seat belt and quickly disappeared into the back of the plane, returning about a minute later with the nurses, Chief and Sparky. In the interim, Harry began flying a circular course, staying well-off the sopped-in French coast.

"Listen up everyone," said Harry, "I've been thinking about this fog situation." He paused as he sought the best words. "I've calculated it cost Uncle Sam a good 250,000 bucks to train me, and it's my opinion if we turned around now and went home because the weather's not perfect, well, that just makes no sense to me. I have a flight instructor rating which, if you ladies don't know, means I teach pilots to fly. I'm perfectly comfortable flying strictly by instruments and have probably experienced worse weather conditions than what we're facing today. I think we must consider whole blood has a limited life, not to mention how many of our men might die if we don't at least get our two tons of blood to Orly today. Who knows when this fog will lift and how much blood might go to waste while we wait? It could be tomorrow, but what if it's not? Since I arrived in England I've lost more flying days to fog than I can shake a stick at, and I'm tired of it." Harry paused as he made eye contact with each person. "I'm asking all of you to trust me. Let me fly us to Orly. I promise I'll get us there in one piece, but I need all of you to be in agreement and to understand there is a risk, so if anyone has any qualms, speak up, and we'll turn back."

Al was the first to respond:

"Count me in Harry!"

The two nurses shook their heads in the affirmative and walked back to their seats, whispering to each other. Whatever their thoughts might have been, they didn't choose to share them, nor did Harry ask.

Harry turned to Chief and Sparky: "How about it?"

"We're in." Chief paused as a smile came across his face. "And who knows, maybe we can spend the night in Paris after all."

"Ok, let's get to Orly," said Harry, who re-buckled himself into his seat. He checked his airspeed, 150mph, and calculated a dead reckoning course for Orly.

It wasn't long before he realized the fog extended more than one mile out from the coast. He lacked knowledge of what the coastal terrain was like and didn't recall whether there were cliffs, trees, or houses awaiting him. He had to drop the plane to the point he was flying just above the waves to achieve minimal forward visibility. Though the altitude was perilously low, he could see just far enough ahead to know where he was. If he flew any higher, he'd be in absolute zero visibility, and he believed some visibility was better than none at all. He trusted his instincts, and they told him to hug the waves. Flying above the clouds was out of the question as there could be German fighter aircraft present.

Before he could shake a leg, a wall of tall trees announced he'd reached the French coast. He had to immediately pull up and gain altitude. He just barely cleared the tree-tops. Al breathed an audible sigh of relief as they proceeded inland while Harry focused on the gauges, maintaining course, and keeping the wings level.

They were soon flying in zero-zero visibility conditions, and the fog, which appeared bright white/grey when he initially approached the coast, had suddenly turned into varying shades of grey, from light to dark. Harry could barely see beyond the tips of his wings, and for the first time in his career, he entertained the thought he might have made a miscalculation of what he was capable of doing. He considered the possibility he was biting off more than he could chew as they flew further and further into France. Lang's words describing them as risk-takers came to mind, and he wondered what manner of trouble Lang might be getting himself into.

He called for Chief and Sparky to come forward and ordered them to post themselves on either side of the cabin and maintain a look-out for possible geographical markers, any type of ground feature he might use to navigate their course to Orly. He told Al to keep his nose plastered straight

The above is similar to what Harry and Al witnessed as they desperately peered through the windscreen searching for landmarks while navigating through a severe fog. Courtesy photo of U.S. Army Veteran Tommy Anderson, Owner – Coyote Mountain Publishing, 941 Cole Street, Norco, CA 92860.

ahead, while Harry primarily focused his eyes on the gauges, being careful to keep the wings level, indicating they were flying straight and true.

The fog was so dense he didn't dare let his eyes wander from the instruments for more than a few seconds at a time. Frequently unable to see his own wings, the gauges were his reality; it was like being locked into an instrument flight trainer. With hardly any time to react in the event they suddenly encountered a hill, tree, or power line, Harry decided to accept the risk and continued flying at altitudes as low as 100 feet. The ground was barely, though not always, visible at that altitude and provided a chance for Al or the crew to spot a landmark.

He remembers briefly glancing at Al and thinking to himself Al's face had turned "white as plaster". Al's forehead was practically glued to the windscreen as he stared into the wall of solid fog. Harry estimated there was probably about 20 feet of clearance between the treetops and the plane and knew he couldn't stay that low indefinitely as he assumed there would be a limit to his good luck.

As he barreled across the countryside, he learned the density of the fog would vary slightly with the terrain as they flew across shallow valleys then followed the tree lines up gently rolling hills. The fog would thicken in the valleys and lighten up a bit when climbing over hills. Harry gradually lowered his airspeed until it was down to a mere 120mph. He knew all too well that even at such a reduced speed, there would be little margin for error in the event an obstacle suddenly presented itself. He was relying on his instincts.

They flew deeper into France, never having a precise fix as to their location. Harry, realizing the fog was worse than any he had previously experienced, again began having doubts. He knew since the Group's mission had been aborted, there would be no fighter support should he decide to climb above the fog and turn for home. Harry had seen enough German fighters on their recent runs to realize they could pose a genuine danger. He decided the last thing he wanted to do was get everybody killed by a German fighter plane and decided to stay in the "soup". He redoubled his determination to reach Orly and deliver his vital cargo intact, praying his instincts would save the day, and pray he did.

Despite his best efforts, he found his mind had wandered, as if it also was in a fog. Suddenly he was back in pilot training at Bergstrom Army Airfield. He fondly recalled a young gentleman of a sergeant would put him through the wringer in setting up ever more difficult instrument flying scenarios. The sudden appearance of a barn, its light grey stone walls contrasted by a dark brown roof poking out from the fog, brought him back to reality.

Nearby was a river his memory raced to identify. In his gut, Harry felt he was drawing close to Orly.

After another fifteen minutes of flying blind, he realized they were overshooting an airfield. Neither he nor Al realized it until they were directly overhead because the airstrip had been completely enshrouded in the heavy mist. They were elated, for they assumed it was Orly, and he immediately began to bank hard to his left.

He tried his best to keep the airfield within view, off the end of the left wing tip, but couldn't quite manage to do so. He throttled back the engines and lowered the landing gear as the plane slowed to safe landing speed. He intended to swing around and immediately set-up an approach. His intention was to fly straight in for fear he might get lost and not find it again. He attempted to establish radio contact with the tower but was met with static. He didn't have time to worry about it.

As he maneuvered into position, he thought to himself he'd performed plenty of zero-zero landings in simulators. But this was real life, not a simulator, and he had five human beings relying upon him to get it right. There was also the fact he was transporting 4,000lbs of whole blood to consider. He hardened himself to the task, kept his eyes on the instruments, and finished executing the 180-degree turn.

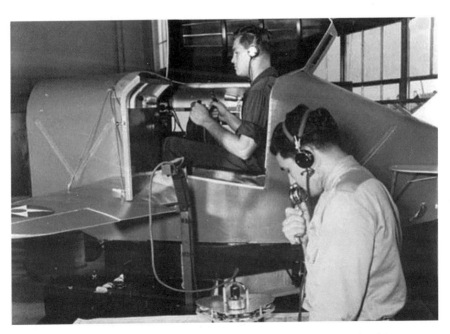

A U.S. Army Air Force Link Trainer similar to the model Harry trained in.

He quickly found himself back in the fog bank but remained focused on the instruments while Al desperately searched for any sign of a break in the fog. Trusting his intuition, Harry edged ever lower until they were finally beneath the fog. The problem was, they were only about 10 to 15 feet above the ground and dangerously close to catastrophe.

He and Al held their breath when the runway suddenly appeared from behind the grey/white veil. It was not more than a few hundred yards straight ahead of them. The maneuver had worked perfectly. The hours upon hours of additional voluntary instrument flight training he put-in had paid-off. Or at least he thought they had.

"Harry, that's it!" Al was nearly shouting in a combination of excitement and relief. "It looks to me like there are bomb craters on our left, so stay as far to the right as you dare."

"Hold on tight!" Harry yelled back into the cabin with excitement.

He conducted a perfect landing, utilizing the right side of the runway, and slowly rolled to a stop. The combination of heavy fog and the fact the cockpit of a C-47 points skyward when on the ground meant he wasn't sure where the taxiway was located, so he decided to wait for instructions.

In less than a minute, he was greeted by a Jeep being driven by an RAF corporal who guided him to what proved to be a relatively nearby aircraft hangar. When the plane slowed to a stop, Harry had Al cut the power to both engines. As the twin 1,200 horsepower engines wound down, he noticed a large hole had been blown right through the center of the hangar's roof, and one of the bullet-riddled sliding doors was collapsed. Al mentioned it looked to him as if the Germans had put up a fight before pulling out.

An RAF captain came running to the plane. Harry stuck his head out the side window as Al leaned towards Harry to better overhear what the captain had to say.

"Hey, Yank! Where'd you come from?"

"Greenham Common and I'm looking for Orly. Is this it?" asked Harry.

"That's brilliant! You flew through all this muck, so you must be one damned determined Yank, but this is not Orly. Come on down, and I'll set you up with a proper map." The captain began to walk towards the plane's still-closed hatch but paused to say: "By the way, my name's Ferguson, and the good news is you're not more than twenty minutes flight time from Orly. But the bad news, I'm afraid, is this whole part of the country is in the thicket."

Harry deplaned and followed Ferguson into the hangar, where he pulled out a map and laid a route to Orly. An RAF sergeant appeared with a tray of tea and biscuits and politely invited them to help themselves. Harry thanked him but asked the sergeant to take everything over to his aircraft. He explained his crew would be more than happy to see him. Harry didn't think to mention there were two nurses on board, and, as it developed, the site of the nurses took the sergeant "for a loop".

When the sergeant returned, empty-handed, he reported to Ferguson the plane was full of medical cargo and "two bloody nurses". Harry then explained their mission to Ferguson, who shook his hand and bid him good luck. Harry returned to the plane, armed with a new map and feeling quite rejuvenated.

"Al, fire 'em up and follow that Jeep. Orly is our next stop!"

"You got it, Harry," said Al as he restarted the engines.

About five minutes later, and after making several attempts to contact the Orly flight tower, Harry successfully established contact and requested they switch-on their range approach system.

The Orly tower immediately complied with the request and switched-on the electronic signal system. It immediately began broadcasting a Morse code homing signal from the center of Orly's runway. Harry pressed his earphones into his head as tightly as he could in an attempt to drown out as much engine noise as possible so he could clearly distinguish the signals.

It was only by correctly interpreting Orly's Morse code signals that he could steer a course to the airfield. Harry focused his ears on the signals and his eyes on the instruments. He instructed Al to temporarily assume the controls so he could concentrate on translating the Morse code. Until it was time to land Al would execute course corrections whenever Harry directed him to do so.

When Harry heard the Morse code signal, "da-dit" (dash-dot), he knew it meant he was too far to the right of the runway, and, in turn, he'd direct Al to bank a little to the left. When he heard a "dit-da" (dot-dash), he knew he had wandered too far to the left and would instruct Al to bank a little to the right. Al executed a string of modest course adjustments as Harry focused on keeping the plane rock-steady on the transmitting beacon. The entire time Al was desperately searching for the Orly airfield and praying he could spot it through the unrelenting fog.

After about ten minutes Harry discovered he was dead on-target when they flew directly over Orly's outer compass locator. At the time, he was flying at an altitude of about 500 feet with absolutely no visibility when he again made contact with the Orly tower and advised them he was coming in and intended to shoot a range approach landing. The tower, to Harry's surprise and consternation, reported there were scores of four-engine C-54 cargo planes stacked up above the airport, from 4,000 to 12,000 feet, all of them in a holding pattern waiting for the fog to clear.

Harry suddenly faced an overhead air traffic situation he had not anticipated. When the aircraft circling above heard the chatter between Harry and the tower, a number of the C-54 pilots conveyed their distinct displeasure. They were upset Harry had flown in below them and was intending to land while they were forced to remain aloft, flying in circles. A few of them voiced particularly harsh words, directed at Harry, who they considered to be an unauthorized and dangerous interloper into their airspace

Harry ignored their chatter and advised the tower his plane's cargo was whole blood and a pair of nurses. In response, he was given clearance to land. Of course, he still had to locate the runway before he could make a final approach for a successful landing. He calmly continued to direct Al, who guided the aircraft according to how Harry interpreted the "dit-da" and "da-dit" signals. There was no visual input upon which either of them could rely.

Harry soon advised Al he was assuming the controls and descended to 300 feet while slowing the plane to about 90mph. He lowered the landing gear to further reduce his airspeed. By lowering his speed, Harry was buying himself a little extra reaction time as the fog was still so thick that neither he nor Al could see much beyond the nose of the plane.

In a few more moments, he flew directly over the inner compass locator. At that point, he knew he should be flying at an altitude of 400 hundred feet by the book, but with zero visibility, he ignored the book and took the plane still lower. He and Al were desperate to catch a glimpse of the ground.

Harry maintained a course he believed would lead directly to the center of the runway. Al called out airspeed and altitude as Harry focused on locating the runway. He knew he had, at best, not more than a minute of flight time before reaching the runway and chose to take a chance and descend just a little more in the hope he'd break through the fog.

But there was no break-through to be had, so he decided to drop down to a mere 50 feet. That's when he concluded the fog was the most tenacious he'd ever experienced and wasn't about to lighten up. He was worried, but determined to stay the course and follow his instincts.

Harry was all too aware of the fact that should he approach the runway too far-off from dead-center, in either direction, he could plow into a hangar or even the tower. The instruments were telling him he was dead-on, so he didn't flinch.

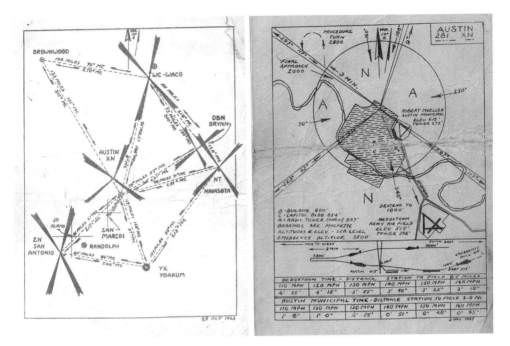

This is the type of pilot navigation aide Harry relied upon while seeking Orly airfield. He originally employed the above-aide when flying into Randolph Field in San Marcos, Texas.

Realizing he needed to descend still further, he advised Al he was taking her down to about 25 feet and told him to keep his eyes and ears open. At the new altitude, Al reported he was observing occasional traces of the ground below them, and he wasn't spotting any trees; it was all farm fields. He continually updated Harry until he suddenly blurted out: "There's the runway!"

Harry had no more than a couple of hundred yards of visibility, which proved to be just enough to allow him a little leeway to correct his approach. In moments, Al let out a shout of joy when he realized Harry had brought them directly into the center of the runway. The innumerable hours of practicing blind landings using the range approach system paid off.

Harry landed without incident, but once on the ground he couldn't see where he needed to go due to the combination of thick, wet fog and the upward angle of the cockpit. He notified the tower, which dispatched a Jeep driven by a sergeant wearing a colossal grin who proceeded to lead them to a nearby hanger.

Al switched off the engines while Chief opened the hatch and jumped the roughly 42 inches to the ground. Sparky pushed their home-made wooden, two-step stool towards the edge of the hatch where Chief slid it out and set in on the tarmac, which made exiting the plane a little less hazardous. He was all smiles as he assisted the nurses from the aircraft to a waiting Jeep.

Almost simultaneously, a pair of half-tracks pulled alongside the plane carrying about ten soldiers who jumped out and wasted no time unloading the scores of crates containing the desperately needed whole blood. For Harry, it was mission accomplished.

It began to rain just as Harry and his crew walked into the Mission Briefing hut. Between the unrelenting fog and the rain, he suspected they'd be spending the night in Paris. He was greeted by an Army Air Force major who, with a big smile and a handshake, enthusiastically said: "Unbelievable bit of flying, lieutenant!"

"Thank you Sir," replied Harry.

Thinking in terms of staying overnight, Harry tried to plead his case and said, "I understand you're planning to load a whole bunch of casualties and nurses onto my plane, but what about the weather? It's looking worse than ever out there." Harry tried his best to sound doubtful.

The major laughed and replied: "You just flew here from England in duck soup, and you made it in one piece. With a planeload of casualties, my guess is you'd find your way back home no matter how bad the weather. Besides, they say it's sunny on the other side of the channel."

The major stopped smiling as he continued: "Take a four-hour break, then get yourself up and outta here. But whatever you do, fly low. We've had reports of German fighters all day long, so don't take chances, and whatever you do, don't climb above the fog! It's a long way between here and England, so stay low and be smart about it."

Harry considered the situation a moment before answering. "Thank you Sir. I appreciate the break, and I'll certainly follow your advice. If there's nothing else, then I'd like to go bring my crew up to date."

A lieutenant had just then approached the major, who threw Harry a quick acknowledging nod of his head indicating a job well done. As soon as he could, Harry left the hut and disappeared into the rain and fog.

There were occasional flashes of lightning accompanied by an extended series of rolling thunder as a storm was bursting upon them. By the time he reached the plane, it was empty, save for the crew. He briefed them on the situation, and afterward, they ran to what served as a canteen. While they were taking their break, they heard but did not see a long column of tanks passing nearby. Chief mentioned, "If this weather keeps up, those guys might be having some supply problems of their own."

The respite coming to an end, Harry filed a flight plan with airport operations indicating his intended destination was an airfield by the name of RAF Grove. At the time, it was being used to serve a hospital located near London.

He conducted his usual pre-flight inspection, taking no short-cuts despite the steady rain. When he climbed aboard, he slowly made his way through the cabin, assuring the wounded men and the nurses he'd have them safely in England in short order.

He counted twenty-eight litters and was impressed by the fact the casualties were neither moaning nor complaining. None of his passengers had even asked him about the fog. Harry assumed it was because they were all very much aware he'd flown through the same bad weather to get there in the first place, and returning them to England was a given. He looked back at his decision to ignore the abort order and decided he'd made the correct choice because the mission needed to be completed, and the evidence to back him up was occupying his cabin. However, he did harbor a fear he might be in trouble for disobeying the abort order, a fear he quickly banished from his thoughts.

In a few minutes the control tower directed him to the take-off point, and Harry advised them he was ready to proceed. Though he could locate

As a C-47 gains speed, the tail lifts from the ground, and the pilot can see the runway. The reverse tricycle landing gear necessitated the use of Follow Me jeeps to guide the pilot to wherever he was going while taxiing, for the reason the cockpit pointed up to the sky when parked or moving at low speeds.

the centerline of the runway, his visibility was limited to not more than 100 yards as the rain continued to mercilessly pound at the windscreen. With the centerline of the runway barely visible, he was able to "pull the corker" and begin to accelerate.

He did his best to keep the plane dead-center on the runway as he encountered numerous deep puddles of water. When he achieved sufficient speed, he began to execute what turned out to be a nice smooth and straight take-off. When "Wee Junie" slipped into the air, he could hear Al exhale. They briefly glanced at each other and smiled. They could hear their passengers cheering as they left Orly behind them.

He commenced a slow climb and steered a west/northwest course. When they unexpectedly broke out of the fog, it was as if someone had suddenly switched-on a bright white spotlight and was shining it directly into their eyes. The patients in the back cheered at the sight. But the break in the fog didn't last for long. As he continued to gain altitude, they soon found themselves ensconced in zero-zero conditions yet again. Despite the weather, Harry breathed a sigh of relief, for if the fog cleared, then he'd possibly need to contend with German fighter planes. He was fully aware his C-47 was an unarmed transport, lacked Red Cross markings, and would have been easy prey for some lucky Luftwaffe pilot.

When he arrived over England, it was pitch-dark. Between the war-mandated black-out of all ground lighting and the heavy cloud cover, it appeared to Harry as if they were flying through a black void. Whether he looked up, down, or sideways, everything was black.

The cockpit itself was lit solely by the glow of the instruments. There were covers fitted over the cabin windows, which blocked the cabin lighting from leaking out where an unfriendly pilot might spot them. The nurses were forced to keep their lanterns set at a bare minimum for fear a little light might, nevertheless, leak through the window covers with potentially devastating results.

It was by sheer dead-reckoning he calculated they were close to the English airfield RAF Grove, at which time he sought to make radio contact. He successfully conversed with the Control Tower and requested assistance from "Darky", an instrument guidance system the British had developed. The control tower operator assigned him the call letters Queen Dog Mike, or QDM for short.

As he neared the general vicinity of the airbase, he spotted an extremely bright-white, perpendicular marker/light indicating the point Harry needed to fly over to remain on course. As he crossed the marker, he noted they were flying at 200 feet, and yet everything ahead of him was still dark. The wartime blackout rules made sure no pilot, friend or foe, would have an easy time locating any potential targets.

It wasn't much longer before the runway lights came to life. To Harry's great relief, the landing strip was dead ahead. He glanced at Al and noticed he was smiling, though his focus was also on the approaching runway. Harry was careful to make an especially gentle landing for the benefit of the wounded men aboard, none of whom had any idea how treacherous the flight had actually been.

They were met by a Follow Me Jeep and guided to a hangar where a bunch of ambulances were lined up, their rear doors open and facing the spot the C-47 was expected to park. When the plane finally rolled to a halt, and before Al cut the engines, the patients began clapping and calling out their appreciation. When Al had cut the engines, they went to the edge of the flight deck, poked their heads into the cabin, and wished the men a quick recovery and the nurses some badly needed R&R. They returned to the cockpit where they could stay out of the way while Chief and Sparky directed the unloading operation.

Less than an hour later Harry was landing at Greenham Common. Their home base was enjoying clear weather as they had flown out of the fog shortly after departing RAF Grove. Harry followed the Jeep, parked the plane, and cut the engines. Chief hadn't even popped open the hatch when another Jeep, being driven by a highly agitated sergeant, raced up to the plane. He furiously signaled towards the cockpit by holding his arms over his head and waving them back and forth. Harry stuck his head through the opening to hear what he had to say. In what Harry considered to be a "smart-alecky" tone of voice, the sergeant shouted:

"Colonel Donalson wants to see you right away, lieutenant!"

Harry climbed down from the plane and hopped into the front passenger seat of the Jeep. "What's going on?" Harry asked.

He was met with no response, irking him a little more. He wasn't accustomed to sergeants being so outwardly unfriendly and hopped out of the Jeep before it came to a full stop without saying another word to him. As soon as he entered the Quonset hut housing Donalson's office, the conversations among the officers and staff scattered about the room promptly ceased. Harry walked to Donalson's doorway, and before he could announce his arrival, Donalson's aide, without so much as looking at Harry, slowly rose from his seat, knocked on the colonel's door, and went inside. A few moments later, he returned and in an emotionless voice said:

"The colonel will see you now, lieutenant." The aide didn't even look Harry in the eyes, almost as if Harry was a dead man. Harry was apprehensive as he moved forward into the office; he knew there might be some disapproval of his unauthorized trip to Orly. Between the attitude of the sergeant in the Jeep, the sudden quiet when he entered the hut, and the eye-avoidance of the colonel's aide, he was beginning to feel queasy.

Cap under his left arm, Harry walked into the office and approached Donalson's desk. He sensed a tension in the air and held his salute as the colonel stared at him. Donalson made him hold the salute just long enough to make Harry a little more uncomfortable than he already was. Donalson was tapping the rubbery end of a pencil on his desktop while staring at the wall behind Harry.

"Sit down lieutenant." Donalson's voice sounded to Harry as if he was feeling a bit hostile towards him.

Donalson slowly rose from his chair while motioning for Harry to remain seated. He walked behind Harry, who was twisting his neck as he followed Donalson. Donalson, however, never so much as glanced in Harry's direction. He pointed to a large chalkboard listing of all the planes in the squadron.

"Do you see where your plane is?" He pointed at a line towards the very bottom of the board where "Wee Junie" was listed.

"Yes, Sir." Harry's voice was almost a whisper.

"You, your crew and your passengers have been reported as Missing in Action and Presumed Dead. The only plane out of 126 that took off this morning and didn't return with the rest of us!" Donalson paced back and forth several times before returning to his chair.

"You've put me in a helluva bind lieutenant." Donalson paused a moment as he appeared to be having trouble maintaining his composure. His face was bright red, and Harry thought he looked as if he was getting ready for a fight. "You know the long cord that comes out of the side of the plane, to your left, and is attached to a little contraption called a microphone? You can actually speak to people with that. Ever try it?" Donalson made no attempt to disguise his sarcasm. Harry realized he was not expecting an answer, so he remained quiet and anxious. He remembers being so uncomfortable his palms were sweating. "It would have been nice if you'd have used the damned thing!"

Donalson leaned halfway across his desk, getting within about 18 inches of Harry's face: "What you did today warrants a medal, though I know you weren't hunting for one. Of course, if I put you in for a commendation, you'd likely be court-martialed for disobeying a direct order. And make no mistake, lieutenant, you'd be looking at Leavenworth, and then you could kiss your airline pilot dreams goodbye."

Harry sat silently, trying his best to appear calm. Right about then, he figured he was in more danger than at any time during the day's flights. Donalson noticed Harry's discomfort but didn't say anything that would allow him to feel better.

Donalson poured himself a glass of water from a steel pitcher on his desk, gulped it down, and slammed the empty glass on the desktop, further rattling Harry, who flinched in response.

"Dammit lieutenant! If you pull a stunt like this again—" Donalson shouted when suddenly he found himself at a loss for words. After a long pause, he continued: "Now, just get the hell out of here! We have a full day tomorrow, and I'm going to need every pilot and crew I've got, including those recently back from the dead."

Harry stood and saluted. Donalson simply waved one hand at him, indicating Harry to get out. "Thank you Sir," said Harry, who wasted no time leaving. As he opened the office door, he noticed everyone was hanging close-by, no doubt listening. Several of the officers smiled at him as he practically ran from the building.

Apparently, Harry did know how to make use of the microphone. Candid photo captured by Al, his co-pilot, not long after the flight to Orly.

He hopped a ride in a Jeep back to "Wee Junie", where his crew was milling around, happy to see him return, still sporting his first lieutenant bars.

"Harry," said Al, "we heard the colonel was glad to learn we are ok, but they said he went into a bit of rage when he found out what we'd done. Is everything okay?"

Harry took a deep breath:

"Yeah, everything's swell, but next time I get a notion to ignore orders, just shoot me and be done with it."

*The C-47 manufacturer rated the plane as capable of holding fourteen litters and three nurses. Harry maintains his aircraft was configured to accept twenty-eight litters, while Donalson, per Harry's recollection, mentioned eighteen litters. Harry said that "when push came to shove, we crammed everyone and everything" into our plane.

Chapter 12

Operation Market Garden

This photo was snapped by Harry's crew chief shortly before taking off on day two of Operation Market Garden. Note the carefully laid-out tow rope attached to Harry's plane. Carl Cary's plane is to the right.

On the evening of September 16 1944, Harry, his close friend Carl Cary and about a dozen of his fellow officers, a combination of C-47 and glider pilots, were lounging in the Officers' Club. Rumors of a major operation had been circulating for well over a week. The scuttlebutt indicated they were going to be flying behind the front lines into Holland as part of a big push to end the war by Christmas. One time when Harry, Carl, and Al were exiting a local pub, a few of the patrons told them to have a good time in Holland. Al mentioned they probably were not going to Holland for the reason too many people thought it to be true and had to be a misinformation campaign to fool the Germans.

Nobody had proof of what was cooking at headquarters. To the two friends, it was just pure speculation. They knew something big was in the offing, but had no idea how enormous the operation was going to be.

Recently Cary had been flying as Harry's wingman. He found it comforting to look to his right and see his pal flying where he was supposed to be and know he'd never miss a course change. Cary had the same sentiment for Harry. Their friendship and trust in each other's flying abilities lent a degree of assurance when flying into less than comfortable situations, especially during instrument flight conditions.

Each of them had recently experienced several instances where their planes absorbed minor hits from ground fire, but nothing serious. At least not yet. They mused death had come closer to them on some of their excursions into London, where they heard the explosions of German V-1 rocket bombs exploding in the near-distance, than it had come to them while flying missions. Cary basically took the place of Lang in Harry's day-to-day life, and the two of them spent a lot of time together, while also sharing an appreciation for the practice of instrument flight.

The light banter in the Officers' Club on the evening of 16 September 1944 was abruptly interrupted when a staff sergeant strode into the center of the room and politely announced:

"Gentlemen, may I have your attention please, I have important news."

The room immediately went quiet as the Staff Sergeant continued.

"There's going to be a maximum effort tomorrow. Jeeps will pick you up for breakfast at 0600 hours, and the briefing will be at 0700 hours. That's all, thank you."

He left as quickly as he came, allowing no time for questions. A few glider pilots, veterans of D-Day, shared their opinions to the effect they expected the next day's objective would be Holland. They claimed to know about a British plan for an all-out effort to win the war in one decisive blow, and the kick in the teeth was about to be leveled against the Germans in Holland.

Rumors of a pending assault on Holland was not a genuine surprise. What was more of a surprise was the fact the locals in town appeared to possess more information than did Harry and Cary. He immediately recalled the recent incident when they were leaving their favorite pub. Harry considered the information leaks, if accurate, to be a bad omen.

Veteran glider pilots believed the operation was going to be a big one, and offered some practical tips for the C-47 boys. Their suggestions ranged from how to dodge German anti-aircraft fire to taping a pair of machine gun clips together for faster reloads should they find themselves in ground combat. They called the taped gun clips banana clips.

Harry had never before considered bringing a machine gun along to supplement his Colt side-arm in the event he had to abandon the plane. Al, on the other hand, always carried a carbine on board. Harry had not given much thought to the possibility of finding himself in a ground combat situation as a consequence of having been shot down. However, after listening to the glider pilots' descriptions of witnessing C-47s being shot down over France, back in June, he abruptly changed his mind. He decided to seek out some heavy artillery in the form of a Thompson sub-machine gun.

The two friends quickly returned to the Quonset hut serving as their temporary housing. A hut they shared with about a dozen other pilots. They had considered the problem of the C-47's lack of armor a couple weeks earlier and realized their flak jackets could easily be separated into two separate armored pieces. A partial solution to the absence of armored cockpit protection was then simple: split a flak jacket into two parts. They laid one half of the jacket on the floor beneath their feet and sat on the second section. They already wore flak jackets to protect their respective torsos, so it proved to be a matter of acquiring two additional jackets, something the supply sergeants never questioned. Consequently, the first item to address when they returned to their tent was making certain they each had two flak jackets ready for the morning's mission.

Harry was particularly impressed with the glider pilots' concept of taping machine gun ammo clips together. He decided to borrow a Thompson machine gun and planned to stow it in the cockpit come morning. Both men cleaned their side-arms, and Harry did, in fact, tape a few machine gun clips together. He practiced loading and unloading the banana clips and realized he could reload much more quickly than with the standard single clips.

The two men shot the breeze for a bit as neither could sleep. When the clock approached 2300 hours, they decided they needed to do whatever they could to get some shut-eye, so both men agreed to call it a night. Cary had taken part in the D-Day drops, but for Harry, this was his first real action. According to Cary, the pending operation was going to be on a "grand scale".

Harry had a difficult time sleeping, which in itself was not particularly unusual. As he tossed in bed, he rationalized he probably wasn't the only person having a tough night. Knowing he probably had a lot of company didn't help. He was excited and nervous, making sleep nearly impossible. While he could hardly wait to get it on, he also knew he'd need to be at his best and finally managed to sleep maybe two hours. When he woke up at 0500 hours, he was so anxious to get going, the lack of sleep proved to be a non-factor.

On the morning of September 17 1944, the Mission Briefing hut was jam-packed with C-47 and glider pilots, along with co-pilots. There was a loud buzz in the room as everyone was anxious to learn the details of the day's mission. Harry looked around and thought the atmosphere closely resembled a locker room before one of his high school baseball games and the analogy relaxed him a little.

He turned to face Cary, sitting to his right, and said: "Have you ever been on such a great team in your life?" Cary just smiled back. Harry looked at Al, to his left, and noticed both of his legs were doing the shakes. He put his hand on Al's shoulder, who seemed to snap out of it as his legs calmed down, and he gave Harry a slightly embarrassed grin. Harry knew Al needed a cigarette and wondered why he wasn't smoking.

An elevated stage at the front of the room was dominated by a large map of Western Europe hanging on the wall. Concentrically larger red circles were drawn around three cities in Holland: Eindhoven, Nijmegen, and Arnhem. As Colonel Donalson appeared from a doorway to the right of the stage, Staff Sergeant Kane called out:

"Gentlemen, attention!"

Everyone immediately jumped to their feet and stood silently at attention as Donalson smartly walked to the center of the stage, where he came to an abrupt halt. Staff Sergeant Kane then announced:

"At ease!" The assembled pilots proceeded to take their seats. All eyes were peeled on Donalson, just as he liked it.

Donalson paused for a moment as he looked around at the eager faces of the men gathered before him.

"Gentlemen, as you know, Third Army's been running flat-out across France, and we've been hard-pressed to keep them supplied with fuel and ammo. Recently," he paused a moment as he appeared to be searching for the right words, "we've been devoting every extra minute of free time practicing glider tows and paratroop drops. Believe me, I'm aware of the strain on all of you from the extra work, but your efforts are about to pay off."

Donalson, by nature, was in the habit of frequently pausing when addressing his men so he could establish eye contact with as many of them as possible. He hesitated yet again as he took his time looking around the room. Harry remembers he found himself momentarily staring Donalson straight in the eyes.

OPERATION MARKET GARDEN

"Men, today, we are participating in the single, largest airborne assault the world has ever witnessed. This is history in the making, and every plane and every pilot we can muster is taking part in this momentous endeavor, an endeavor the Top Brass believe can bring a rapid ending to this damned war!"

He was temporarily interrupted by a spontaneous eruption of cheers.

Harry, standing, is in the center. The man wearing the parachute is Lieutenant Colonel Clement G. Richardson, 438th Troop Carrier Group, 89th Squadron. Harry was flying one of the lead planes on the first day of Operation Market Garden, September 17 1944, the day this photo was snapped. Harry's co-pilot, Al, is standing to the far right. In front of Al is his crew chief, "Chief", and in front of Harry is his radioman, "Sparky". Harry and Al are wearing "wheel hats". The "wheel hat" features a hard visor. After many flights wearing headphones, the hat would take on a permanent droop. The saucer-shape of the hat resulted in the term "wheel". It also served as part of their dress uniform. LTC Richardson is wearing a "flight" cap. Harry says they put up 247 aircraft on the first day of Market Garden. He was 21 years old at the time. Harry appears to have aged quite a bit since the photo taken of him in front of the Texas State Capitol building.

Donalson described Operation Market Garden in enough detail so the men understood their specific mission and how it fit into the overall operation. He explained they would be dropping elements of the 101st Airborne near a Dutch town by the name of Eindhoven and pointed to the first and lowest of the three red-circled cities on the map.

When Donalson was finished, he turned the briefing over to a captain from "G2", the intelligence unit. The G2 captain assumed a position in the center of the stage and looked around for a few moments. In a monotone delivery, he proceeded to advise the group the majority of the anticipated German anti-aircraft weaponry would probably be installed on barges docked in the various canals they'd be flying over, going to, and coming from their objective. He pointed to multiple channels on the map and asked they make a mental note of them.

He proceeded to address what was in the back of everyone's minds. Donalson said casualty projections, based on intelligence gathered from a combination of the Dutch Underground and aerial reconnaissance, had been calculated. He paused a few moments before delivering the bad news.

The anticipated casualties on this first day were expected to run between 12 and a whopping 18 percent. Harry did some quick math in his head and realized the G2 captain was saying they anticipated about thirty-five to forty-five of the pilots, along with their respective three and four-man crews, would not be here at the end of the day. He calculated nearly 180 men might fail to return, not counting losses among their paratrooper/passengers.

That was a very sobering thought, one he immediately chased to the back reaches of his mind. His numerous conversations with Lang, regarding death and legacies, were temporarily forcing themselves into the foreground of his thoughts, causing him to become just a bit queasy.

The next officer to speak was a lieutenant colonel from the Army Air Force's climate services division. He painted a pretty rosy weather picture for the round trip and pointed out they should have no difficulty locating the drop zones. He hesitated when he realized what he had just said and clarified his statement to mean: "at least no weather-related difficulties."

To Harry, it appeared the colonel had temporarily overlooked the fact they were flying behind the enemy lines. And other, non-weather related issues might come into play. Their attention could be diverted by anti-aircraft fire or even German fighter planes. Weather was likely to be the least of their concerns.

Upon completion of the weather briefing, Donalson took the stage and wished the men good luck. Jeeps were waiting outside to taxi the pilots to their aircraft, and Harry was so anxious to get moving he ran to his Jeep with Al close on his heels.

The driver whisked the two men to "Wee Junie", and as Harry performed the exterior preflight inspection, Al took care of matters inside the cockpit. By the time Harry finished the review, which included his standard search for any sign of sugar granules, a line of paratroopers had formed near the hatch and were waiting to commence loading. As Harry walked past them to board his aircraft, several of the paratroopers threw him salutes, which was not necessary. Smiling, he obliged them by returning their greetings. The paratroopers were very aware it was up to Harry to safely drop them at the intended landing zone and appeared to be showing their respect.

Harry could appreciate what was likely going through their minds because he attended the Fort Benning Parachute School and was keenly aware of what they were about to do. He knew he couldn't control what would occur once the paratroopers jumped from his plane, but he was damned determined to make sure to drop them precisely on target and as low as feasible so they would spend minimal time in the air where they could be exposed to ground-fire.

As Harry entered the flight deck, he noticed Al had already laid one of their two-piece flak jackets on the floor beneath their feet with the other piece on their respective seat bottoms. Harry smiled as he noticed Al also had stowed both machine guns in the cockpit where they could quickly grab them and sling them over their shoulders in the event they were forced to bail out.

On the flight to Eindhoven, Harry encountered anti-aircraft fire now and again, but nothing close enough to his plane to be particularly concerning. Chief popped his head in at one point to report a piece of shrapnel had come through the floor, but nobody had been hit. He also took comfort at the regular fly-bys of P-51 Mustang fighter planes and didn't observe so much as a single German fighter plane on the round-trip.

Conditions over the target area had proved to be very good, and he proceeded to drop the paratroopers at an altitude of slightly under 500 feet so they'd be hitting the deck directly in the center of the Landing Zone. As he continued on his course, he looked behind him as best as he could manage and realized there were hundreds, maybe thousands, of parachutes in the air.

As he made the return flight, Harry found he was feeling a little let-down. He'd been expecting the mission to be far more difficult than it had been and realized he was feeling a bit guilty at how easy the trip had proven

Second Lieutenant Carl A. Cary, one of Harry's two best friends, is taking off from Greenham Common towing a British Horsa glider. Note the formations already aloft in the background. Photo courtesy of Robert A. Cary. The precise date is unknown.

to be. Harry thought he might be experiencing those feelings because he was flying back to the safety of England while the men he dropped over the target zone were quite possibly engaged in life-or-death struggles. Either way, he decided he'd talk about his feelings with Cary later that night and discuss with him what emotions he had experienced.

When he landed at Greenham Common, he was not immediately free to return to quarters, at least not until after a thorough debriefing. The location and type of German anti-aircraft installations were near the top of the list of questions the G2 officers posed. They made no mention of casualty reports and, in a way, Harry didn't want to know. The debriefing session lasted about twenty minutes, and Harry hoped the information he provided would prove useful for the next day's mission.

That evening many pilots were gathered in the Officers' Club and made an informal estimate of the planes lost. They came to the conclusion G2's loss predictions were high. The consensus opinion was total losses looked to be under 5 percent for the first day, putting everyone more at ease concerning the prospects for day two.

OPERATION MARKET GARDEN

Most of the men thought the first day was likely the most dangerous for the reason they assumed the enemy would be worn down after that. Harry didn't understand the rationale, but certainly hoped they were correct. In Harry's way of thinking, he figured the Germans would likely anticipate further Allied reinforcements being sent, and the Germans might be more prepared than on the first day. However, the overall mood was decidedly upbeat, and the pilots were looking forward to continuing the campaign.

The following morning Colonel Donalson briefed the pilots on the mission for Operation Market Garden, day two. Harry discovered he was assigned to tow a single glider and would be flying deeper into Holland, near a town called Nijmegen. He understood there was a vital highway bridge over the River Waal and ran through Nijmegen which the Allies needed to quickly capture. He knew some of the gliders were transporting artillery pieces and jeeps, along with a variety of equipment, munitions, and paratroopers, but didn't know what might be inside the glider he'd be towing until he actually saw it. Donalson reported things had been going pretty well on the ground-end of the operation, which drew loud cheers. He made no mention of any delays or difficulties the ground forces might have experienced.

Having been certified as a glider pilot, he couldn't imagine what it'd be like piloting a glider loaded with a cannon or a Jeep onto an unpaved landing zone from perhaps only 200 or 300 feet of altitude. He truly hoped the glider pilots, especially the pilot of the glider he'd be towing, had sufficiently practiced such maneuvers in the weeks leading up to Market Garden. However, his primary focus was on the delivery of his glider to the point where it could make a safe landing in the correct location. What happened once the glider was released from his plane was out of his control. As it developed, the glider he would be towing was to be loaded with paratroopers of the 82nd Airborne.

A captain from G2 presented the assembled pilots with good news as they expected casualty rates of only 5 to 7 percent, or roughly 50 percent less than the loss rate they predicted the first day. The G2 captain said they were expecting enemy resistance to be even less concentrated than on day one. Harry noted his tone of voice conveyed optimism, quite unlike the monotone presentation of the day before. Donalson finished the briefing with his usual "good luck and stay alert."

While being driven to their plane, Harry and Al shared the opinion G2 may have failed to take into account the first day was likely a surprise assault. They believed it was possible the Germans would be waiting for them.

Second Lieutenant Carl A. Cary is in the center. The men standing immediately to his right and left went down with him a few hours after this photo was taken. Second Lieutenant Buck Arnott, on the far right, usually flew with Cary, but for unknown reasons, did not receive flying orders on that fateful day, September 19 1944. The officer on the far left was Second Lieutenant James A. Lawhorn and served as Cary's co-pilot in place of Arnott on that day. The two crew members who also perished were Tech. Sergeant Richard K. Rockwell, the crew chief, and Staff Sergeant John D. Hines, the radioman, both in the second row. Photo courtesy of Robert A. Cary.

However, they both agreed G2 probably knew more than they would ever know about the German defenses awaiting them and decided it was better to drop the topic and, as Al pointed out, not risk jinxing themselves.

From the first day Harry met him, Al had proven himself to be superstitious. He never failed to follow the same routine the night before any mission. Al would make a hand-written list of everything he'd need for any given mission, right down to his socks, boots, and good-luck charm. Upon arriving at the plane, the first thing he did was get on his knees below the fuel caps and examine the ground. If it had rained during the night, he would run his right forefinger on the pavement and taste it for traces of sugar.

As Al stepped through the hatch, he always patted the outer skin of the plane, just above the hatchway. He always shook shake hands with Chief and Sparky before proceeding to the cockpit where he laid out the flak jackets on the floor and seat, first for Harry, then for himself. Al always brought a carbine with him. He'd clean it each evening and stowed it beside his seat. Finally, he carried a lucky rabbit's foot, except his wasn't a fake. His rabbit's foot originated from his last small game hunting excursion before enlisting in the army. Harry never really gave Al much grief over his "crazy idiosyncrasies" and figured: "Who's to say, maybe they helped."

Harry and Al's speculation the casualty rate could prove higher than G2's estimate turned out to be correct. Unbeknownst to them, Adolf Hitler had sensed there was an opportunity for a German victory at Market Garden and had ordered well more than 1,000 fighter planes, including the ferocious Messerschmitt 262 jet fighter, be immediately redeployed to Holland. They didn't know it yet, but day two of Market Garden wasn't going to be easy.

Towing a glider was a great deal more complicated than merely flying a C-47 loaded with paratroopers or munitions. How easy or difficult glider towing would be depended in no small part on the skill level of the glider pilot. If the glider pilot was good, he'd fly on an even-keel, remain a little below the tow-plane, and slightly off-center. If he was inexperienced, or perhaps just plain nervous, he could be all over the place; up, down, left, right, making Harry's job of maintaining the formation much more difficult. The C-47s also flew in a completely different formation than they'd typically employ. Rather than a three-plane, V-shaped formation, they would fly in a four-plane diagonal-right configuration referred to as "echelon-right."

When towing a single glider, Harry could fly at not more than 115mph with the throttles wide open. He'd maintain an altitude of about 400–500 feet, which allowed the glider pilot all the time he'd need to safely land once he cut loose from Harry's aircraft. One of the dangers of flying very slowly, and so close to the ground, was that any German soldier toting a rifle could take pot-shots at them. Acerbating the situation, the C-47 didn't carry enough fuel to safely make the round-trip, so temporary plywood fuel tanks were constructed and installed at the front of the cabin. As many as nine 200-gallon tanks might be installed, depending on whether it was a single or double glider tow and how far they were traveling.

On the second day of Market Garden, Harry had a pair of 200-gallon plywood gas tanks installed in the cabin, a few feet behind him. A well-placed incendiary bullet or cannon fire from a German fighter, or searing hot shrapnel from anti-aircraft shells could strike the tanks and cause the immediate disintegration of the aircraft.

Needless to say, Harry made sure the first fuel that the engines consumed was sourced from the temporary wood fuel tanks. Once empty, Chief and Sparky would take axes to the tanks and discard them out the hatch as quickly as they could unless they were under orders not to do so. On that day, they were under orders not to dispose of the tanks. Even if he was able to drain the tanks of fuel, the trapped vapors within the tanks could be highly explosive.

Harry discovered the Germans were much better prepared on this second day. Anti-aircraft fire rose to greet them from fixed ground emplacements, roll-back roof-tops, and the anticipated anti-aircraft barges on the canals. He still remembers how shocked he and Al were as the first time they witnessed the roof of a house literally roll back to reveal an anti-aircraft emplacement.

At times the sky around Harry was flooded with black and white puffs of exploding anti-aircraft shells. Harry was lucky none of the shots directly hit his plane, though there were several uncomfortably close calls. From the corner of his eye, Harry caught sight of a pair of Messerschmitt 109s lining up to attack a nearby formation. He realized he was gripping the wheel so hard his fingers were hurting and had to force himself to relax.

Eventually, the glider Harry was towing cut loose as planned. Chief stuck his head out the open side-hatch and watched the glider execute a safe landing and immediately conveyed the fact to Harry and Al.

As Harry turned for home, he and Al were nearly startled out of their seats when a German Messerschmitt 262 Jet fighter roared past their nose. The open side windows allowed the full effect of the screaming jet engines to penetrate the cabin, having an unsettling effect on the entire crew. The jet was so quickly out of sight, they almost questioned what they'd just witnessed.

Chief stuck his head into the cockpit and shouted: "What in the Sam Hill was that?"

Harry was still anxiously searching to see where the Messerschmitt might have gone and didn't immediately answer as he feared the much-dreaded jet fighter could be circling back to target them. Once satisfied they appeared to be safe from attack, Harry turned around to face Chief and calmly said:

"Nothing to worry about."

Chief shrugged his shoulders and returned to the cabin. Once they were safely on the ground, Harry told him what had happened, and Chief replied he was glad he didn't know it at the time.

September 19 1944, was day three of Market Garden. It would prove to be the last time Harry would see his close friend and wingman, Carl Cary, alive. The morning mission briefing included a significant increase, from the prior day, in the anticipated casualty rate to as high as 18 percent, which would prove to be painfully accurate. The weather report was exceptional, but even a decent weather prediction could be a two-edged sword.

Good weather would make hitting the drop zones easier, but the planes would be much more visible to German fighter planes and anti-aircraft gunners. Harry would prefer low-lying, scattered clouds. Though he had reasonable grounds for concern, he didn't allow his thoughts to linger on the potential dangers ahead; he had become a believer in positive thinking.

His assignment for the third day of the Operation was glider tow. Harry huddled with Cary and the remaining two pilots who'd be flying in his four-plane echelon-right formation to be sure they were all on the same page. Harry didn't know the other pilots as they had recently arrived from Stateside. He stressed to them the importance of staying in the formation and not wandering, no matter what. He advised them to keep focused on Harry's plane, ignore all else, and everything would work out swell.

As usual, Harry was piloting the lead plane in the formation. Cary was positioned a bit behind him and to his right. A little behind Cary, and to his right, was plane number three, and the fourth, with the least experienced pilot, was the last plane in the echelon-right formation. It was Harry's opinion that the fourth position was the safest spot for an inexperienced pilot. From there, the pilot had a clear view of the entire formation and, should he wander from his position, it was unlikely he'd interfere with the balance of the group. He also was aware the last plane was the least likely to be targeted by the Germans.

With more than 2,000lbs of the additional aviation fuel needed for the operation and a loaded glider in tow, the C-47's airspeed was significantly reduced along with the potential altitude. Harry felt as though he was a flying gasoline can that anyone with a rifle could shoot at.

Inherently, he was a risk-taker, but hauling hundreds of gallons of additional gasoline stored only a few feet behind him did cause him some reflection. He recalls quietly reciting a couple of prayers to himself. As he did so, he noticed Al was vigorously stroking his rabbit's foot as an unlit cigarette dangled from his lips.

Harry's plane was a prime target of the Germans for the simple reason he was flying the lead plane in the formation. It didn't matter whether it was a German fighter plane or ground fire; he'd been taught the enemy tended to concentrate their fire on the lead plane in any formation. It was Harry's understanding that the Germans believed if they were to shoot down the lead plane, it could send the balance of the formation off-course, not to mention the fact it would likely have a disheartening effect on the remaining pilots and their crews. It was one of the reasons he and Al improvised additional armor for their cockpit.

The flight to Nijmegen proved much more eventful than the previous two days combined. They saw American and German fighters performing impressive aerial maneuvers while engaged in combat, though no Messerschmitt 262 jet fighters appeared. There was anti-aircraft fire originating from locations where previously there had been none. Harry knew they were in for a rocky ride.

At one point they witnessed a roof roll back atop a two-story house to reveal an anti-aircraft battery that definitely was not there the day before. He wondered how many more new emplacements awaited them.

There were times the ride was outright rocky, like a carnival ride. Al went so far as to compare the experience to being on a roller coaster at Coney Island. As they progressed to their destination, Al kept a watchful eye over the balance of the formation. To Harry's delight, the planes stayed in a pretty tight grouping.

When they achieved the target zone, Harry's glider was cut loose over what appeared to be a large, mostly flat meadow outside of Nijmegen, where numerous gliders had landed earlier. He noticed smoke rising from several locations, indicating there may have been ground engagements in the recent past.

With the release of his glider, Harry's plane immediately began to increase both in speed and altitude. The anti-aircraft flak was again becoming very heavy, and his unarmed and unarmored aircraft continued to experience numerous near-misses. He had to wait for Chief to advise him all of the gliders were released before he could open up the throttles.

Suddenly puffs of black and white smoke appeared just ahead of them. The exploding shells were so close that they actually flew directly through the smoke. Harry recalls being rocked by nearby anti-aircraft bursts more severely than he'd ever before experienced. Later, a post-flight inspection would discover dozens of shrapnel holes in the nose cone, wings, tail, and fuselage.

Chief was just entering the cockpit when Al shouted: "Oh my God!" He was pointing his right hand, still holding his rabbit's foot, straight through his open side-window towards Cary's plane.

When Harry followed Al's outstretched arm, he realized Cary's cockpit was filled with white smoke, blocking both Cary and his co-pilot from view. As he and Al watched in horror, Cary's plane began to lose speed and altitude while simultaneously slipping out of the formation and falling off to the right. In a few moments, Cary's plane rolled over on its right side, went into a dive, and crashed in a ball of flames.

Cary's glider, however, made it safely to the landing zone. It was at that moment Harry realized they'd just flown beyond the range of the anti-aircraft guns. The difference between survival and death had been a matter of seconds.

Harry still cannot describe the despair and helplessness he felt when he saw Cary's cabin full of smoke. In a way, he was relieved he'd been unable to see into the cockpit. Harry wanted to remember Cary as he had been, not as he might have looked in the final moments of his life. Neither Harry, Al, nor Chief noticed any parachutes, confirming Cary and his crew had all perished.

He ordered the remainder of the formation to close up, and they continued on their return route to England.

By the time Harry was released from the day's debriefing and could return to his quarters, he realized someone had already cleared out Cary's belongings. There was no evidence Cary had ever been there. "That's war," Harry mused, for there was simply no time to mourn the dead as he must be ready to again fly into combat, unarmed, tomorrow. And if the third day was a sample of what awaited him, he figured he'd need all the rest he could manage.

September 20 1944, heralded the fourth day of Operation Market Garden. For the first time, Harry was not transporting troops, but instead was going

The tail section of Second Lieutenant Carl A. Cary's C-47 having been shot down while flying as Harry's wing-man during Operation Market Garden on September 19 1944. There were no survivors. Photo courtesy of Robert A. Cary. The serial number on the tail was one removed from Harry's own serial number, a coincidental acknowledgment of their friendship.

to be dropping supply parapacks to British paratroopers who'd been cut off and surrounded by Germans near Arnhem, Holland. He was not fully aware of the desperate situation the British paratroopers at Arnhem were facing. All Donalson said at the morning briefing was they were to drop supplies to a group of paratroopers who had managed to get themselves isolated and needed to be resupplied from the air.

Donalson told them Pathfinders' paratroopers were going to be installing a radio-wave beacon they could follow all the way to the drop zone. With electronic guidance, Harry anticipated there'd be no trouble locating his objective. He did, however, expect strong German resistance on what would be his deepest incursion into Holland to date.

The parapacks were attached to the fuselage, which Chief would release on Harry's order. Parapacks were long metal tubes containing anything from medical supplies and food, to ammunition and everything else a paratrooper might need. In addition, crates filled with ammunition and supplies were stacked on the cargo deck. Chief and Sparky were to literally kick the boxes from the aircraft after the parapacks were released. They kicked the crates out, rather than push them, to minimize the risk of falling out of the plane themselves.

Harry successfully dropped the supplies in the designated zone and rightfully assumed they landed in the hands of the British paratroopers. He enjoyed perfect flying conditions and had quickly located the drop site with no difficulties. Even the Germans cooperated that day as they met almost no resistance. It was not until decades later, when he viewed the movie, *A Bridge Too Far*, did the thought occur to him the Germans may have been the recipients of his supply mission that day. All he knows for sure is he dropped his cargo precisely on target, amid perfect flying conditions.

On both September 21 and 22 1944, weather conditions over many of the airbases prevented the launching of any additional missions. The squadron took advantage of the time to rest their pilots and aircrews while over-worked ground crews rendered the requisite maintenance and repairs to the planes. Regardless of the weather, many of the aircraft in his group were beat-up and badly in need of repair. Harry's mechanics complained there was a parts shortage, and they would likely need to scavenger parts from some of the damaged aircraft to keep the other transports flying.

There were holes in his plane's nose cone, wings, tail section, and fuselage from small-arms fire and anti-aircraft flak. Al said he felt engine number two needed some attention because it didn't sound right to him. The crews confirmed Al's suspicion and repaired it.

Harry learned early in their relationship Al possessed an uncanny ear for an aircraft engine and trusted his opinion when an engine didn't sound right. After that, the mechanics were also believers in Al. Every now and again, they might ask his opinion on engines they were putting back together. If the engine didn't sound right to Al, they'd keep working on it.

September 23 1944, was Harry's fifth and final day of flying missions in support of Operation Market Garden. The highlight of the mission briefing that day was a prediction for still higher casualty rates. A good weather report and the news they would be towing single gliders that day rounded out what had become ever-shorter mission briefings. There had been little mention of the progress the ground forces had been achieving, which Al and Harry felt was kind of odd. Scuttlebutt was indicating what had been the most massive airborne assault in history was failing. Hearing the stories caused Harry to wonder whether Cary's death had been in vain, not to mention the casualties on the ground.

As Harry and Al walked towards their waiting Jeep, Harry sighed as he knew it was going to be another low altitude, low-speed mission. It was the same type of assignment that resulted in the death of his good friend.

Many planes were out of commission either due to damage, lack of parts, or having been shot down, so it was a notably smaller squadron that was mustered on the airfield that morning; gliders dutifully lined up behind their respective planes. Harry had no complaints about the visibility, other than there was "too much visibility", as they awaited clearance for take-off.

Due to unexplained take-off delays, Harry found himself with a little extra time, so he wandered back to the glider he was going to tow. He recognized the pilot, a man named Milt, as someone he'd shared an occasional beer with and walked over to greet him. Rather than the self-assured man he remembered, he found someone who had what he termed "the stare". It was the expressionless appearance most glider pilots bore on their faces when they first arrived at Greenham Common following the Normandy operations.

Harry hesitated, then decided he should go ahead and convey his greetings. "Hey, Milt, keep an eye out today as my crew chief tends to spit his tobacco out the hatch."

Milt didn't immediately respond and momentarily continued staring into space. After a few seconds of delay, he slowly turned his head and looked at Harry. It was still a few moments more before he expressed recognition, causing Harry to wish he'd remained quiet. Milt put on a faint smile and said something about it wouldn't be the first time someone spat at him. They made some small talk, which came to an abrupt stop when it appeared the day's operation was ready to get underway. Harry never saw Milt again, though he knew his glider landed in one piece that day.

Shortly after releasing Milt's glider, Harry began to lead his squadron in a slow left bank to begin the journey home. Harry had just finished watching Milt safely land when the plane shook. Then it shook again, only more violently. They were taking anti-aircraft fire and were still at only 400 feet in altitude and slowly accelerating from what had been a treadmill-like 110 mile per hour pace.

Harry ordered the formation to go full throttle and get the hell out of there. No sooner had the words come out of his mouth than appeared a gigantic flash of white light directly in front of the windscreen. It was as if a spotlight had been suspended in mid-air and was pointed directly at him.

The serial number of Harry's plane was 21-00769, something Harry considers to be a reminder of how close to death he had been. Photo courtesy of Robert A. Cary.

At the same moment, he heard what sounded like hail hitting the nose cone. A crack formed at the lower edge of his windscreen and began to slowly work its way upwards. In less than a minute, the damage reached the top edge of the glass, causing Harry to worry the entire windscreen was in danger of imploding into their faces.

He told Al to check on the other planes in their formation. Al looked out his window and responded they appeared to be "A-OK". As quickly as it began, the anti-aircraft fire had ceased. He would never know if it stopped because they outdistanced the anti-aircraft batteries, or if they had been taken out by ground troops. It didn't feel to him as if they'd flown that much further.

Later that evening Al advised Harry that immediately following the explosion, he thought Harry looked as if he'd seen a ghost. Harry admitted he had, in fact, seen something and believed it was the ghost of death. From that moment forward, Harry began to think he'd survive the war and had some manner of an angel watching out for him. He was soberly aware that if he had sped up just a moment sooner, his plane would likely have been shot apart, and he would have gone down with it. Eventually, he would describe the scary event during a phone call from Lang, who agreed with Harry's conclusion. Lang, however, told him he was still haunted by the feeling he was living on borrowed time. Both men would prove to be correct.

Following Market Garden, things got back to normal. Most days were spent conducting supply runs to forward airbases and, sometimes, grassy meadows adjoining supply dumps. Paratroop and glider training was routinely worked into the schedule.

In early October, Lang flew a P-47 into Greenham Common for a visit. Harry heard the plane's distinct engine and ran out to watch it land. When Lang jumped from the wing and onto the tarmac, Harry was already well on his way there. Lang ran over to him and immediately presented Harry a cigar with a pink ribbon around it. Harry was initially taken by surprise as neither man was a smoker, but then he realized Lang was following an army tradition as it announced the fact he had become a father. He told Harry that Lillian had given birth to a baby girl, and both mother and daughter were doing real swell.

They went into Newbury and had a celebratory dinner of Shepherd's Pie and "war cake", a cake-like concoction made without the use of butter and other severely rationed ingredients. A few days later, Harry learned he was the father of a healthy baby boy, Daniel Michael Watson. The two men's life paths were nearly mirroring each other, leaving Harry to contemplate perhaps both of them were destined to return home.

W...N, Harry E. Jr.

89th Troop Carrier Squadron
Office of the Operations Officer

Sortie Record

DATE	TYPE OF PLANE	FLYING TIME	PLACE OF ORIGIN & DESTINATION	TYPE OF MISSION	REMARKS
1944 9/17	C-47A	6:00	Greenham Commons, England,- Holland	Paratroops	
9/18	C-47A	5:30	Greenham Commons, England - Holland	Airbonre Glider Tow	
9/19	C-47A	5:10	Greenham Commons, England - Holland	Airbonne Glider Tow	
9/20	C-47A	6:00	Greenham Commons, England - Holland	Parachute Re-supply	
9/23	C-47A	5:35	Greenham Commons, England - Holland	Airborne Glider Tow	
12/24	C-47A	5:15	Greenham Commons, England - Bastogne	Parapack Re-supply	
12/26	C-47A	5:20	Greenham Commons, England - Bastogne	Parapack Re-supply	
7 Missions		38:50	Total Hours Combat.		

CERTIFIED TRUE AND CORRECT:

Arthur A. Christy

ARTHUR D. CHRISTY,
1st Lt., AC,
Ass't S-3.

1945 3/24	C-47A	3:55	Reims, France- Wesel, Germany	Paratroops	

CERTIFIED TRUE AND CORRECT:

Allison S. Perry Jr.

ALLISON S. PERRY, JR,
CAPTAIN, AIR CORPS,
OPERATIONS OFFICER.

Official Sortie Record of Harry's Market Garden Mission.

As the war dragged on, the routine became one of ferrying supplies to the front lines all across France. On October 25 1944, Harry was to fly the trailing plane in a four-plane, diamond-shaped formation. It was to be a simple freight haul of signal core wire to Lille, France.

Captain Vanesse, a man he had not previously flown with, wanted to lead the flight himself. For reasons Vanesse did not disclose, he didn't brief Harry and the other two pilots before taking off regarding the weather, the course, or anything else. Harry felt the failure to take the time to conduct at least a minimal mission briefing was unusual because he was aware they would likely encounter heavy, though probably broken, cloud cover en route. He had studied the weather forecast himself, as he always did.

One of Harry's buddies, Bob Avent, was assigned the number two position in the formation; Harry doesn't recall who was flying in the number three spot. Harry was in the fourth position at the center-rear of the four planes. From his seat, he could observe the entire formation. They took off and assembled with no issues, at least not immediately.

After not more than fifteen minutes of flight time, Vanesse decided to take the squadron up and through the cloud layer. Harry adhered to his training and experience. As soon as he found himself totally immersed in the clouds, he carefully stuck to the instrument flight prescribed course of action. As he says: "You don't do anything. You don't change your power setting or your airspeed, and you keep your eyes on the instruments. You don't ever look outside as it can confuse you because all you can see is grey, so you have no reference as to which way is up and which way is down."

As the four planes broke through an opening in the cloud layer, he caught sight of Avent's plane. He was off to the right and a little too high above him. Harry realized Avent had just flown beyond a vertical position because he was looking at the top of Avent's plane.

As far as Harry knows, there was nothing Avent could have done to save the plane once he flew beyond the vertical position. It appeared the cargo of signal core wire had broken loose during the ascent, slid to the rear of the cabin, and likely caused Avent to lose control of his aircraft. There were no survivors from the subsequent crash. Harry suspected the cargo broke loose because of Avent's potentially overly-steep angle of ascent, but nobody would ever know with certainty. It could just as easily have been improperly secured.

Upon return to his base, Harry was debriefed and explained what he witnessed and why he thought the plane had become doomed. Harry and his co-pilot were the only eye-witnesses and were directed to sign-off on their account. By the time Harry returned to his bunk, there was no trace that Avent had ever been there. He was reminded of when he lost Cary the month prior and, for a little while, had some difficulty putting the two events out of his mind.

Chapter 13

Battle of the Bulge

Harry was in the Officers' Club at Greenham Common somewhere around the middle of December 1944. The club was decorated for Christmas, and the atmosphere was upbeat. It was damned cold outside, and the radio was playing popular tunes courtesy of "Axis Sally".

Sally suddenly interrupted the music with a message directed at American units located in Belgium. She was welcoming members of the United States Army 28th Infantry into captivity. One of the officers shouted, "Shut her up!" Someone immediately walked over to the radio and changed the station to the BBC.

A few minutes later, a second lieutenant, clearly a youngster recently arrived from stateside and eager to fit in, rushed through the door, and exclaimed the Krauts had launched a major offensive and were pushing us back to the English Channel. He was met with jeers and boos, not to mention a couple mugs of beer tossed in his direction. Try as he did to convince his fellow officers he wasn't kidding, he eventually gave up and walked out in a huff.

Harry and Golden Lang, who had flown in for one of his short visits, again utilizing a borrowed P-47 Thunderbolt, were sitting at a table with about four other officers. Harry was enjoying something he had grown very fond of, black tea and crumpets. Over the course of the next half an hour, many of the pilots in the club left, leaving Harry and Lang practically alone.

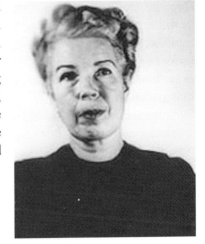

"Axis Sally" was an American. Her given name was Mildred Gillars.

As the two men considered the possibility that the young lieutenant had been correct, Lang said he had a pretty accurate view of what German industry and its cities looked like from his B-24 and thought the kid was "all wet". The two men laughed it off. It wasn't too much longer before Lang received word he was being ordered back to his base and had to cut short his visit. When the two friends departed the club that night, neither knew it would be the last time they'd ever see each other.

Reports coming into Greenham Common regarding the battle taking place in Belgium were not encouraging. As December progressed, Harry thought it was odd he didn't find himself flying any missions in support of the battle. Colonel Donalson advised him the weather over where the action is simply wasn't fit for flying supply missions, so they mostly flew practice runs. While the battle raged, Harry was performing formation flying maneuvers and practicing instrument landings. They conducted no missions across the English Channel. Harry and his fellow pilots were growing frustrated at the lack of action when suddenly, there was an abrupt change in their routine.

Early on the morning of December 24 1944, an urgent order came down from Army Air Force Headquarters. Harry's squadron was to immediately engage in what was described as an emergency munitions run to resupply the 82nd Airborne near a town in Belgium none of the pilots had ever heard of, Manhay.

The briefing conducted by Colonel Donalson was tense and short. A captain from G2 explained the front lines were very fluid and stressed the importance each parcel be dropped precisely on target because "our 82nd Airborne boys can only hold the landing zones just long enough" for us to drop our loads. He made it clear the situation on the ground was getting desperate.

G2 explained Manhay was a critical crossroads that the Germans very much wanted to make their own. He said various SS Panzer units were massing for an attack, and without our supplies, the 82nd would either be over-run or forced into a retreat-under-fire. He did mention the likelihood that any interference from the Luftwaffe was, at best, remote but cautioned that the Germans did have mobile anti-aircraft units in the vicinity.

Donalson stated he'd be leading the formation himself that day. As it developed, his plane was in the lead position of a set of three, three-plane formations. Each V-shaped formation had Three C-47s, for a total of nine aircraft in each. Harry was assigned to fly the lead plane in the second group. His nine planes were followed by a third group of nine, for a total of twenty-seven aircraft. It was all the strength the squadron could muster.

Every manner of supply item that could be found had been crated, parachutes affixed to them, and quickly loaded onto the planes. The drop would require each crew chief to kick the crates through the hatch, and a parapack loaded underneath the plane would be released separately. A parapack could hold heavier weapons, such as bazookas, that wouldn't fit into a crate.

Due to the critical need for accuracy, they were flying at altitudes varying from 300 to 600 feet while maintaining tight formations. Accuracy was paramount, and as they approached the target zone, Donalson led the group still lower to assure maximum accuracy.

Harry's plan was to begin dropping the supplies immediately after Donalson's plane commenced its supply drop. The result would create one continuous drop, from the first plane through to the last. The signal for Chief and Sparky to begin kicking out the crates was simple, as it was similar to when they would drop airborne paratroopers, they'd utilize the existing jump-warning lamp.

As they approached the drop zone, the plan was for Harry to order his co-pilot to switch-on the two-color signal lamp located over the open hatch. The first lamp was red, signaling they were closing in on the target, and, in response, Chief and Sparky would get ready kick-out the crates. When they reached the target zone, Harry would order the co-pilot to switch the signal light to green. The green light indicated Chief and Sparky were to immediately begin kicking the crates through the hatch as quickly as they could, after first releasing the parapack.

Due to the strain of so many planes and crews flying missions, Harry had been experiencing a "revolving door" of youngsters and glider pilots for his co-pilot position. Co-pilots were being juggled throughout the squadron, sometimes being temporarily transferred in from other airbases. Al had been assigned a C-47 of his own the month prior, so the cohesiveness Harry enjoyed with his co-pilot had pretty much been destroyed. He considered himself fortunate to have retained Chief and Sparky as the balance of his crew.

Harry was aware there'd been a definite manpower drain in the pilot pool due to continuing losses of planes and crews coupled with the ever-expanding theatre of operations. To make matters worse, new pilots were no longer arriving as quickly as they did before Market Garden so Harry, and every other pilot, had to make adjustments to their routines.

Harry had been anticipating yet another new co-pilot for this mission and was under the impression he was to report to Harry on December 23 for a practice run. The new man, however, didn't show up on the 23rd, and Harry could learn nothing of his whereabouts. Even Donalson was at a loss to explain the man's absence and assigned a glider pilot to serve as Harry's co-pilot on the day's practice run.

On December 24 1944, his replacement co-pilot, a young second lieutenant by the name of Fred,** finally made an appearance. He arrived very late and Harry had already completed the pre-flight checklist, the plane had been loaded, and Harry was standing around outside the hatchway, wondering when the guy would decide to make an appearance.

Just when Harry was prepared to give up and seek out a glider pilot, Fred showed up. He sheepishly offered what Harry considered to be one of the lamest excuses he ever heard. Fred swore an oath he'd been told Harry's plane was still in a repair hangar. Fred was taking a walk when he noticed the name "Wee Junie" and realized it was his assigned plane. He offered no explanation for his failure to report the day prior or for missing the mission briefings on both mornings.

Harry didn't think much of Fred's story, and not one to waste time, ordered Fred to get in there and fire up the engines. In short order they were being led by a "Follow Me Jeep" and were quickly off the ground. It didn't take long for the twenty-seven planes to form up and begin the journey to Belgium. Harry, however, had a funny feeling about his new co-pilot. He believed Fred was either in over his head, or had been hoping to be excused. He appeared to be very nervous. Either way, Harry knew he wouldn't be turning the controls over to him, not even for a minute.

Following Donalson's nine plane formation proved to be relatively easy. Now and again they'd make a minor change in altitude or execute a modest course correction. Harry was paying his usual close attention to their progress, having ordered Fred to keep an eye out for German fighter planes. There were no beacons to guide them to their destination that day. Therefore they were navigating strictly by visual flight rules. The successful completion of the mission was based on their ability to identify various geographic features as they flew over them.

Eventually, Harry identified some key landmarks he'd memorized and was aware they were approaching the drop zone. Knowing Donalson was likely doing the same, he instructed Fred to flip on the red lamp to alert Chief and Sparky to get ready. He heard the signal lamp lever click, confirming his order had been followed.

About a minute or two later, Chief came into the cabin. He advised Harry the parapacks, along with all of the crates, had been successfully

---

** Harry recalled the man's actual name, but because he may still be alive, declined to reveal it for purposes of publication.

cleared out. Harry, alarmed, turned and looked at him, but before he could say a word, Chief said:

"Hey! Why's the colonel's dropping his load so late?"

Harry screamed so loudly at his co-pilot his verbal eruption actually drowned out the drone of both engines: "What the hell did you do?"

Harry had never before experienced such anger in his life. Fred had the nerve to tell him he thought he'd skip the red warning light and go straight to the green "drop" signal. In response, Harry unconsciously flicked open the leather flap covering his revolver and momentarily laid his right hand onto its wooden handle. He realized the likely consequences of the early drop and was beside himself.

Harry opened his side window, stuck his head outside and looked behind him. The groups following Harry had interpreted his drop to be the cue to release their own loads. Save for Donalson's nine planes leading the formation, everyone else had dropped too soon, quite possibly into the Germans' hands.

Fred began to offer an explanation, but Harry cut him off and told him to shut the hell up. Harry again put his hand on his gun and advised him that he was lucky he didn't shoot him right then and there. He ordered Fred to "get the hell to the back of the cabin", and told Chief to keep an eye on "the bastard". Fred quickly unbuckled his seat belt and hurried out of the cockpit. Later that evening, Chief confided to Harry that he'd never seen Harry's face turn so red, so fast.

Harry could hardly wait to land and get into the debriefing room. That's where a second lieutenant from G2 recently in from the States informed Harry that Fred was of German descent and could even speak and write the language. He explained the G2 colonel had been considering utilizing Fred as an interpreter. Due to the pilot shortage, he had not yet done so.

To the shock of the G2 lieutenant, Harry went, in his own words, "practically nuts". He screamed at the young officer, "With the Krauts dropping spies all over the place, you send me out on a critical mission with a German?" The G2 lieutenant appeared as if he had just experienced a revelation. Fred was sitting only a few feet from Harry and hadn't said a word in his defense. Given Harry's state of mind, it was likely a smart decision on Fred's part to keep quiet.

Next thing Harry knew, the G2 officer stood up and declared the briefing to be over. Enraged at the lack of action, Harry jumped upright, his right hand on his holster, and threatened to shoot Fred right then and there as a being a spy. Without hesitating, Fred immediately ran and stood behind the lieutenant who meekly told Harry he'd "take care" of Fred. Harry never saw hide nor hair of either of them again.

Harry believes it was a good thing he didn't have the luxury of time to contemplate the unfortunate events of the day because early the following morning, Christmas Day, they were scheduled to make another supply run. The Christmas Day mission was to drop desperately needed ammo and food to the beleaguered 101st Airborne at Bastogne.

While conditions at Bastogne on Christmas morning were acceptable, the squadron was advised at the morning mission briefing the whole of England was sopped in. Donalson delayed the mission as long as possible before finally tossing in the towel and canceling the drop due to the continued bad weather.

Harry spent the day milling around the Officers' Club with a few of the other pilots, gathering whatever information they could about the status of the boys at Bastogne. The news they heard wasn't too encouraging. They learned the Luftwaffe had made an appearance in force and had pounded Allied positions. The report caused Harry to feel all the worse over the botched supply drop to the 82nd the day prior.

He considered the plight of the paratroopers on the ground, fighting for their lives as they watched their desperately needed supplies potentially falling among the Germans. His anger returned, but there was nobody to direct it towards. Instead, he took a long walk around the base to cool off. It was a few days later when he learned the 82nd Airborne, in the face of a fierce German onslaught, had been forced to retreat from its positions the night of December 24. He couldn't help but wonder if the retreat was due to the supply-drop being bungled, and grew angry all over again. It would be decades before he'd learn the 82nd was going to withdraw, regardless.

With Christmas evolving into a day-off, Donalson asked Harry to turn in a detailed written account of the previous day's mission. He advised Harry he'd be looking into the Fred situation.

On December 26 1944, they were advised flying conditions over the drop zone were very good, and the weather over England had also improved dramatically. The planes were still loaded from the day prior, saving significant prep time. One of the pilots mentioned it was better their Christmas presents be a day late than never at all, and Harry agreed.

The entire squadron took off as soon as the briefing was finished. Donalson was flying the lead plane, again with nine planes in his group. Harry followed behind just as he had done on December 24. Harry doesn't remember the name of his co-pilot that day, but he was someone he had known for a few months, could trust, and didn't speak German. The mission was accomplished with a perfect drop, no losses and no drama, except the drama on the ground at Bastogne.

As Harry flew over the drop zone, he noticed dozens of paratroopers scattered all around the area, jumping up and down while waving their arms at the planes. He interpreted the scores of waving arms to be a combination of alerting the aircraft to their presence, as well as the expression of happiness. As Harry watched the paratroopers, he was sincerely hoping they'd be out of their jam in short order.

They encountered no anti-aircraft fire or interference from German fighter planes, though the radio chatter did include a Messerschmitt sighting in the general vicinity. The return trip to Greenham Common went smoothly. After landing and enduring the usual debriefing, Harry decided to spend an hour in the Instrument Flight Instruction Hut. They were not called on again to return to the Battle of the Bulge in 1944.

On December 27 1944, Harry's long-time Squadron Commander, Colonel John M. Donalson, was transferred and replaced by Colonel Lucion M. Powell. Powell immediately started the squadron on a strenuous ten-day training regimen where they practiced day and night landings, instrument flying, low-altitude night navigation, formation flying, and more. Harry considered the man to be a fly-by-the-book officer and rather much liked him. He never learned whether Donalson ever followed up on the Fred situation.

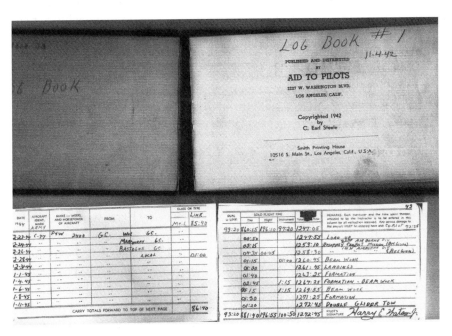

Harry's Pilot Log for the relevant period.

Chapter 14

Emergency Evacuation

Towards the end of August 1944, the Allied armies captured a large airfield at Reims, France, and renamed it A-62 Reims. Engineers immediately cleared the field of damaged Luftwaffe aircraft and made ready to receive Allied air units.

Despite the fact it had routinely been the target of Allied bombing efforts, the landing strips, tarmac, and support facilities were not in poor condition. The engineers, therefore, wasted no time laying down a 5,000-foot long, pierced steel planking, all-weather runway. No sooner was the task complete then they quickly laid out a second 5,000-foot dirt runway, immediately increasing the airfield's traffic capacity to better suit the Army Air Force's immediate needs.

It wasn't long before A-62 Reims proved to be too small to accommodate all the ever-expanding air transport needs. In response, it was decided to add a second airfield near Reims. Army engineers, despite the fact it was the middle of one of the more severe winters on record, set to the task of constructing an Advanced Landing Ground named "A-79" Pronses, France. The new forward airbase greatly facilitated supplying the front lines of the Allied armies and was destined to become Harry's new home base.

In late January 1945, Harry's Squadron was transferred to the just completed airbase at A-79 Pronses, France. The immediate result was to place them hours of flying time closer to the front lines, saving wear and tear on the aircraft and lessening the fatigue issues rampant among the pilots and aircrews. With the Allied armies advancing across Western Europe on three broad fronts, Harry's unit was immediately tasked with ferrying supplies and transferring essential personnel. It didn't take long for him to appreciate the shorter flying distances.

Harry felt all hell was breaking loose as the daily missions were scattering the squadron across the entire Allied front, from north to south. Planes were continuously being sent out in groups of one, two, or three on

Harry at A-79 Pronses, France. Note the pierced steel planked runway and the light snow cover.

urgent resupply runs. Harry thought his squadron was more closely akin to an aerial fire brigade, rushing supplies and men on short notice whenever, and wherever the need, or fire, arose. Even the Italian front was calling for urgent resupply.

It was on an afternoon when the squadron was down to only five planes fit for immediate service when a call came into A-79 seeking an emergency evacuation of an army mobile field hospital. Harry, along with four other pilots, and their planes, were the only available pilots. The problem was they were not at A-79; they were at A-62, Paris-Reims having been sent there on a late afternoon freight haul the day prior, necessitating they remain overnight. There were no available planes at A-79, so Colonel Powell transferred the evacuation orders to Harry's group at airbase A-62 Reims, France.

Harry was meeting with the other four pilots in his squadron to review the day's planned mission delivering various types of parts and fuel. They were occupying a table in the base mess hall when they were urgently summoned to the Mission Briefing hut.

Harry was first to arrive and was about to open the door when a good friend of his and fellow pilot, Jack Sale, beat him to it and held the door open for him, a broad smile on his face. Sale enjoyed kidding him about Harry's senior pilot status and never missed an opportunity to make the point, even one as simple as holding a door open. Harry and Jack took seats in the front row and waited while the remaining three pilots, along with all the co-pilots, settled themselves in.

A large map was set-up on an easel, and the men had barely finished settling in when a captain came rushing onto the stage. He assumed a position alongside the map and asked everyone to gather in close. Clearly flustered, he explained a mobile field hospital nearly 200 miles distant was in grave danger of being overrun.

The hospital had been caught in the cross-hairs of a localized, but effective, German counter-attack mounted by a mechanized SS unit. The captain explained he had no idea of the size or exact composition of the German counter-attack, but he knew it was SS, and there was no time to waste. There was no reason for him to explain that the SS was known for killing prisoners, especially wounded and medical staff; it was common knowledge among the aircrews, yet he did so regardless.

He reminded the men it was an SS unit that was responsible for the massacre of 84 GIs at Malmedy last December, and he hated to think about what might happen should they successfully capture the mobile hospital.

He could offer only minimal information as to the conditions they might encounter once on the ground. He explained the adjacent meadow had been mowed, and it was intended to accept C-47s. However, he didn't have specific information about the landing field, nor did he possess any reconnaissance photos. He didn't even have any knowledge as to whether planes had ever landed there. In short, they'd find out what they were up against when they got there.

He explained that they better "get 'em all the hell out of there" as fast as feasible and fly them directly to Greenham Common. He also mentioned that once in England, they could take a breather and remain an extra day for some R&R. Harry assumed the extra time in England was the captain's way of rewarding them for what he presumed would be a successful, but possibly perilous mission.

The weather wasn't expected to be great, but the captain did anticipate visibility should be relatively acceptable all day. He said there was no time for the Pioneers to set up direction beacons, so there'd be no instrument guidance and strongly suggested they pay close attention to the various landmarks he had already circled on the map. He then appointed Harry, the senior pilot in the group, to lead the five plane squadron. Harry was easily the youngest of the pilots involved in the rescue effort, but it was flying experience that counted, not age.

The men took some time studying the map while quietly talking among themselves. Harry was busy memorizing notable ground features between Reims and the mobile hospital while waiting for additional copies of the chart to be delivered, delaying the trip by about twenty precious minutes. He hoped the delay wouldn't cause them any problems and, once he was comfortable with the topography, took his personal copy, marked a proposed course on it with a pencil, and reported to the captain he was good to go.

The captain did have one piece of good news; a pair of P-38s had been diverted to A-62 Reims to serve as escorts on the flight to the mobile hospital. He told Harry as soon as they were formed-up, the fighter escort would take places above and behind them. The problem was, he couldn't confirm whether there would be any escorts for the return trip and advised Harry that in all events he should stay low, both going and coming back.

Harry picked Sale to fly as his wingman, then assigned the remaining pilots to their respective positions in what would be a five plane, V-shaped formation. The captain indicated he had nothing further to add and bid them good luck. Harry proceeded to lead the men out to the Jeeps, which whisked them to the waiting planes.

Pilots and co-pilots were in short supply at the time. Harry doesn't recall the name of his "co-pilot du jour", but he does remember the man was a glider pilot. With nothing much to do except wait for the next glider mission, he'd been pressed into emergency service to fly with Harry.

When he was initially assigned to Harry a few days prior, it was intended he'd only be flying a freight haul to Paris, not embarking on an emergency evacuation that required landing in a cow pasture. Harry liked the man, and since he hadn't heard any complaints about him and he'd performed well on the flight to Paris, he felt reasonably confident the glider pilot would work out.

Within half an hour, the five planes were in the air, escorts in place, and the group was bound for the mobile field hospital at about 200mph. There were scattered low-lying clouds, but not thick enough or low enough to prevent Harry from identifying the various landmarks. He kept the formation tight and flying at about 400 feet. He thinks they'd been flying for just over one hour when the mobile hospital came into view, dead ahead, just as he planned.

Before take-off, he advised the group that upon arriving at their destination, they'd perform one fly-over, then he would lead them into the cow pasture, which proved to be a little less than 50 yards off to the side of the hospital tents. As he flew over the hospital tents, he noticed each tent was identified by a large red cross on the canvas top. Red Cross markings or not, Harry was aware the SS didn't have a reputation for acknowledging the non-combatant nature of field hospitals.

The condition of the landing field proved worse than anticipated. Shortly after touching down, he struck a particularly deep hole disguised by tall grass, which caused the plane to jolt so hard he thought he might have cracked his landing gear. Once his squadron was safely on the ground, he directed them to follow him in a single file.

There wouldn't be a Follow Me Jeep, forcing him to slowly taxi in the direction of the tents. It was his intention to pull up as close to them as possible to facilitate loading. The upward angle of the cockpit didn't make it easy for him to see where he was going, but the tents were just tall enough to afford him a pretty good idea of where they should park. Harry had been careful to maneuver the squadron, so the hatches faced the tents. His intuition was signaling him time might soon prove to be of the essence.

When Harry rolled to a bumpy and somewhat abrupt stop, he ordered his co-pilot to cut the engines, check out the landing gear, and join him at what he assumed was the mobile hospital's Command tent. He gathered Chief and Sparky together and ordered them to follow him. The three men rushed to the Command tent, and as Harry was about to enter, he literally ran into a major who was on his way to meet them. The major, a medical doctor, introduced himself as the senior officer and said he had everyone ready to commence the evacuation.

Harry took a moment to glance around the camp and didn't see any stretchers being carried towards the planes. The major noticed the concerned look on Harry's face. Anticipating Harry's thoughts, he assured him he still had enough staff on hand to properly execute the evacuation. He also explained they were suffering from a manpower shortage because earlier in the day, he had sent the least seriously wounded and non-essential personnel to the rear in a combination of Jeeps and trucks.

Harry suggested the major might consider taking the most seriously wounded to his plane as he would likely be the first to take-off and, presumably, the first to land. Harry explained he intended the planes would take-off in the same order they were parked so the major could determine the urgency of each patient's situation and deliver them to the appropriate aircraft. Harry said the respective planes' crews would handle the final loading; all he had to do was get the wounded men to them. The major agreed and quickly strode towards the nearest hospital tent.

Harry paused long enough to survey the situation and decided it was, at best, organized chaos. In anticipation of his arrival, the medical staff had commenced piling empty stretchers in stacks outside of each hospital tent. In a few minutes, several men on crutches began slowly making their way to the planes under the direction of two nurses who appeared to be in charge of determining the order in which the patients were to be loaded.

Despite the advance notice of their arrival, about five minutes passed before the first litters on the most grievously wounded casualties arrived at his plane. Soon, nurses and doctors were directing stretcher-bearers and pinning sheets of typing paper on each casualty's chest with a number on it, indicating the aircraft each patient was to be taken.

Realizing the process was going to take more time than he'd hoped, he made a quick assessment of how much longer evacuation might continue, then checked his watch. Though he didn't know precisely how many casualties and staff were going to be evacuated, he feared the process could easily take two hours, maybe more. Alarmed at the slow progress, he fought back a desire to prod the stretcher-bearers himself. He considered how he might feel if he was critically injured and being jostled around on a stretcher and decided not to rush the process, at least, not yet.

There was no distant gunfire to be heard, so he decided they may have more time than he thought. Nevertheless, he immediately pitched in to help. Afterward, he would consider that maybe he should have forced the staff to conduct themselves with more urgency, but at the time, there was no apparent urgency. The absence of gunfire was something he took to mean the incursion was not very close to them.

They had been on the ground a good twenty minutes when a Jeep came flying up the road, diverted to the Command tent where it skidded to a halt. Harry was helping carry a litter, but when he saw the Jeep barreling in, he traded positions with an enlisted man and dashed to the Command tent, arriving at the same moment as the major.

An infantry captain jumped out of the passenger seat and raced directly to them. Without waiting to hear what the captain had to say, the major suggested they should move the conversation into his tent. The major, for whatever degree of privacy it might have provided, closed the flaps behind them.

Once inside, the captain explained the entire sector had been quiet for a few days when, just before dawn, they found themselves under an artillery bombardment. Next thing he knew, about half a dozen Panzers were behind them; they'd been encircled. They fought their way out but were under orders to pull back and form a defensive line on the other side of a small river a few miles beyond the mobile hospital. He told the major he'd better move fast because there were SS not all that far behind him, and nobody wanted to be here when they arrived. The captain didn't even stick around to help and took off like a "bat out of hell".

Harry decided it was time to return to his plane and check with Chief about how things were proceeding. As he approached the hatch Chief stuck his head out to greet him, but before he could say a word, their attention was diverted by a loud noise much like that of a locomotive at high speed. The roar was coming from behind Harry, who was looking directly at the Chief when his eyes suddenly drew wide-open. Harry swiveled around, half-expecting to see German tanks coming up the road, but the road was empty. It was at that moment he realized the commotion was coming from above.

He found himself facing a German Messerschmitt 262 jet fighter about to fly directly over his plane! The Messerschmitt swept past them, climbed to gain altitude, then dipped its left wing and began to circle back towards them. The noise from the twin-jet engines was deafening, increasing the fear factor the two men were experiencing.

156

Harry remembers being struck by how graceful the swept-back winged aircraft looked as it circled the camp, and for the briefest of moments, he was enthralled. He could easily discern the Nazi logo emblazoned on the jet's tail section, sending a chill up and down his spine. He was momentarily mesmerized when he realized the German pilot was lining-up to strafe the row of five sitting duck C-47s. Mesmerization immediately changed to alarm.

A good example of what Harry witnessed when he looked up at the "262".

He knew there was nothing he could do about the men already loaded onto the planes. He took off running towards the encampment, screaming as loud as he could: "Hit the dirt!" He remembers hearing someone else was yelling: "Take cover!" Harry realized, in a millisecond, it was a better description and began yelling, "take cover" himself.

Maybe thirty seconds elapsed since they first heard the roar of jet engines. Harry, along with virtually everyone else not aboard the planes, had thrown themselves to the ground. Despite the danger, Harry had to see for himself what was transpiring. He swiveled onto his back so he could determine what the Messerschmitt was doing. To his horror, the plane was on a perfect flight path to strafe the five transport planes neatly lined up tail-to-nose with its four, nose-cone mounted MK 108 cannons. He remembers unconsciously pushing himself up on one knee to get a better view as the Messerschmitt bore down on them.

As he watched the jet fighter, he suddenly recalled examining the four cannons mounted in the nose of the disabled Messerschmitt 262 parked in a hangar the summer before and thinking about how devastating they could be. And there he was, staring at a fully operational 262 bearing down on his squadron, about to unleash all four deadly cannons against his defenseless planes and the helpless occupants within.

When the Messerschmitt reached the far edge of the meadow, someone began firing at it with a Tommy gun. Undaunted, the jet bore down on them, flying directly over Harry's plane at no more than 50 feet, the ground shaking from the roar of its twin jet engines. However, the pilot didn't open fire. Harry immediately assumed the pilot was sizing-up the potential resistance he might encounter and believed he would return because he knew he wasn't in danger of being shot down by ground fire. He could take his time and devastate everything in sight.

Harry found himself feeling helpless, awed, and angry, all at the same time as he watched the Messerschmitt clear the meadow, gain altitude, and bank to the left. It was evident he was positioning himself for a second approach and was soon bearing down on the row of C-47s, possibly the easiest targets he'd ever been presented with. Harry returned to a prone position.

Ever since staring down the barrel of the German tank back in France the prior summer, and surviving a near-miss during Market Garden, he'd been considering the possibility he was going to survive the war. However, with the Messerschmitt about to unleash its fury on them, its engines screaming like banshees from hell, Harry realized he was probably going to die along with a lot of other people. He considered the likelihood of being killed while hugging dirt and grass in a cow pasture. He never imagined his life ending under such circumstances.

He propped himself by his left elbow and stared at the jet, knowing cannon shells would soon be flying towards him. Except the Messerschmitt pilot didn't fire, he continued flying, right past the parked planes, towards the horizon and then quickly disappeared into the distance. The only explanation Harry could fathom was the Luftwaffe pilot had no stomach for shooting-up hospitals.

Everyone was back to work in an instant. Harry rushed to rejoin in the evacuation process, which was moving slowly, though not as slow as it had been before the appearance of the Messerschmitt. Transporting men with grievous wounds was tricky under any conditions, let alone when trying to hurry across the uneven ground of the cow pasture.

Harry grabbed the front of a stretcher while a medic grabbed the other end, and a second medic held a bottle of what he assumed was blood over the casualty. They worked their way to his plane as quickly as they could, being careful to dodge the various rocks and small depressions they encountered. Harry found himself keeping one eye on the ground in front of him and another eye scanning the sky.

His co-pilot didn't find any damage to the under-carriage and was waiting in the cockpit. Harry called to him that he needed to start warming up the engines.

Before they embarked on the mission Harry had instructed all the pilots to begin warming-up their engines when the last of the wounded were being loaded. One thing he didn't want to experience was to be sitting on the ground waiting for the engines to warm up because they had waited until all the wounded were snugly aboard.

Not more than five minutes passed, and the C-47s were still being loaded. Harry was ascertaining the over-all progress as the major ran from tent-to-tent, helping to facilitate the final evacuations. Suddenly he heard a single-engine airplane overhead. Harry glanced skyward and immediately recognized a German Fieseler Storch "Stork" reconnaissance plane circling the hospital base. He had a bad feeling about the Stork's arrival and shouted instructions to anyone who could hear him to speed up the process while he pointed towards the Stork. The major called out to him in response: "We're almost done!"

Harry again looked for the Stork and realized while it had gained some altitude, the pilot was still observing the evacuation while lazily circling the camp. He called out to the major, pointed skyward towards the Stork, and said: "That can't be good!" The major looked up, saw what he was pointing to, and shouted orders urging everyone to step up the pace.

The Fieseler Fi 156 STORCH (Stork) performed multiple roles for the German Army. It gained a measure of notoriety as having been the aircraft utilized to grab the Italian Dictator Benito Mussolini from where he was held prisoner on a boulder-strewn mountaintop near Gran Sasso, Italy in 1943. The Stork could land on a 100-foot runway and, fully loaded, only required 250 feet to take-off as it proved at Gran Sasso.

159

It was less than a minute later when the unsettling scream of incoming mortar rounds pierced the air and sent everyone scattering for cover. Harry noticed the Stork had increased its altitude to avoid being struck by the mortar shells. There were still about a dozen evacuees remaining, but they had to wait because running through an open field during a mortar bombardment wasn't a good idea.

The first five or six mortar shells landed well-off to their left. Then a second round began pouring in well-off to their right. Harry glanced up and noticed the Stork was still maintaining its observation of the base and was probably directing the mortar bombardment, accounting for the corrections the mortar crews were making.

Mortar shells were soon dropping everywhere among them. For the first time in his life, Harry found himself fighting off panic. He knew he had to get ahold of himself. He looked around and noticed a large bomb crater with a bunch of legs sticking out of it, so he jumped in and landed on top of a doctor and a pair of nurses, all of whom were scared crazy. Harry, doing his best to appear calm, assured them the attack wouldn't last long. In reality, he had no idea whether the bombardment could last two minutes or an hour. He had never come close to experiencing being shelled but felt he needed to do his best to prevent them from fleeing and getting caught out in the open. After all, he reasoned, they're basically civilians, and he was the professional and needed to act the part. As it turned out after only about fifteen or sixteen rounds, the mortar fired abruptly ceased.

Harry knew enough about mortars to recognize if they were within mortar range, the SS couldn't be very far away. As he crawled out of the crater, he was relieved to find all five planes were intact. The same couldn't be said for some of the hospital tents as the remnants of several of them were blazing away. Whether there were any occupants in the flaming tents was something he'd never know. Harry barked out orders for everyone to get up and get moving. The evacuation continued at a frantic pace as the major rushed from tent to tent in a desperate attempt to make sure nobody was being overlooked.

After a few minutes, the major approached Harry as he stood outside "Wee Junie's" open hatch. Despite the cold weather, his face was covered in sweat, and he appeared to be a bit shaken up, though still in remarkably good control of himself. He advised Harry they were about as ready as they could be and gave Harry the approval to "please get us the hell out of here".

He followed Harry onto his C-47, but as soon as Harry stepped into the cabin, he was met with obstacles. In addition to the roughly eighteen litters of wounded, every nook and cranny was packed with medical supplies and personnel. It was necessary to wind his way around nurses and doctors before finally reaching the flight deck. He decided to forego donning his parachute because he didn't want to take the time. With the plane crammed as full as it was, he rationalized he wouldn't be getting out in an emergency anyway.

The engines had been warming for several minutes by the time he strapped himself into his seat. He checked all the gauges, and when his co-pilot advised him they were ready to "get the hell someplace else," he released the brakes and began to slowly taxi into position.

The remaining four planes joined in behind him as the procession taxied towards the end of the airfield. Unfortunately, the field was a patchwork of mowed and partially leveled grazing land, replete with small rocks and shallow holes, making the process of maneuvering into take-off position more time consuming than Harry desired. He also had to take into consideration the condition of his passengers, coupled with the fact he couldn't afford to lose any planes due to damaged landing gear. Harry basically "felt" his way to the end of the strip at an agonizingly slow pace.

He radioed his pilots they'd take-off in a staggered formation, right-to-left. Then he directed Sale to set up towards the right-hand side of the field while Harry taxied into a position on the opposite side. He intended to get the planes off the ground as quickly as he could, and taking off two at a time was, in his opinion, the best way to accomplish his goal. He decided he'd wait for Sale to get a little bit down the runway and then start forward himself. Each plane was to repeat the procedure, and once in the air, they would form-up with Harry.

As Harry initiated his take-off run, he had Sale clearly in sight, just ahead and to the right of him when another mortar bombardment commenced. For a moment, Harry thought the mortars were landing among the tents, but just as Harry was about to "pour on the coal", and precisely when the rear wheel of Sale's plane was lifting from the ground, Sale's C-47 exploded in a ball of flame and black smoke.

A mortar had struck Sale's plane directly amidships, instantaneously turning it into a blazing inferno. Harry watched in horror as a fireball rose about 100 feet into the air, and the aircraft careened off to the right side of the makeshift runway. Its left propeller came barreling across the pasture, just missing Harry's plane. Sale's stricken C-47 came to an abrupt halt when the landing gear collapsed. He didn't observe anyone escape the blaze and didn't believe anyone could have made it out.

Following a successful take-off, he commenced a gentle turn to the south, affording him a view of the planes taking off behind him. All of them made it and followed him as he circled around and flew over the base at about 200 feet. He had an excellent view of Sale's burning plane and confirmed there was nobody anywhere around it, nor did he observe any bodies. What he did notice was that the black plumes of smoke were rising skyward and probably serving as a direction beacon for the approaching Germans. The Luftwaffe spotter plane was nowhere to be seen.

Satisfied he wasn't leaving anyone behind, he took a couple of deep breaths before straightening his course and heading directly for England. He was relieved he didn't need to make a decision to return. If they had observed any survivors, he was fully aware that deciding whether he should turn back would have been extremely difficult. All four planes were jammed-full with wounded, and the German Stork was likely still observing from a distance.

There were no fighter escorts for the return flight, and after experiencing a Messerschmitt 262 way too up close, Harry, Chief, and his co-pilot were constantly scanning the skies for signs of enemy aircraft. He took advantage of the low-lying clouds and kept the formation down on the deck until they were over the English Channel when he led the formation up to 3,000 feet so he could get his bearings.

In a matter of a few minutes, Harry was advising the control tower at Greenham Common they were 40 miles out and confirmed Greenham was aware his four planes were loaded with scores of casualties. From the sound of the voice of the air traffic controller, Harry thought they may have heard he'd come under attack as the controller sounded both surprised to hear from him and, at the same time, relieved. Harry's suspicions were confirmed when another voice came over the radio advising him they were told to anticipate five planes, not four. Harry didn't elaborate and simply repeated there were only four planes in his squadron.

A veritable fleet of vehicles was awaiting them. All four planes were able to accomplish soft landings, were met by Follow Me Jeeps, and promptly guided to what was row upon row of ambulances and troop transports equipped to accommodate stretchers. Harry remained in the cockpit while the litters of casualties were carefully carried from the cabin.

Once all the planes had been unloaded, Harry was quite happy to learn nobody aboard was the worse for wear and none of the wounded had died during the flight. He was the recipient of many "thank-yous", "God bless yous" and notes passed to him from some of the survivors.

He was not looking forward to the debriefing, which meant reliving the destruction of his friend's fully loaded aircraft from mortar fire. To this day, he says he was never so shocked and devasted as when he witnessed Sale's plane explode into flames not more than 200 feet from him.

He still remembers the feeling of helplessness that was amplified as he watched a propeller flying across his path. Harry was feeling shaken to his bones, sick to his stomach and, at the same time, fearful of also being blown apart himself. He made a conscious effort to execute the smoothest landing at Greenham Common he'd ever performed for the benefit of the many casualties on board. It was something Sale wouldn't get the opportunity to do. As with his late friend, Carl Cary, he was glad he wasn't able to see Sale's face at the moment his plane exploded.

That evening he decided to take his mind off the events of the day; he had long ago discovered the best way of doing so was to sit down and write a letter to Junie. His letters seldom included details that might alarm her and instead focused on responding to her most recent letter to him and his continuing love for her and baby Daniel. She didn't learn details of his various scrapes with death until well after the war. In letters from Junie, Harry observed just how incredibly small Junie could print as she made use of every space in her efforts to relate to Harry all the events transpiring back home.

They spent the next day in England where Harry and the aircrews from the four remaining planes decided to travel to London for the day. The time off was something they all appreciated, but the still fresh memory of Sale's

A C-47, perhaps caught on the ground at the wrong time.

aircraft exploding right before his eyes was still haunting Harry. He spent fruitless hours considering what he could have done that would have put Sale's plane in a different location. He thought maybe he should have delayed the take-off a few more moments, or maybe realigned the planes' take-off positions. No satisfactory answer presented itself to him, and he had nobody close enough to him to share his reflections.

A day later, when he finally returned to his quarters at A-79, he discovered all of Sale's belongings were gone. Even the photo of Sale and Harry, smiles on their faces while standing outside of Sale's plane, was nowhere to be seen. Harry had been hoping to keep the photo as it was the only picture he had of them.

Chapter 15

A Second Market Garden

For five consecutive days commencing March 10 1945, and concluding March 14 1945, Harry found himself conducting practice paratroop drops over target zones near Chalon, France. Nobody really knew what was up, the scuttlebutt speculated a new push into northern Germany was in the works. Some of the more connected sergeants speculated a second Market Garden operation, intended to sweep the Allies across the Rhine and into the northern plains of Germany, was in the offing.

A captain, whose name Harry no longer remembers, believed they were simply practicing for an assault on Berlin because we'd already captured a large bridge over the Rhine at Remagen. Berlin, in his opinion, presented the only logical target. Harry thought he'd like to experience what Berlin looked like and hoped the captain was correct.

Throughout the five days of practice drops, American fighter plane escorts were abundant. Harry didn't observe any German fighters, though he did talk to a pair of C-47 pilots who'd experienced coming under attack. The weather had been cooperative throughout the practice regimen, and Harry was sure his drops had been precisely on target.

The practice drops came to a halt as suddenly as they had begun. From March 15 through March 19 1945, they didn't fly a single mission. It was the most prolonged non-weather delay Harry experienced. Nobody was complaining over the unexpected break as scuttlebutt ran more wild than usual. The conclusion most men reached was an offensive being referred to as a Second Market Garden was going forward, and they were experiencing delays while final preparations were being made. Others speculated a secret deal to end the war had been concluded. In any event, the time off for non-weather related reasons was unprecedented, though much appreciated.

The situation changed abruptly on the afternoon of March 23 1945. The entire squadron was alerted there would be a priority mission briefing early the next day. Scuttlebutt confirmed the final big push to end the war that the men had been expecting was about to commence.

Early the next morning, the mission briefing room was packed. Precisely on time, Colonel Powell quickly strode in from a side door and assumed a position at center stage. Behind him was a large map propped up on a makeshift easel.

Powell wasted no time and immediately announced they were about to be a part of an offensive operation even more significant than Market Garden. He explained it was going to be the most incredible single airborne operation in history, and it was all happening on that day, and, unlike Market Garden, only on that day.

He stated they were among thousands of pilots who'd be participating and pointed to the map upon which various drop zones had been circled in red ink. All of the drop zones were beyond the front lines and inside of Germany proper.

Harry recalled the Market Garden briefings, the loss of Cary, and experienced a brief episode of déjà vu-like chills. Unconsciously he briefly removed his cap, ran his fingers through his half-grey hair, and returned it to his head before realizing he'd even done so.

Powell explained the plan called for them to drop their paratroopers near a German town by the name of Wesel. Wesel, and the vicinity surrounding it, was circled in red on the map.

Harry immediately realized Wesel was east of the Rhine River. He considered the possibility the paratroopers were going to try to gain control of any bridges over the Rhine and other rivers in the area. He assumed the paratroopers would be expected to hold until relieved, just as it had been planned the prior September in Holland. Harry hoped if he was right about what was planned, that it wouldn't be so evident to the Germans as he thought it was to him.

Powell described the overall offensive that Field Marshal Bernard Montgomery had coined, "Operation Plunder". When he said Operation Plunder, it became necessary for him to pause as more than a few chuckles swept across the audience, along with a handful of derogatory remarks directed at Montgomery. Powell, always a man to put business first, only paused a few seconds.

Eventually, he turned the briefing over to a G2 intelligence officer who presented a very optimistic intelligence report. He pointed out they were going to make a daylight assault to assure accuracy and explained they were definitely not anticipating strong German resistance, either in the air or on the ground, as "we" overwhelmingly outnumbered the Germans. To Harry, the whole presentation sounded very similar to the initial Market Garden briefing. He took the G2 advice regarding the degree of German resistance with a large grain of salt. The memory of Cary's smoke-filled cockpit came back to the forefront of his thoughts and all he wanted to do was get to his plane. But he had to wait.

Another officer came onto the stage and presented the weather report. He stated conditions should be "rather optimal" for the entire four-hour circuit. Powell took over again and asked if there were any questions. Harry doesn't recall if there were any but does remember Powell told them he'd be leading the formation himself and wished them all good luck.

Harry arrived at his plane just as the eastern sky was beginning to turn light. He had completed his pre-flight inspection when Chief and Sparky arrived, followed shortly after by his most recent co-pilot, Dave. Dave was a chatterbox and was hoping to get himself to Paris because he'd traded for a stack of French Francs and heard he could make a "small killing" selling them on the Paris Black Market.

Harry knew what he was talking about but played stupid in an attempt to just get the guy to clam up. He was still thinking about Market Garden and Carl Cary and strongly desired to lose himself in the roar of the engines and the wind slapping against the windscreen in front of him.

The squadron would be flying in a series of nine plane formations, each comprised of three V-shaped groups. Harry was to pilot the lead aircraft in the second group, behind Powell's first formation. If the weather report proved correct, all he had to do was follow Powell's group ahead of him.

Out of habit he always kept track of where he was by continuously checking for landmarks. Identifying a landmark gave him the assurance he was on the correct course and made it possible for him to point at a spot on a map and take heart in the fact that area represented where he was at the time.

They took off shortly after dawn and proceeded to Brussels, where they rendezvoused with another squadron and jointly set their course for drop zones a little northwest of Wesel. As Harry approached the area of the drop zone, he witnessed several large formations of C-47s, including groups of the larger and relatively newer C-46 aircraft, on the far horizon.

He'd never seen so many planes in the air at the same time. It looked to him as if they were all converging on the same map coordinates. As they drew closer to their destination, it slowly became apparent the other squadrons were actually following different courses. Later he'd discover there were so many planes converging on the area surrounding Wesel it would take well over five hours for the last of the aircraft to reach the drop zones.

Each formation progressed as planned. What wasn't planned was a fairly widespread ground haze that somewhat concealed some of the drop zones. There would be several missed drops as a consequence.

Harry made his paratroop drop "on the dime" and returned to base with no incidents. After landing and going through a relatively short debriefing, he and three other pilots managed to wrangle a Jeep. They drove into a small hamlet near the airbase where they beelined for a corner tavern they'd become particularly fond of. Harry toasted to the memory of Carl Cary and Jack Sale. Following Harry's toast, each pilot took a turn toasting to one, or more, of their fallen comrades.

Early in the evening, Harry was still at the tavern eating dinner when a few frazzled-looking pilots came in and sat at the bar. They ordered drinks, gulped them down, and immediately ordered a second round. A couple of the pilots from Harry's squadron walked over to them and asked if they had any news about the day's drops. One of them, a captain, was about to take his second drink when the question was asked. He realized the men in the bar didn't know of the disaster that had transpired only hours earlier.

He sat up straight, downed his drink, and proceeded to describe a horrific scene of planes and men plummeting to the earth. His squadron, along with a few others, had encountered intense anti-aircraft fire, and that more than thirty transports had been shot down. One or two hundred planes were damaged.

The captain went on to explain that everything had been going swell when suddenly there were anti-aircraft explosions all around them. He said he'd never before experienced such heavily concentrated anti-aircraft fire, and it was as if it came out of nowhere. He also had no idea as to the total number of casualties; all he knew was a lot of men had perished. He returned to his drink, and nothing more was said as the room went quiet.

Following Operation Plunder, Harry found himself with two unexpected days off. He then spent three consecutive days making run-of-the-mill freight hauls to Reims. On March 30 1945, he found himself embarking on another paratroop drop into Germany. It wasn't a major operation, and it went off without a hitch. He didn't encounter any anti-aircraft fire or spot any German fighter planes. The flight, both going and coming, had been quiet, and everything went smoothly. He considered the possibility the Germans were close to capitulation.

Chapter 16

Midnight Flight to Nuremberg

It was shortly after 2300 hours on April 10 1945, at the hastily put together, but by then operating smoothly, United States Army Air Base Number A79 near Reims. Harry was relaxing in his tent after a tiring day of flying supplies to Patton's Third Army. He was catching up with the progress in the war as he read an April 10 1945, issue of Stars and Stripes. He was just about ready to snuff out his reading lamp and bed down for the night.

As he began to reach for the lamp, he stopped and softly growled for the quiet surrounding of his tent was being rudely interrupted by the commotion of a Jeep skidding to a halt. Almost before the grinding sound of tires sliding across loose dirt and gravel stopped, he heard the driver jump from the Jeep and quickly shuffle to the entrance of his tent. Harry assumed the man was trying to make as much noise as possible to be certain Harry was awake.

"Lieutenant Watson, are you in there?" Harry recognized the voice to be youngish-sounding and a bit squeaky.

The "Cathedral of Lights" at one of the annual Nazi Party rallies in Nuremberg, Germany.

For a moment Harry considered not responding. However, he figured if somebody needed to see him that late at night it must be important, although it still didn't change his mood as he was definitely feeling grumpy.

"Come on in!" Harry barked with just a bit of an edge to his voice.

He was facing a nervous private who appeared barely old enough to be in uniform. The teenager was anxiously transferring his weight from his left foot to his right foot and back again, causing Harry to wonder whether the kid was going to make himself sea-sick.

"Spit it out private. Why are you bothering me when I'm about to hit the sack?"

"Lieutenant Sir," the kid was staring at the ground as he meekly answered, "Captain Beard wants you down at Mission Briefing right away."

Harry realized Beard never called upon him this late in the day unless something out of the ordinary was about to come down. "Relax kid, I'm not known to bite. Let me grab my flight jacket, and we'll be on our way."

Visibly relieved, the private responded: "Thank you very much, lieutenant sir. I'll wait for you in the Jeep."

Harry quietly chuckled at the young man's formal language. He settled himself into the Jeep, and when the private inexplicably hesitated before starting the engine, he admonished him to shake a leg.

A few minutes later, Harry found himself as the only person sitting in the large Mission Briefing room. After a couple of minutes pondering what could be transpiring so late at night, Captain Beard quickly walked in accompanied by a lieutenant whom Harry knew was attached to G2, Army Intelligence.

Harry's curiosity inched up quite a bit at the site of the G2 lieutenant. His appearance was a sign this wasn't going to be an ordinary mission – assuming he was being sent on a mission. The thought crossed his mind that perhaps this meeting has to do with the "Fred" incident the prior December. The idea was quickly extinguished, for Beard wasted little time getting to the point.

Beard explained he had an extraordinary, top-secret mission for him to undertake immediately. Harry's interest surged as he'd never before been directed to conduct a top-secret mission and didn't even know anyone who had been. Beard said Harry's plane was being readied, and his crew would be waiting for him. He pulled a map from his pocket, spread it on a nearby table, and motioned for Harry and the lieutenant to draw closer. As the three men huddled around the table he pointed to a location near Nuremberg, Germany, a city Harry knew was still controlled by the Germans.

Beard pointed to a small red circle on the map, which represented his landing field. He explained the targeted airfield was nothing more than a grassy meadow with no lighting. He said G2 reported it to be a relatively flat meadow and should easily accommodate a C-47. Harry remembers Beard frequently paused as he glanced at the G2 lieutenant from time to time. Beard motioned Harry to draw closer to the map, pointed to it, and said: "This is where you're going to land, yes, and I am aware it is behind enemy lines."

Harry examined the map, noting the landmarks in the area, and took a deep breath. Satisfied with the layout of the landing site, Harry told Beard he could land just about anywhere and didn't foresee any problems. Harry, referencing the fact the proposed unlit landing field was firmly behind enemy lines, asked if he could delay his take-off until daylight. Harry was not thrilled with Beard's response:

"Sorry lieutenant, no such luck. I need you on your way, pronto! Timing's the key."

Beard told Harry that as he approaches the meadow paratroopers will mark the center point of the landing field for him. He advised him to conduct a fly-over first, and when he was ready to make his final approach the paratroopers would do whatever might be possible to mark the boundaries of the meadow. The fact the moon was a waning crescent that night meant the landing area would be pretty dark. Harry kept to himself the thought a fly-by wouldn't be all that revealing.

Beard had been leaning over the table, reviewing the map the entire time as if he might glean some hidden information. He eventually took a seat, glanced at the G2 lieutenant for a few moments, and proceeded with the briefing. Harry couldn't help but think something was being left unspoken, for he felt the number of times Beard looked over at the G2 lieutenant was, at best, peculiar. He wondered what they knew, and he might like to know. Recollections of his earlier missions refueling tanks and rescuing a field hospital flashed across his mind, momentarily drawing his attention away from the pending mission.

Beard told him G2 was there for a good reason; Harry was about to engage in a top-secret mission. He ordered Harry to keep his crew in the dark and say nothing of the mission's purpose. He said when Harry reached his destination, he wanted him on the ground and back up again "quicker than a rabbit". He also advised Harry not to kill both of his engines when he lands and should be prepared to depart as soon as his passengers were safely aboard. Beard told him that with a little luck his cargo would already be there, waiting for him. Beard added:

"I cannot stress how important it is you get back into the air as fast as you can! You're picking up some top Nazis, and they won't be happy about it, understand?" Harry shook his head in the affirmative and focused on the map as chills ran down his spine.

Beard explained how specially trained members of the 194th Glider Infantry Regiment had landed in the vicinity of the meadow, specifically to pick up a very special Nazi before he could disappear. He said "that Nazi" was going to be the most critical element of Harry's human cargo and was someone the Allies had been tracking for quite some time. Harry was to transport his "cargo" to Greenham Common. Though he mentioned the Nazi was someone named von Papen, "the idiot who put Hitler in charge", it didn't yet mean much to him, but the idea he was going to swoop in behind enemy lines and scoop up some Nazi "scum" was exciting.

Beard instructed Harry to fly low, both coming and going, and he especially didn't want any radar-equipped night-fighters to detect his flight. Those fighters possessed armament aimed upwards at a 45-degree angle and could drop behind and below Harry, without him ever knowing it. Such an encounter would likely prove deadly. He apologized about the fact he couldn't spare any fighter escorts because all the fighter planes were off covering bombing missions, but did say a lone plane was less likely to draw attention. He then asked him if he had any questions.

Harry was well aware of the night radar-directed Messerschmitt 110s having had a close encounter with one of them in the not so distant past. He harbored absolutely no intentions of further pressing his luck and knew the lower he flew, the less attention he'd attract. After his unauthorized flight to Orly, he made a promise to himself to avoid risk-taking, unless it was absolutely necessary. However, the Orly mission left an indelible impression on his commanding officers; they could count on him when it came to sending him on a risky mission. He took another look at the map before turning to face Beard.

"Understood. I assume I can take the map with me."

"That's correct," Beard said. He went on to say he couldn't spare Harry a navigator as he didn't have enough of them to cover the next day's operations. He said it was "reason number one" why he chose Harry, who he then called "the best seat-of-the-pants pilot I have and the only one with an Instructor's rating to boot." He paused a moment and caught Harry off-guard when he added: "And it's no secret you're a self-avowed risk-taker."

He told Harry he'd demonstrated what he considered to be an almost uncanny ability to fly in pea soup and not only safely reach his objective, but get his plane back intact. Beard did make a bit of a confession when he said:

"Sorry Harry, but this is how it has to be. And under no circumstances are you to use the radio until you're over the Channel on your flight to Greenham Common." Harry appreciated being called by his first name, a rarity for Beard.

Beard attempted to lighten the situation by referencing the Orly episode when he told Harry he'd been led to believe Harry wasn't much for using the radio in the first place so that the radio silence restriction for the mission shouldn't pose a problem. Beard couldn't hide a smile as he stood and motioned to the G2 lieutenant who said:

"Those are your orders lieutenant, and I can tell you they come straight from the top. If you go down, you'll probably be on your own for a bit because you'll be on the wrong side of the front line. I've sent along survival kits, rations, and side-arms for all four of you. And remember, the army doesn't like news about missions-gone-wrong, so don't take unwarranted chances." He paused as if he had another thought, then stood straight, looked Harry in the eyes, and said: "Good luck lieutenant!" Harry considered everything he'd seen and heard for just a few moments and replied.

"If there's nothing else captain, I'd like to get going."

Beard told him he'd covered everything he needed to know and added: "Just get in and out as fast as you can, and I'll see you in a few hours." Beard began to leave when he suddenly stopped. "Hold on a minute Harry. You know if you don't want to take this mission, you could elect to decline."

Harry saluted and responded: "I appreciate the offer, but time's wasting."

"Good luck Harry!" Beard said.

Realizing he couldn't remember Beard ever calling him by his first name once, let alone several times, Harry smiled and replied: "No problem Sir, I'll be seeing you soon." He quickly left the building and joined the young private who'd been waiting for him in the Jeep.

Harry asked the private to drive him to his tent, where he grabbed whatever he thought he might need, including a Thompson machine gun and a sack of "banana clips". When Harry emerged, he leaped into the front passenger seat, and they immediately sped off to his waiting aircraft. He and Dave, his co-pilot, had by then flown several missions together, and Dave had proven to be very capable.

Dave, along with Chief and Sparky, had been milling around outside the hatch while they waited for Harry's arrival. As Harry approached, Dave was the first to speak up.

He queried Harry about what the hell they were doing flying off in the middle of the night. He complained, somewhat bitterly, why was it that nobody appeared to give a hoot that they'd been flying all over the continent and just maybe might need a little shut-eye.

Harry was short of sleep himself and in no mood to listen to senseless griping. In response to Dave's comments, he said: "Damn it, nobody told me the war was over, so unless you know otherwise, I'd very much appreciate it if you'd quit yacking and crank up the engines."

Harry cast an angry look towards the men and scolded them to get moving. He made it clear they should have been off the ground already and was in no mood for dilly-dallying around. Not accustomed to seeing Harry in an angry mood, Chief and Sparky immediately went about the procedure of prepping for take-off. Harry does recall they were muttering under their breath as they climbed aboard, but he chose to ignore them.

As soon as Harry completed the pre-flight checklist, he climbed aboard, and Chief swung the hatch closed behind him with a loud clang. Before taking his seat, he secured his Thompson nearby, adjusted the flak jacket on the floor to better cover his feet, and strapped himself in.

Dave asked where they were going, again mentioning it was the middle of the night. Harry told him they were heading to a meadow somewhere near Nuremberg. He pulled the map from his jacket pocket, handed it to him, and explained their objective was circled in red. Harry remembers Dave blinked a couple of times as he stared at the map. His eyes opened wide when he realized the destination was behind enemy lines. Harry braced for a complaint, but Dave remained silent.

Harry allowed himself a moment to absorb the reassuring roar of the twin engines and checked the gauges. Satisfied all was in order, he waived out the side window to the Follow Me Jeep, indicating it was time to lead him to the end of the unlighted runway.

Once Harry had maneuvered "Wee Junie" into the center of the airstrip, he "poured on the coal" and lifted off without a hitch. He quickly climbed to about 500 feet and set an initial course slightly south of due east. There were scattered clouds overhead and no fog, making navigation much less complicated. The downside was they'd be more easily spotted by any nearby German night fighters.

Dave soon noticed their course heading and mentioned he thought Nuremberg was a bit north and east, not south and east. Harry remembers he sounded confused as he had memorized the map himself and had a pretty good idea of what their flight path should look like.

Harry told him he was correct, but he had absolutely no intention of signaling their ultimate destination to the Krauts. Harry said they were going to drift south until they reached the front lines, then they were going to abruptly change course to zero degrees and bee-line for the meadow at full throttle while continually changing their altitude. "I'm taking no chances."

After considering Harry's explanation, Dave pulled some pieces of metal from his flight jacket and shook them around in his right hand.

"What's that?" Harry asked.

Smiling, Dave replied: "Some of the shrapnel the mechanics yanked out of our nose after the last paratroop drop. If we'd been flying just 24 inches lower, these babies," he continued to shake the bits of metal, "would've been in our skulls."

Harry laughed and told him they weren't going to be flying in a formation so he could change course and altitude as much as he wanted, whenever he wanted. He also mentioned the last thing they needed was for some lonely Kraut 'AA' gunner to lock in on them, so "Don't sweat it."

He tried to think of something witty to say to help keep things loose because he could sense Dave was very nervous. He believed a nervous co-pilot was a man who could be subject to making silly mistakes.

"You know something Dave, my dad called me a bonehead once in a while, but never a metal-head, and I have no intention of giving him cause to come up with a new moniker for me." Dave smiled but didn't laugh. Instead, he kept watching in all directions for any unwelcome air traffic.

After less than an hour Harry calculated they were just about over the front lines and turned due north. Until then they had been at cruising speed, but once committed to his new course he fully opened the throttles. He wanted to get to their destination as fast as feasible. They had more than enough fuel to make a pair of round trips, so there was no need to conserve gas.

About half an hour passed when Harry decided the meadow should be nearby. He throttled back the engines, lowered his airspeed to 110mph, and dropped to an altitude of only 200 feet. He and Dave were searching for a signal from the ground but had spotted none so far. They were flying over a patchwork of farmland, scattered forest, and meadows, but no marker light was to be had. Suddenly Sparky poked his head into the cockpit.

"There's a light at three o'clock; I think that could be our signal."

They immediately looked towards three o'clock and spotted a single white beam pointing skyward, as if it were a small spotlight outside a drive-in theatre beckoning to its patrons. Harry realized it must be their marker for if it was a truck or some other vehicle, its light would be shining on the ground, not straight up into the air.

He believed the light had to be the marker they were looking for, but first, he needed to conduct a fly-over. Harry executed a gentle right turn until the beam of light lay dead ahead and dropped to 150 feet. As he flew over the meadow, he burned a picture of it into his mind and proceeded to make a second right turn as he intended to waste no time and come in for a landing on his next approach.

He recalls Dave saying he wasn't comfortable with a single fly-over. He complained he couldn't see a damn thing where they were supposed to land and expressed hope those were American paratroopers down there, not Krauts.

The marker light was growing ever closer as Harry dropped the landing gear and made ready to land even though he had no side-marker lighting to delineate the outline of the runway. He kept them pointed at the middle of what he assumed would be his landing field.

"I thought you said there'd be some kind of runway lighting," Dave complained, "this could be a trap!"

"Don't worry, those guys aren't going to take any chances. Just wait, the lights will be there when we need them." Harry's voice was perfectly calm as he dropped the plane below 100 feet and cut-back the throttles.

The beam was growing closer by the second but remained surrounded by darkness. Just as he began to consider aborting the landing and circling around to try again, the left and right sides of the meadow were suddenly defined by numerous pairs of headlights. They were coming from what would prove to be a hodge-podge of cars and trucks. Smiling, Harry looked at Dave and said:

"No sweat. I told you they'd come through." Dave, not one to be easily satisfied, remained quiet.

Harry set the C-47 onto the grass with a series of hard thumps and was soon at taxi speed. As they bounced around on the extremely uneven turf, one of the vehicles lining the field blinked its lights a few times, pulled out of line, and cut towards the left side of the plane. Harry remembers saying, "that's either our Follow Me Jeep or a German trap." He immediately regretted openly venting his thoughts, for Dave quickly replied:

"Let's hope they're on our side, and this isn't a trap because that's no Jeep!"

The Follow Me vehicle appeared to be an open-top Opel, lacking any manner of military markings and too closely resembling a German staff car to suit Dave. Harry was feeling a little anxious about the Opel himself and wished he could be sure who the hell was driving it. He momentarily considered that it might, in fact, prove to be a German staff car loaded with German troops.

He ordered Dave to cut the power to the number one engine as he slowly taxied to a halt alongside the now-parked Opel. In the pale moonlight, Harry discerned there were four men in the Opel, at least two of whom were carrying rifles. Though Harry had tested for perfect night vision, in the shadowy moonlight, he couldn't determine which army they were with and chose to assume they were Americans.

"Chief, drop the stairs and see what those boys have waiting for us," Harry said.

"On my way!" Chief said as he quickly strode through the cabin and opened the hatch. He dropped the stairs and disappeared into the darkness in the direction of the Opel as a second civilian vehicle pulled up alongside it.

Harry stuck his head out of his open cockpit window and noticed several infantrymen wearing camouflage uniforms along with four Military Police walking towards them. He wasn't expecting to see any MPs; he was under the impression this was a commando operation, and he thought it highly unlikely they'd have taken any MPs along for the ride.

The MPs stood out because they were wearing bright white helmets. Suddenly Harry remembered back to the prior December when German soldiers disguised as MPs during the Battle of the Bulge had infiltrated the front lines. Harry unhooked the Thompson and gently set it across his lap. His action was not lost on Dave, who pulled out his service pistol and cupped it in his hands. Dave unstrapped himself and joined Sparky near the open hatch.

Harry found himself staring hard at the combined group of infantry and MPs as they slowly approached the plane. When they drew close enough to discern details, he realized there were three men in civilian clothing walking among the MPs. Harry concluded they must be the prisoners he'd be transporting and assumed one of the three prisoners must be his guest of honor. Realizing it wasn't a trap, he let out an audible sigh of relief. He noticed Dave return the pistol to his holster.

Chief was standing with his hands on his hips at the base of the flight stairs he'd rigged up specifically for this mission, almost as if he was about to conduct an inspection. Harry realized he had a poor vantage point from the cockpit seat and decided to stand in the doorway at the edge of the flight deck, affording him a good view of the entire cabin.

He was keenly disappointed when he observed an elderly man dressed in very fancy civilian clothes climb aboard. The man didn't meet his expectations of what a high-ranking Nazi was supposed to look like. He wasn't wearing a Nazi armband or uniform and sported no medals. He looked as if he was dressed to attend a beer hall party. The civilians accompanying him were equally non-descript and similarly attired. None of them bore Nazi armbands, lapel pins, or uniforms. Chief, the last to board, closed the hatch behind him, worked his way up to Harry and whispered:

"They say this old Nazi is someone named von Papen, Franz von Papen. That MP over on the left told me he was the key Kraut in putting Hitler in charge way back in the '30s. But I gotta say, he doesn't look like much to me." Chief pointed at the passengers: "The one to his right's his son, but I don't know who the other guy is." He added as far as he could determine, "everybody's set," so they could get moving any time Harry was ready.

Harry instructed Chief to get their passengers ready for a bumpy take-off. He jumped into his pilot's seat, returned his Thompson to its cubby, and told Dave:

"Fire 'em up and let's get the hell out of here!"

Harry followed the Opel to the center of the meadow where, once the driver had the plane lined up, he switched off his headlights and disappeared into the darkness. Pressing the brakes hard, Harry increased the throttle because he wanted to be off the ground in a hurry. One of the paratroopers had told Chief they couldn't be sure if the far end of the meadow was clear of land mines, and Harry had no intention of finding out himself as he planned to lift-off faster than he'd ever done before.

The plane shuddered as the engines roared in response to the sudden flow of fuel while the brakes fought to hold "Wee Junie" in place. The entire airframe was violently shaking while Harry waited for his makeshift runway's marker lights to illuminate his path.

Almost immediately after he began revving the engines, the vehicles lining the meadow switched on their headlamps. With a satisfied grin, Harry released the brakes and pushed the throttles into the full-open position. "Wee Junie" immediately roared down the meadow, the vehicles lining each side flicking off their lights as he passed.

Franz von Papen, second from right, disembarking after his midnight flight from Nuremberg. The man to the far left is probably his son, Captain Franz von Papen Jr. His coat matches Harry's memory. The individual with the cane is not identified. Harry said the army staged this photo, which explains the lack of a white helmet on the MP. He recalls they were not wearing dark glasses when they came on board "Wee Junie".

"Here we go!" Shouted Harry, as much for his own edification as for his passengers. He pulled back on the wheel and lifted off. Harry banked left and glanced towards the meadow to discover it had already returned to darkness. He proceeded to take the plane to 400 feet when Dave asked him if they were going to take the same round-about course home as they did on their way in.

Harry replied: "Nope! We're going straight home, lickety-split!" A few minutes later, Harry was focusing on the compass when Dave asked:

"So just who is our guest of honor?"

Harry smiled and said: "Just another Nazi, no big deal."

"Allow me to say how manly and humanly great of you I think this is. Your courageous and firm intervention have met with nothing but recognition throughout the entire world. I congratulate you for all you have given to the German nation by crushing the intended second revolution."

Franz von Papen in a letter to Adolf Hitler on July 12 1934. Source: Office of the United States Chief Counsel for Prosecution of Axis Criminality. Publication in 1946

Chapter 17

Who was Franz von Papen?

Franz Joseph Hermann Michael Maria von Papen was a German aristocrat who served as a German military attaché during the pre-World War I years in Washington, D.C. During that time, he traveled and became quite familiar with the United States ... and began to earn a reputation as being a spy.

On December 28 1915, the U.S. declared him to be a "persona non grata". In April 1916, a U.S. Federal Grand Jury indicted him over his part in a plot to destroy a key canal connecting Lakes Ontario and Erie. However, before he could be arrested for suspected acts of sabotage, the German Embassy quietly shipped him back to Germany.

In addition to the canal plot, he attempted to purchase and ship weapons to Germany. He commenced a campaign intended to sabotage and/or bomb businesses owned by citizens of the Allied nations. He attempted to buy-up all the hydraulic press machines in the United States to prevent artillery shell production destined for the Allied powers. He even concocted plans to invade Canada and start a revolution in Mexico.

Upon returning to his homeland, the German High Command promptly dispatched him to Palestine with the title "Chief of Staff". He was made an officer with the rank of major in the Fourth Turkish Army as part of his cover. It was the beginning of what would be a long-term entanglement with Turkish affairs.

While in Palestine, he continued his covert espionage work and became involved in plans to start revolutions in both Ireland and India. His goal was to disrupt the British and Allied war effort during World War I; however, his various plans proved unsuccessful, and most, though not all of them, failed to progress beyond the drawing board.

Following World War I, he plunged himself into the German political scene and was elected to the Reichstag, which was similar to a Parliament. Von Papen also wasted little time in acquiring ownership of a newspaper, the *Germania*, and used it as a forum to propound his far right-wing opinions. He was aware of how effectively the Italian Fascist Dictator Benito Mussolini had manipulated his political views via the press and sought to duplicate Mussolini's success for himself.

Despite the outside appearance of being no more than a minor player in German politics, he managed to secure himself an appointment from the aging President of Germany, Paul von Hindenburg, to the lofty position of Chancellor of Germany on May 31 1932. Von Papen then sought to solidify his post and reduce his opposition. With his rise to Chancellor, the indictment in the U.S. was dropped and never resurrected.

Realizing the Nazi party was achieving a solid following, he sought to gain the Nazis' good graces by lifting the ban on the Nazi party's Sturm Abteilung, or "SA". At the time, the SA was little more than an organized gang of street thugs employed by the Nazis to intimidate and sometimes eliminate political opponents. Von Papen believed he might also benefit from their tactics. Thus he cozied up to the Nazis, and Adolf Hitler in particular.

The lifting of the ban on the SA did gain him the attention of Adolf Hitler. However, von Papen's principal political enemy, General Kurt von Schleicher, was not yet ready to capitulate. He managed to put together a robust political coalition. He convinced von Hindenburg to force the resignation of von Papen before he could successfully exploit his growing ties to Hitler and the Nazis. General von Schleicher succeeded him as Chancellor on December 3 1932. His reign didn't last long.

Von Papen proceeded to successfully lobby the support of the majority of Germany's industrial leaders, who were all anxious to profit from the rearmament of Germany, as proposed by von Papen and opposed by von Schleicher. Von Hindenburg was convinced by von Papen to appoint him to the post of vice-chancellor and to name Adolf Hitler, the new German chancellor over von Schleicher.

He is said to have told von Hindenburg not to worry about Hitler's more extreme views

Paul von Hindenburg was the President of Germany and, in response to von Papen's request, formally appointed Hitler as Chancellor.

and assured von Hindenburg he could keep Hitler under control. As the world would shortly discover, von Papen utterly failed to control Hitler.

On June 30 1934, despite his attempts to ingratiate himself to Hitler, von Papen barely averted being murdered during what came to be called the "Night of the Long Knives". Kurt von Schleicher, the political opponent of both von Papen and Hitler, would be permanently removed from the German political scene when he was among more than 100 political and military figures who were murdered during the Night of the Long Knives. Three days later, von Papen resigned as vice-chancellor, after which Hitler appointed him to the post of ambassador to Austria, a position he held until that country was merged into Germany.

From 1939 until 1944, von Papen served as the German ambassador to Turkey. He was charged with preventing Turkey from joining the war on the side of the Allies using any means possible. Hitler realized it was unlikely he could convince Turkey to join the fighting on behalf of the Axis powers as Turkey had done in 1914, yielding disastrous results for what had previously been an empire. Von Papen was successful until very late in the war when Turkey joined the Allies in the struggle against Germany.

In September 1943, while still serving as Germany's ambassador to Turkey, he became embroiled in a multi-country plot to end the war right then and there through the ouster of Hitler. The secret plot never got further than the desk of President Franklin Roosevelt, who took no action, and World War II dragged on.** Fortunately for von Papen, Hitler never learned of his treacherous plan and, in 1944, awarded him with the Knight's Cross of the Military Merit Order for his service in Turkey.

Franz von Papen was put on trial at Nuremberg for conspiring to start World War II. While he was found not guilty of any conspiracy against peace, for which he had been indicted, the German government separately convicted him of other offenses. In May 1947, he was sentenced to eight years in prison as a major offender. He appealed the sentence and won his release in January 1949.

In 1959 Pope John XXIII returned von Papen's previously lost title of Papal Chamberlain and also anointed him a Knight of Malta. He was also awarded the Grand Cross of the Pontifical Order of Pius IX.

He eventually died of natural causes on May 2 1969, while residing in West Germany.

** Bauer, Yehuda *Jews for Sale? Nazi-Jewish Negotiations, 1933-1945*, New Haven: Yale University Press, 1996, pages 125 and 134.

Grand Cross of the Pontifical Order of Pius IX. Courtesy of Wikimedia.

Franz von Papen standing trial at Nuremberg, Germany, in September 1945.

MIDNIGHT FLIGHT TO NUREMBERG

During the night of April 10 1945, First Lieutenant Thomas McKinley, along with members of the 194th Glider Infantry Regiment, the 550th Airborne Glider Infantry, and a handful of Military Police penetrated behind enemy lines. Having been tipped-off that von Papen would be at his hunting estate, their intention was to capture von Papen and hold him until he could be tried for war crimes.

Lieutenant McKinley burst into von Papen's lodge to find him having dinner with his son, Captain Franz von Papen Jr and others. He invited Mc Kinley to have dinner with them and was afterward brought to the meadow where Harry was waiting.

"But Hitler didn't strive for the annihilation of the Jews – he stressed that fact in public life and in the newspapers. Hitler merely said at the beginning that Jewish influence was too great, that of all the lawyers in Berlin, eighty percent were Jewish. Hitler thought that a small percentage of the people, the Jews, should not be allowed to control the theater, cinema, radio, et cetera."

Franz von Papen, as told to Leon Goldensohn, March 30,1946.
"The Nuremberg Interviews" by Leon Goldensohn, 2004.

Chapter 18

Victory in Europe

In late April 1945 and into May, the Germans continued to resist the Allies with a resolve Harry didn't understand. In one stretch during April, Harry made supply hauls into the front lines of the Allied advance, carrying everything from gas, diesel oil, and foodstuffs to towing gliders and ferrying troops. He did not encounter even a single Luftwaffe plane.

It appeared to him that Germany was in ruins and nary a day passed when someone didn't pass along word the Germans had surrendered. Unfortunately, the daily mission briefs never mentioned anything about the war ending, and it continued to drag on. He and Lang hadn't communicated in a couple of months as both men were pretty occupied with the war and had been unable to wrangle free time when they could get together.

Then Harry received the news he'd been anticipating since his days back in Taft, California, when he and Lang were still far removed from combat. Colonel Powell summoned him to his office with no clue as to the reason. Ever since his unauthorized flight to Orly, anytime Harry received an order to report to Squadron HQ, he always felt a slight twinge of apprehension, and that occasion was no different.

He hadn't flown a mission the day prior and assumed he was being sent on another short-notice supply haul because back-to-back days off were not the norm. When Colonel Powell's aide directed him into Powell's office, Harry was surprised; as soon as he entered, Powell abruptly stood and, without saying a word walked around his desk, looked him in the eyes, and handed him a telegram. Harry instinctively knew it was a conveyance of bad news. He was correct: Golden Lang had been killed. Harry recalls the date was April 23 1945.

Fifteen days later Germany would surrender, and Harry would find himself wondering what the hell kind of justice would have caused Lang to be flying, what he assumed was a combat sortie, when the war had already basically been won. He felt it was a senseless death and recited a silent prayer for Lang, his wife, and his daughter. He sent Junie a letter advising her of Lang's passing.

On May 7 1945, Harry made a return flight to Nuremberg. Rather than a covert landing in a meadow, he was guiding his plane onto a smooth runway at the Nuremberg airport, in broad daylight, at a landing field flying the stars and stripes. He was ferrying a plane-load of Jerry cans filled with gasoline and took-off flying a plane loaded with recently liberated British prisoners of war.

There had been a temporary canteen set up inside one of the hangars, and each of the men was drinking hot tea and eating chocolate bars. Harry thought they looked as close to walking skeleton-men as he'd ever seen, though they indeed were in a happy and talkative mood. Harry remembers a British paratrooper exclaimed how pleased he was to once again find himself in a "Dakota".

The former POWs booed when Harry announced he was taking them to Brussels for medical attention. That's when he learned somebody had,

An undated photo of Golden Lang standing in front of his B-24 Liberator. The B-24 had a notoriously narrow, 18-inch wide passage through which the pilots would need to maneuver so they could reach the main cabin and bailout in an emergency. Most pilots would find it necessary to remove their parachute, a tricky task when under pressure, simply to make it into the cabin where they could proceed to jump from the plane, after managing to first get the 'chute back on. (Source: First Lieutenant George Franklin Bowles, World War II B-24 Liberator Pilot.) (Photo courtesy of Lieutenant Harry E. Watson.)

in error, earlier advised them they were being flown to England. Several of his passengers vociferously complained they'd been told they were going home.

Harry had never been booed before, except perhaps in a baseball game, but could certainly understand their position. As he stood on the edge of the flight deck facing his passengers, he didn't know what to say. He offered an apology and said he'd call ahead and confirm he was to take them to Brussels.

His statement appeared to appease his passengers but didn't result in a change in destination. The war with Germany would not be officially declared at an end until the following day. Consequently, he was still operating under radio silence rules, but he broke the rules and sought confirmation he was to deliver the British POWs to Brussels. The orders were quickly confirmed, leaving him with about two dozen unhappy passengers.

On May 10 1945, he flew his first group of former American POWs. He picked them up in Munich, where they had been held in Stalag VII-A and brought them back to A-79, Pronses. They appeared to be in the same walking-skeleton condition as the British POWs had been, except these men were elated to be going to France.

Over a period spanning four consecutive days, he found himself ferrying former prisoners of war, British, American, and French, all of whom were in dreadful condition. He couldn't fly fast enough to suit him as he wanted those men out of Germany as quickly as he could safely manage. The sight of smiling skeleton-men was burned into his memory forevermore.

Gary was Harry's newest and youngest co-pilot to-date. Gary didn't even need to shave and was barely 19 years old. His first day in Europe was the second-to-last day of the war, and Harry described him as at best immature. It wouldn't be long before he'd discover Gary was a "money-grubbing bastard."

One day they picked up a plane-load of former Russian POWs. Harry quickly realized their attitude was much more sullen than that of the former slave laborers he'd recently ferried from Germany to France. While Chief was getting the Russians settled in, Harry noticed Gary was going from one Russian to another. Each of them appeared to be handing Gary what looked to him to be money. Harry called him over and asked what the hell he was doing.

Gary told him they were voluntarily giving him money they'd been provided by their liberators because it would do them no good where they were going.

"You can't take their money!" Harry scolded.

"I'm not taking their money," Gary responded and went on to explain they knew they're either going to be quickly executed once they returned home. If not killed, they'd be immediately dispatched to a gulag where they'd be worked to death. He said they preferred he gets the money, then it go to their executioners.

"What?" Harry exclaimed.

"Yeah," said Gary in a subdued tone, "I guess it's common knowledge Stalin considers anyone who surrendered to be traitors to the Motherland. Apparently, those who aren't shot right away will be sent off to a gulag in Siberia. Either way, they're dead men." He shrugged his shoulders and continued: "I see no reason not to take the money when they're offering it to me."

Harry turned to the Russian with whom Gary had been conversing and asked him if what Gary had said was true. In broken English, he explained his "comrade" was correct. They'd all heard the stories Stalin considered anyone who had been captured by the Germans to be a coward and a deserter, even Stalin's son.

He said Stalin had made it clear any prisoners of war returned to Russia after the conflict was over would either be outright sentenced to death, or relegated to life terms at a gulag in Siberia. He told Harry they all knew what would become of them once they surrendered, and the fact Harry was flying them to an airfield in Russian-controlled Germany meant they were all about to die, or worse. He then pulled some French Francs from his pocket and shoved them into Gary's hand.

"Here, take this too. It cannot do me good where I am being taken."

Gary cheerfully accepted the cash, looked at Harry as if to say, "I told you so", and went into the cockpit.

"I understand their situation, but leave me out of it. That's blood money," replied Harry.

Harry turned to the Russian, grabbed his right hand in a firm handshake, and told him: "I wish you well, my friend, and I pray to God you're wrong."

It wasn't the only time he flew freed Russian POWs back to their former comrades, and the routine was the same each time. The passengers were keen to dispose of anything of value rather than have it fall into the hands of their former countrymen.

The flights weren't always serious. On one trip, Harry was flying a group of reporters. As they passed over a former POW camp, Harry called out to them, "You can see a POW camp off the left-wing."

When the passengers quickly rushed to the left side of the cabin to peer through the windows, Harry dipped the left-wing and shouted out: "Don't do that! Do you want to flip us over?"

The startled passengers quickly returned to their seats. A journalist with the BBC realized the joke, and after they landed, he sought out Harry to compliment him on his sense of humor. As he departed the plane, the smiling journalist turned to look at Harry and said:

"That was a good one, Yank!" Harry simply smiled back at him.

On some days, Harry might make five flights, mostly ferrying Russian and French former POWs and, almost as frequently, former slave laborers who were of a multitude of nationalities. As the calendar progressed further into June, the pace slowed considerably, and they began practicing various routines again, such a glider towing, night landings, and flying by instruments. Harry had long-since accumulated enough points to qualify for a return to the States. He totaled 145 battle points, but volunteered to keep flying until his service was no longer required. 125 battle points was the relevant threshold.

From May 22 through May 24 1945, Harry made at least six trips from his base at A-79 to B-48 at Amiens/Glisy, France transferring supplies and records. After that, B-48 was designated as his new home airfield. The moving of POWs and former slave laborers continued until late June.

Making the decision to remain in Europe was not easy. He hadn't seen June in more than a year and had never met his son, who was born in Taft, CA on October 11 1944. But the reality was the income he was earning as a first lieutenant was good, and the job prospects in California, according to June, were not particularly great. He decided to remain in the service until such time he was ordered to return to the States. He rationalized that it was the most responsible thing he could do for his wife and baby boy.

As June progressed into July, the pace slackened a great deal, and Harry found himself with more and more free time on his hands, giving him the sense he'd soon be getting orders to fly home. When he finally did receive the order to return to the States, on about July 6 1945, he decided to go on a sightseeing tour of the Normandy beachheads.

He lingered over the D-Day landing sites for about an hour before returning to Airbase B-48 for the last time. When he returned, he was assigned the "Southern Route" for his trip to the USA, rather than the route he followed when he flew over from Ohio. The change surprised him because it was a much longer flight across far greater expanses of ocean, therefore much more challenging.

He was transferred to yet another base, USAAF Airfield A-58 near Coulommiers, France, where he would prepare for the long haul to the United States, and eventually a discharge. Once at A-58, he waited several days for his flying orders, which finally came down the pipe on about July 14 1945, advising him he'd begin his nine leg, Southern Route, trip on July 16. When he asked why he wasn't returning via the much shorter Northern Route he had traversed on his flight from Indiana to England, he received a convoluted answer placing the blame on the volume of air traffic "up there".

Harry was offered a choice of eligible co-pilots, and when he discovered his long-time friend Ed Oulette was on the list, he grabbed him. Having Ed along for the ride would certainly, in his opinion, help keep the trip interesting as Ed had a clever sense of humor.

The balance of his crew had accumulated the requisite battle points to qualify for a return home. In addition to Chief and Sparky, he was given the rare privilege of having a navigator with him.

Considering the length of their journey, the presence of a full-time navigator was significant, if not outright critical. Four spare fuel tanks reduced the cabin space by a good 33 percent but left enough room to take along a few battle points qualified fighter pilots, each of whom was happy to be aboard. With the addition of everyone's gear, the cabin was full, leaving few options for comfort modifications.

The first leg of the return flight took him to the British Base at Gibraltar, where weather conditions forced him to land. The weather delayed the continuation of his trip until first light on July 18 1945. He made the hop across the Mediterranean Sea and landed in Marrakech, Morocco, where he barely had time to eat and sleep. The next morning he was off again at first light. He was already one day behind, so the earlier he could take-off, the better.

The next leg of the journey took him across the vast, barren plains of the Sahara desert. After a seven and one half hour flight, he arrived at Mallard Field, Dakar, Senegal. Again, there was just enough time to eat and relax a little before hitting the sack.

With warnings of an incoming "Haboob", he took off at first light on July 20 1945. His destination was Roberts Airfield in Monrovia, Liberia. It was a long day spent flying over impossibly dense jungle for hours-on-end. Upon his arrival in Liberia, the ground crew inspected his plane and made some repairs. The next morning, it was ready for another leg of the journey, an eight-plus hour flight to Wideawake Airfield at Ascension Island in the middle of the Atlantic Ocean. It proved to be a day of flying over

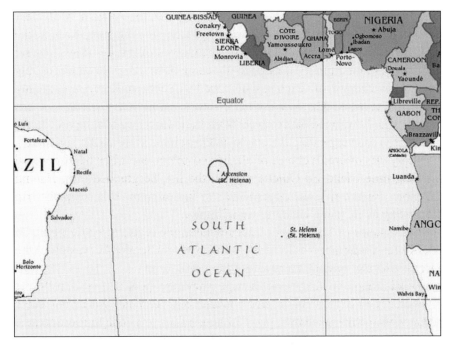

Ascension is a volcanic island located near the middle of the South Atlantic Ocean. The hop from Roberts Airfield in Liberia to Ascension Island was approximately 1,050 miles. It was an additional 1,690 miles to the airbase at Fortaleza, Brazil.

a never-ending expanse of water, which sharply contrasted with the days flying over deserts and jungle. "There are no landmarks in the ocean," Harry said. To him, reaching Ascension Island meant he was edging closer and closer to home.

The hop across the second half of the Atlantic took him to Fortaleza, Brazil. After more than eight hours flying over vast expanses of water, he was flying over incredibly dense jungle. He fondly remembers the gigantic, bone-in steak he was served at dinner that night. When he finished eating the largest chunk of meat he'd ever seen, the waiter asked him if he'd like another one. Harry thought the person was kidding, except he wasn't. Harry politely declined, but Ed, his co-pilot, accepted the offer.

On July 23, he made the seven-hour flight to Atkinson Field in British Guiana. It had been another day of flying over endless jungle, and the humidity and heat were as stifling as he'd ever experienced in his life. The next leg, the eighth, was only a six-hour flight, mostly over the Caribbean Sea.

Late on July 24, he landed at Borinquen Field in Puerto Rico. It was still hot and humid, but Harry didn't care so much as he did earlier, for he knew the next day would find him back in the United States proper. That night he, his crew, and the fighter pilots/passengers all spent a few hours relaxing at a nearby restaurant. He says referring to it as a "restaurant" was probably being generous. Regardless, everyone was in an excellent mood, not just because the next day would take them to the United States mainland, but it also represented what was likely to be the least dangerous leg of the journey.

At first light on July 25, Harry commenced the ninth and final leg of his return flight. For the first time on the long circuit back home, they could spot the occasional large ship plying the ocean below them. Harry took the sightings as signs of civilization. Seven hours after take-off, in the early afternoon of Wednesday, July 25, he touched down at Hunter Field, Hinesville, Georgia.

Once on the ground, he was met by a Follow Me Jeep. He taxied past hundreds of parked planes until he was guided into a spot alongside a B-24 bomber. As he exited "Wee Junie" for the last time, he noticed the B-24 and was immediately reminded of Golden Lang. In a way, he felt it was a strangely appropriate ending to his World War II career. He took a knee to honor his departed friends and proceeded to kiss the tarmac. As he rose, he took one final look at the two planes, parked side-by-side, for he never

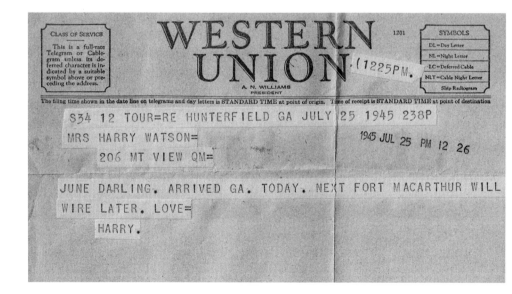

wanted to forget the coincidence. He considered the possibility it wasn't a coincidence and saluted the B-24.

On October 9 1945, Harry had the opportunity to fly a B-24 Liberator, the plane Golden Lang had flown to his death. He spent four hours flying the aircraft around Long Beach, California, imagining Lang as his co-pilot. Harry took his last military flight the next day, in a Vultee BT-13A, the same model he flew as a cadet. He spent about four hours having a blast with the acrobatic plane.

He thought he would become a full-time civilian and leave the military life behind for good. At least he thought it was for good. Colonel Donalson looked him up, established a loose friendship, and talked Harry into joining the Air Force Reserves. It was pure chance he wasn't called up to participate in the Korean Conflict.

Chapter 19

The Post-War Years

Harry as a captain flying for Continental Airlines.

It didn't take long for Harry to realize the post-war job market wasn't exactly robust. He moved in with Junie, his son Daniel and his mother-in-law at her home in Taft, California. They all got along very well, but Harry found himself getting antsy as his airline pilot dream was being put on hold due to a lack of finances. Becoming a commercial airline pilot required both ground and flight school training to achieve the requisite certification.

But just as he found a way to become an aviator back in 1940, he knew he'd discover a path to his goal. He just didn't know when the door would open for him.

In late fall 1945, he managed to gain a position as a "derrick man" on a Standard Oil Company drilling rig. It wasn't long before Standard began to lay-off workers. Harry was lucky and immediately went to work for Union 76 as an assistant in their Bakersfield, California paleontology lab.

Harry had accumulated some savings, and Junie had proved frugal and very adept at making a little bit of money stretch and stretch. In early 1946 the young couple was able to purchase a modest home in Bakersfield, California. The house even featured a nice fenced-in yard for their son and his little puppy to play in. Life was starting to become good, and it was far better than the conditions he grew up around in Courtney, Pennsylvania.

It wasn't long before the opportunity to purchase a hamburger joint in Ridge Crest, California, presented itself. Though the only kitchen experience he ever logged was KP duty in the early years of his army career, Harry jumped on it. He was doing OK in the burger business when, in 1948, he was able to obtain financial assistance from the "GI Bill", which allowed him to pursue his Airline Transport Rating "ATR" certification.

They sold the restaurant at a profit. Having little choice but to leave Junie and Danny behind on a short-term basis, he traveled to Fort Worth, Texas, where he enrolled in the ATR training program located there. On April 15 1948, the day he passed his ATR exam, he was hired by Pioneer Airlines and immediately moved his family to Houston, Texas. Pioneer was soon swallowed up by fast-growing Continental Air Lines, greatly expanding the routes Harry would be flying.

Though the great majority of the flights over his twenty-plus year career with Continental were standard domestic/international affairs, he did have occasion to exercise his sense of humor. During the height of the Vietnam War, he was ferrying a Boeing 707 loaded with Marine Corps fighter pilots. He realized his flight path would take him over Iwo Jima, the sight of a famous Marine Corps battle fought against the Japanese in 1945. As he approached the island, he remembered an old trick. He went onto the intercom and announced: "If you look out your port windows, you can see Iwo Jima."

The entire right-side isle of Marine pilots left their seats to get a glimpse of the famous island. When the co-pilot signaled Harry they were all in place, he dipped the plane hard to the left, giving everyone a good scare. He blared through the intercom: "Hey, get back in your seats! You want us to crash?"

The Marine pilots had already scurried back to their seats only to turn red-faced as Harry kept the intercom on so they could hear him, his co-pilot, radioman, and navigator laughing.

Once he retired from Continental Airlines, Harry dabbled in real estate development. At one point in the early 1980s, he nearly pulled off enough

Left to Right: Harry Watson, R.W. Samuelson, and G. Boatmen while attending ATR training. In a too rare moment of free time, the three men were about to attend a Fort Worth Rangers American Hockey League game at Will Rogers Memorial Stadium in Fort Worth, Texas.

financing to build an entire subdivision of single-family homes, all of them powered by solar energy. It was a revolutionary concept at the time. Unfortunately, the economy took a nosedive, interest rates shot beyond 20 percent, and Harry's plans crashed and burned. Undaunted, he continued to work in real estate and pursued a physically active lifestyle in sunny Southern California.

In the '70s, the stresses and strains of life took a toll on Harry and June's marriage. Harry had been flying around the world while dabbling in real estate and was frequently out-of-town, leaving June to deal with various household affairs on her own. Eventually, Harry and June embarked on separate paths. Years later he discovered a new source of happiness and married again. He and his new wife, Donna, spent more than two happy decades together.

Harry summed up his experiences in the USAAF as having been "a whale of an adventure. No matter how much danger there may have been, it was still an adventure, and I wouldn't trade it for all the money in the world."

Retired Continental Airlines Captain Harry E. Watson with Donna, his devoted wife of more than twenty-four years.

Chapter 20

Harry's Last Flight West

HARRY E. WATSON,
CONTINENTAL AIRLINES CAPTAIN, RETIRED

LAST FLIGHT WEST

I had a dream the other night in which I had the opportunity to not only plan, but experience my last flight west. It was as though I was doing a practice run on the final flight that every pilot takes … his very last.

The first part that I remember of my dream was:

I was sitting in the captain's seat of a 707-320C waiting for take-off clearance on 24R at Los Angeles. I had lived through this scenario many times in my career, and it was a privilege to have the opportunity to take-off with a passenger load of 165 and a crew of 8 bound for new, untold adventures. Once I was cleared for take-off by the tower, and throttles applied, the thrill of the surge of power was an experience that you never forget. A safe take-off with clearance from Departure Control to proceed on course left us with the low, throbbing roar of four powerful engines carrying us to heights never before attained.

Once cleared by Departure Control, we were given a new en route frequency … one I had never used before. Immediately upon dialing in this channel, a cacophony of voices filled the air-waves, all of them easily recognizable of friends and comrades who had taken their last flight west many years ago. To name a few, there was John Fannin, Sam Bickford, Barney Barnwell, Red Stubben, even that of Freddie Gray who was killed on a flight in May of 1962. Most were urging me to try to catch up, all of the congratulating me on this new journey I was undertaking. A loud squawking interrupted my reverie with instructions from the tower to taxi into position and hold.

HARRY'S LAST FLIGHT WEST

I'm very much looking forward to my "Last Flight West". It appears I have already assembled my crew, and we're on the run-up pad of 24R. Instructions from the tower were just given:

"Continental 1 cleared for take-off."

Harry's final "take-off" took place at 9:45 a.m. on Thursday, January 10 2019.

Chapter 21

Letters from Harry to Junie, Danny and God

Harry wrote the following letter over an extended period. Harry's words speak volumes as to the matters pouring through his thoughts during the long course of the war. The following is a transcript. For persons wishing to view the original, it is posted on my website along with his letter to God, which he attached to the main letter.

Undated Letter

U.S. Army Air Force
England

"June Darling"

I have a lot of things to say to you and Danny that might go "unsaid" if I don't do it this way.

I hope you never get this letter because I would much rather tell this in person. But only God himself knows whether I'll ever see you again or not. I've lost a lot of my boyfriends, and me, being just of flesh myself, could very easily have been one of them.

My number has almost come up several times and I believe my luck has been stretched too far. When it happens time and again it starts a guy to thinking and its always about the ones he's left behind.

If you ever get this I will no longer be on this earth. I have no regrets for myself but I do for you. I came into your life and before you had a chance to catch some breath I was gone again/ But with me I took your childhood, your freedom and your life itself because your life would have to be devoted to the burden I left you with, our child. I found you just a smiling, bashful, blue-eyed Irish girl that would steal any man's heart away. And being the greedy man that I am, I jumped at the few months of complete happiness that you offered me. I never knew that God created a woman as alive and wonderful as you my darling, until I married you. I never knew that such a

200

dream could ever really exist. You are all a man could ever ask of in a wife darling and I will never know why God blessed me, out of all the men in the world, with wonderful you. I have no regrets for myself-my life was complete while it lasted. Now its ended but you must go on. I loved you more than I loved my life itself but now that I am gone I want you to forget me. Your life is just beginning and if you enjoy it to the fullest I'll know my life was not given in vain. One thing I do ask – that you give my son "Danny" the fullest advantages that life has to offer. See that he gets the proper education and the chance to choose his own profession or life career. But don't confine him too much. Give him as much freedom as possible but don't let him get into trouble. That's a big order & will probably take a life time to fulfill. But if anyone can do it I know you can. I don't know who your partner in life will be but I'm sure you'll choose the best. **********

This is several days later, a Saturday night in fact. I started this out originally as my last letter to you, but it looks like its turning into my diary, my thoughts and my dreams. And my dreams are always of you so that's about all you'll find in this letter, my thoughts & dreams of you.

You know I want to help but have a guilty conscious when I think of you. There you are, the sweet, adorable, faithful little wife that you are wasting the best years of your life waiting for me. We lost another ship 2 days ago & all the crew. And when I think that it'll be at least 2 years before I see you, well my chances are pretty slim, and I know that all your waiting is in vain. I've only been over here 4 mo. & 2 years seems like an eternity. You know honey sometimes I wish I had never met you, because I think I've brought you more trouble than I have happiness. God knows I've never meant it to be that way. I believe what I'm really trying to do is apologize for the unhappy moments I've caused you. My darling this comes from the bottom of my heart, because your happiness means more to me than anything in the world. I wish I could spend the rest of my life with you. I was never more happy or more contented in my life than I was when I had you beside me. But fate plays funny tricks some times and tears come to my eyes when I realize that I'll never kiss those tender lips or feel your tender embrace again. Your love was the greatest thing that ever happened to me & I miss it now more than anything in the world. ***

"Hello Darling," I'm very lonesome tonight & as always I think of you when I'm lonesome. Sometimes I wonder just what it'll be like when we meet again. I've changed a lot you know, not in age have I grown older, but in every other way & I wonder if you'll love me as before. Even my hair is getting gray. I noticed a few myself one day but today one of the other boys told me that it was very noticeable. He just couldn't believe that I was just 22. Yes honey just 22 & he said I looked at least 28. I wish it wasn't so. But I am still alive and enjoying life so I'm just not going to worry about it.

We've had a few accidents lately & we lost 51 lives all told. I wonder how many broken hearts & lonely homes those 2 small mistakes caused. How many wives are waiting in vain & how many mothers and sweethearts are broken hearted all because of 2 small mistakes. It just doesn't seem fair to wipe out so many lives & cause so many heart aches. War is a horrible thing darling but we never realize it until it strikes close to home. It's hard to lose a buddy honey, just like losing a brother. So many have gone that I just can't believe they'll never come back. Its better just to pretend they've gone home or been transferred. How I wish it were so. ****

Many days have passed since I last wrote in this letter & now I am in France. They're getting us ready to pull a big drop soon & I suspect it will be around the 21-25 of this month [March '45]. There are lots of preparations going on & we're dropping paratroops every day just to keep in practice. Its supposed to be the final blow & I sure hope it is. Everyone seems to think this one will be the roughest yet, all we can do is wait and see. Probably a lot of the fellows will get it this time & if I'm one of them – well that's just the fortune of war. Funny thing though … I never am really afraid when I go through the missions, in fact I look forward to them as an adventure of some sort, or the ending to a good book. They're very exciting & they leave you with the feeling of a hard job well done. Only when you come back to your base & find an empty bunk next to you do you realize the seriousness of this whole thing. This is when the fear of God comes to you & you wonder just what the hell you're doing in a dirty business like this War. It isn't hard for the boys that go down, for them the War is over, it's the family they leave behind that gets hurt. Even if we win the War no amount of money or further happiness can erase the memory of a loved one. We will be victorious but it'll be a very empty victory for some. I sure hope Danny never goes to War and I'm damn glad I have some one like you to watch over him thru life. I only wish I could be there with you because I would like to see the guy-just once.

LETTERS FROM HARRY TO JUNIE, DANNY AND GOD

"Little Letter to God"
(Reprinted exactly as handwritten by Harry when stationed in the ETO.)

Look, God, I have never spoken to You,
but now I want to say "How do You do",
You see, God, they told me You didn't exist-
like a fool I believed all this.

Last night from a foxhole I saw Your sky-
I figured right then that they told me a lie;
Had I taken time to see things You made,
I'd have known they weren't calling a spade a spade.

I wonder, God, if You'd shake my hand,
Somehow, I feel that You will understand;
Funny I had to come to this hellish place
Before I had time to see Your face!

Well, I guess there isn't much more to say,
But I'm sure glad, God, I met You today!
I guess the zero hour will soon be here;
But I'm not afraid since I know You're near.

The Signal! Well, God I'll have to go;
I like You lots, this I want You to know:
Look now, this will be a terrible fight---
Who knows? I may come to Your house tonight.

Though I wasn't friendly to you before,
I wonder, God, if You'd wait at Your door?
Look, I'm crying! Me? Shedding tears?
I wish I had known You these many years.

Well, I have to go now, God, goodbye…
Strange, since I met You, I'm not afraid to die.
I wonder how many other boys felt this same way.
Lets hope it wasn't all in vain.

The End.

Left: Carl and Naomi Cary (Photo courtesy of Robert A. Cary)

Below: Lieutenant Golden Lang with his crew. The date is unknown, and it appears he named his B-24 "Tondeleyo". As odd as it may, or may not, seem, the name was also used on another B-24 lost earlier in the war.

Lang was promoted to fly as the flight leader of his group in February 1944, by which time he'd already completed ten of the requisite thirty combat missions and earned an Air Medal with Cluster. German gunners and fighter pilots tended to focus on lead planes, so perhaps it was only a matter of time before his skills would be overtaken by the odds.

He was in England when his little girl, Jean, was born. Harry believes he never did see his daughter, but on March 28 1944, Lang received a set of her footprints from his wife, Lillie. He described the footprints in a letter to Harry: "They were the most beautiful little footprints I've ever seen in my life."

Lang's courage shall not be forgotten, and I salute his memory,

The author, Marcus A. Nannini.

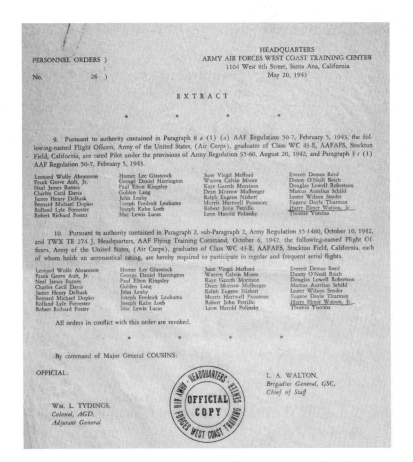

Note both Harry Elmer Watson, Jr. and Golden Lang are listed.

Author Biography
Marcus A. Nannini

Mr Nannini began his writing career when he published his own newspaper in the sixth grade and charged 25 cents per school quarter for the privilege of reading the only handwritten copy of each edition. The newspaper was a modest success.

He was a paid newspaper reporter during his undergraduate years and also worked three semesters as the research assistant to journalism professor Richard Stocks Carlson, Ph.D.

Nannini is a life-long history buff with a particular interest in World War II and the Japanese attack on Pearl Harbor. He once discovered an error in his fifth-grade history book concerning the attack. Nannini's continuing curiosity over several Japanese aerial photographs and the turtling of the *U.S.S. Oklahoma* lead him to write the pending historical mystery/thriller, *NINE MEN DOWN, The Silent Invasion of Oahu.*

Nannini is also the author of the highly regarded WWII biography: *LEFT FOR DEAD AT NIJMEGEN, The True Story of an American Paratrooper in WWII.* Casemate Publishers, Philadelphia, PA and Oxford, UK, March 2019. *LEFT FOR DEAD AT NIJMEGEN* was awarded the *Pencraft 2019 Nonfiction Book of the Year* honor, *IAN's Nonfiction Book of the Year-History,* and entered into the United States National Archives.

Nannini currently writes on a full-time basis. Look for more books from him soon, along with articles he has composed for *World War II History Magazine, History Magazine, and MilitaryHistoryNow.com.*

AUTHOR BIOGRAPHY

Titles from Marcus A. Nannini.

Left for Dead at Nijmegen, the True Story of an American Paratrooper in World War II

Casemate Publishers, Philadelphia, PA and Oxford, UK. (2019)

ISBN: 9781612006963

The order to retreat had been given by Lieutenant Weaver. Gene, being in the most advanced position, didn't hear the order and continued to fire as fast as he could, having run out of hand grenades. Ray Meade, his best friend, did hear the order, realized Gene wasn't pulling back and decided to charge across the roadway to warn him.

Just as Ray took his first step, a shell burst from the German "Eighty-Eight" exploded near Gene and threw his body high into the air, hitting the ground with an audible "thump." Undaunted, Ray continued and found Gene lying face-down. He rolled him over, noticed blood coming from his right ear, and assumed the worst. Gene was left for dead at Nijmegen, the only member of the patrol who did not return.

It was just the beginning of a tortuous eight-month imprisonment at the hands of the German High Command. Eight months spent wearing the same blood-soaked clothing while being forced to perform slave labor. After nearly being killed by friendly fire on numerous occasions, he finally made good on an escape. With the snow-capped Swiss Alps within sight, fate again stepped in to pull him back into the hopelessness of Stalag VII-A.

Coming Soon: The Commander Christopher Pastwa Mystery/
Thriller Series:

NINE MEN DOWN

The Silent Invasion of Oahu

It is 1941, and the Japanese midget submarine *I-16-tou* lurks unseen in the depths of Pearl Harbor, Hawaii. When the shock waves of the commencing Japanese aerial attack wake its crew, they rouse the machine from its silent slumber and begin an attack that will take down a U.S. battleship. More than one American sailor swore revenge for his comrades that day. The crew of the *I-16-tou*, however, was never found.

In present-day Hawaii U.S. Navy investigators Lieutenant Commander Christopher Pastwa and Lieutenant Ania Yamura puzzle over a mysterious skeleton unearthed in Kailua. When it is confirmed to be the body of one of the I-16's lost crew, Pastwa and Yamura begin to unravel a dark secret lurking at the heart of their beautiful island.

This member of the crew might be confirmed dead, but what happened to his shipmate? Creating a still-larger headache for the Navy investigators was their conclusion there might be two more Japanese navy personnel who had swum ashore in December 1941.

GEOGRAPHIC TREACHERY

The Shah's Revenge

Commander Christopher Pastwa and Lieutenant Ania Yamura find themselves being pulled in multiple directions when one of their own turns up as the victim of a torture/murder on a Kona coffee farm located on the beautiful island of Hawaii. As the body count increases and the loose ends multiply, their boss, Admiral Roman Reardon, decides to take a more hands-on approach and joins the team in Hilo where they work closely with Leilani Fuchida, the County Medical Examiner.

Ensign Gary Kida's wedding serves as a reunion of sorts and provides the team with a short respite. But the emergence of a pair of shady characters Reardon met a few years earlier, Cy and the "Aussie" appears to tie into the continuing string of murders. Pastwa corners a small group of traitors and guns most of them down, save one, and he holds the key to the underlying plot. However, it may be too late to prevent a Pearl Harbor Remembrance Day helicopter attack on the *U.S.S. Abraham Lincoln* as she sits in Pearl Harbor, her decks loaded with dignitaries and her entire crew on a sunny Sunday, December 7th.

VIGOROUS BRUTALITY

Pastwa and his Navy team find themselves with their backs to the wall and time running out as a passenger liner 200 miles out from the Big Island is being lined up in the targeting sites of a rogue North Korean submarine.

Index

210

INDEX